Collaborative Research in the Digital Humanities

A volume in honour of Harold Short, on the occasion of his 65th
birthday and his retirement, September 2010

T0299840

Edited by
MARILYN DEEGAN AND WILLARD McCARTY
King's College London, UK

Routledge
Taylor & Francis Group

LONDON AND NEW YORK

First published 2012 by Ashgate Publishing

Published 2016 by Routledge
2 Park Square, Milton Park, Abingdon, Oxfordshire OX14 4RN
711 Third Avenue, New York, NY 10017, USA

First issued in paperback 2016

Routledge is an imprint of the Taylor & Francis Group, an informa business

Copyright © 2012 Marilyn Deegan and Willard McCarty

Marilyn Deegan and Willard McCarty have asserted their right under the Copyright, Designs and Patents Act, 1988, to be identified as the editors of this work.

All rights reserved. No part of this book may be reprinted or reproduced or utilised in any form or by any electronic, mechanical, or other means, now known or hereafter invented, including photocopying and recording, or in any information storage or retrieval system, without permission in writing from the publishers.

Notice:
Product or corporate names may be trademarks or registered trademarks, and are used only for identification and explanation without intent to infringe.

British Library Cataloguing in Publication Data
Collaborative research in the digital humanities.
   1. Humanities--Research--Data processing.
   2. Communication in learning and scholarship--
   Technological innovations.
   I. Deegan, Marilyn. II. McCarty, Willard, 1945-
   001.3'0285-dc23

Library of Congress Cataloging-in-Publication Data
Collaborative research in the digital humanities / [edited] by Marilyn Deegan
   and Willard McCarty.
      p. cm.
   Festschrift honoring Harold Short, Department of Digital Humanities, King's College
   London.
   Includes bibliographical references and index.
   ISBN 978-1-4094-1068-3
   1. Humanities--Research. 2. Group work in research. 3. Communication in learning
   and scholarship--Technological innovations. I. Deegan, Marilyn.
   II. McCarty, Willard, 1945-

   AZ186.C65 2011
   025.00285--dc23

                                                                            2011040781

   ISBN 13: 978-1-138-25451-0 (pbk)
   ISBN 13: 978-1-4094-1068-3 (hbk)

COLLABORATIVE RESEARCH IN THE DIGITAL HUMANITIES

Contents

List of Figures and Tables

Figures

Tables

List of Contributors

Michael Best, University of Victoria, Canada

John Bradley, King's College London, UK

John Burrows, The University of Newcastle, Australia

Melanie Chernyk, ETCL, University of Victoria, Canada

Lynn Copeland, Simon Fraser University, Canada

Hugh Craig, The University of Newcastle, Australia

Richard Cunningham, Acadia University, Canada

Marilyn Deegan, King's College London, UK

Teresa Dobson, University of British Columbia, Canada

Wendy Duff, University of Toronto, Canada

Julia Flanders, Brown University, USA

Alan Galey, University of Toronto, Canada

David Gants, Florida State University, USA

Bertrand Gervais, UQAM/Université du Québec à Montréal, Canada

The HCI-Book Consultative Group

Susan Hockey, University College London, UK

Laszlo Hunyadi, University of Debrecen, Hungary

The INKE Research Team

Karon MacLean, University of British Columbia, Canada

Willard McCarty, King's College London, UK and University of Western Sydney, Australia

Jan-Christoph Meister, Hamburg University, Germany

Janet L. Nelson, King's College London, UK

Elena Pierazzo, King's College London, UK

Steve Ramsay, University of Nebraska, USA

Geoffrey Rockwell, University of Alberta, Canada

Charlotte Roueché, King's College London, UK

Stan Ruecker, Illinois Institute of Technology, USA

Susan Schreibman, Trinity College, Dublin, Ireland

Lynne Siemens, University of Victoria, Canada

Ray Siemens, University of Victoria, Canada

Kathryn Sutherland, University of Oxford, UK

Colin Swindells, University of British Columbia, Canada

Melissa Terras, University College London, UK

Charlotte Tupman, King's College London, UK

John Unsworth, University of Illinois, Urbana-Champaign, USA

Christian Vandendorpe, University of Ottawa, Canada

Claire Warwick, University College London, UK

John Willinsky, Stanford University, USA

Vika Zafrin, Boston University, USA

Foreword

This volume is dedicated to the work of Professor Harold Short, who retired as Director of the Centre for Computing in the Humanities (now the Department of Digital Humanities), King's College London, in September 2010.

Harold was Director of the Centre for more than 20 years (its gradual beginnings make the figure approximate). Under his guidance, it grew from a service unit of four people to a full academic department of more than 40 staff, with taught undergraduate and postgraduate programmes, a doctoral programme and numerous collaborative research projects, raising many millions of pounds to support them. Collaboration was and is the watchword of Harold's approach to digital humanities. In the Centre he built a team that continues to collaborate with academics and technical specialists in many disciplines all around the world. The influence of the Centre, and now the Department, is pervasive. Many wish to emulate its (and his) success.

Harold was also Chair of the Association for Literary and Linguistic Computing for 13 years (1997–2010), and was one of the prime movers in establishing in 2005 the umbrella organization, the Association of Digital Humanities Organizations, which has provided an ever-growing international framework for the digital humanities. It is a huge credit to his professionalism and his personal collegiality that a number of organizations have been and continue to be brought together in a loose but fruitful alliance, and it has involved several years of diplomacy on the part of Harold and others in a continuous and continuing process.

The book you have in your hands or on screen began in a thoroughly conventional way, when one of the editors remarked to the other that a book honouring Harold had to be done: a collaboration to celebrate a man who has championed collaboration, and done so in a typically self-effacing way, enabling others and helping to build the field for generations to come. So it happened. Gathering contributors together was not difficult, nor persuading the publisher.

We would like to thank the contributors to this volume for working together harmoniously and, for the most part, in secret, to produce something worthy of the man we honour. We would also like to thank Dymphna Evans, the publisher at Ashgate, for her help and patience. There are also many other people who commented on the endeavour over the three years of its realization – too numerous to name, but we are grateful to them all. It has been a truly collaborative enterprise.

Marilyn Deegan and Willard McCarty

Chapter 1

Collaborative Research in the Digital Humanities

Willard McCarty

> When a new freedom comes into being, the kind of thing it leads to depends largely on the characters of the people who first enjoy it. And, character being a less rigid thing than an already fixed and limiting set of traditions, the element of chance in the determining of events becomes unusually large ... Thus it follows that any fitting account, or, to put it more solemnly, any adequate history [of how this new freedom was used] must deal largely with persons and their characters. It cannot avoid regulations and other academic events but it would be superficial and misleading if it confined itself to them. It must have as its topic certain people: by what accidents they became involved ... what ideas they had, and how they translated them into action.
>
> Tillyard (1958): 11–12.

This is a *Fest* (celebration) in the form of a *Schrift* (publication) honouring the professional career of an extraordinary man, Harold Short, by looking at his work and, beyond it, to the digital humanities which he has done so much to establish, in the style and with the trajectory that he has helped to give to the field. But it is also a *liber amicorum*, a testament of friends to the enduring and improving difference he has made through an inseparable combination of love, imagination, thought, patience and stubbornness: love, in energetic devotion to our subject and to many of its practitioners; imagination, technical, intellectually critical and administrative; thought, in puzzling out the implications of computing and attending to all the details of implementing it collaboratively; and, yes, both patience and plain stubbornness in the face of uncomprehending resistance to new ideas and ways of working. He reminds us that at the centre of all that we do are people, some very special people.

This introduction attempts to point toward the significance of what Harold has done. It does that in a densely referential style which, given my admiration for clear and simple language, needs some comment. Hence a brief personal note. At some point in my career, when I noticed that this density was on the rise, I was forced to consider what it might be a symptom of: pride? insecurity? hostility? weakness of argument? After rigorous self-examination, I drew a blank. But, I realized, whatever the besetting sin, this style has a real function: to manifest the degree to which our computing is not merely *in* but more essentially *of* the humanities; to articulate the connections with the ideas and questions which inform the digital humanities and which it transforms; rather more militantly, to oppose with a great arsenal of evidence a tendency of the field to become boringly workaday, rule-bound and mindlessly industrialized; but finally, joyously, to suggest how fertile the ground is that Harold has prepared and tended all these years in London, removing stones, adding compost, turning over the soil, watering, protecting, tending the flowers as they emerge. 'Human nature is a garden', Lorraine Daston has written (2010). This is especially the case for someone so much at home in his adopted country.

The Collaborative Imagination

'Collaboration' is a problematic, and should be a contested, term. It is often used nowadays to denote what Peter Galison has called a transcendental virtue (2004: 380), that is, a good without qualification, which, having enhaloed its object, has nothing much to teach us. Harold has given collaboration real, specific and effective meaning in the only way this could be done, by working with colleagues across the disciplines and by creating an environment greater than himself in which collaboration is institutionalized – given, as Mircea Eliade said of ancient burial practice, a stone body so that the soul is able to continue to act in the world once it has gone on to presumably better things (1978: 116). As we know all too well, monuments are broken down, stones carried off and used for other, lesser or at least different purposes. This is why recognition, here and in other ways, is essential to the project. The stone body he has built is a house for us to live in and take care of and pass on to the next generation of digital humanists.

True collaboration within a group happens rarely. Even rarer, I expect, is collaboration that is manifested in group after group of individuals, as has been instantiated at what Harold named the Centre for Computing in the Humanities (CCH) – now, signifying its success, the Department of Digital Humanities (DDH) – at King's College London. I suspect that Harold's style of bringing these many collaborations about makes the subset even smaller. It is the style of an 'un-boss' – someone who makes it happen and administers its progress, but who steps back as often as possible to become just one of the boys and girls, or perhaps more accurately, *primus inter pares*. Creating an academic department for a new academic discipline requires an administrative imagination – itself so rare an attribute as to seem oxymoronic, if not cruelly euphemistic – even more magnanimous. Harold has fulfilled both by building this house, not according to the usual template, but in response to the needs of the activities and people it is meant to house. Its success tempts us immediately to take this house as an institutional model (which seems to me the best so far in our relatively short history). But to do so in those terms is to treat it as a finished product, and so ultimately to solidify a liberating institutional development into a rigidly inhibiting structure. Eliade's metaphor must be laid aside for a more adequate one.

In his yearly lectures on the Bible at Victoria College, Toronto, Northrop Frye would commonly refer to a story in the book of Jeremiah in which Jehudi, secretary to King Jehoiakim, is commanded to read the prophet Jeremiah's words of denunciation to him from a scroll:

> Now the king sat in the winterhouse in the ninth month: and there was a fire on the hearth burning before him. And it came to pass, that when Jehudi had read three or four leaves, he cut it with the penknife, and cast it into the fire that was on the hearth, until all the roll was consumed in the fire that was on the hearth. (Jer. 36: 22–3)

Frye comments in a book that arose from his lectures on the Bible:

> This must have been a papyrus scroll: parchment, besides being out of the prophet's price-range, would have been tough enough to spoil the king's gesture. The king's palace totally disappeared in a few years, whereas the Book of Jeremiah, entrusted to the most fragile and combustible material produced in the ancient world, remains in reasonably good shape. The supremacy of the verbal over the monumental has something about it of the supremacy of life over death. Any individual form of life can be wiped out by the smallest breath of accident, but life as a whole has a power of survival greater than any collection of stones. (1982: 200)

The moral I draw is that Harold's Centre, now a department, is best regarded as a current form of an idea in process of development. Taking CCH/DDH as a finished model or template diverts attention not only from the process of modelling the idea but also from the modeller, who always plays an essential but often ignored role. 'The model relation is inherently ternary', Marvin Minsky reminds us (1996), and this is best seen *when it is happening* rather than after the fact. Especially because computing is present-participial in nature, our attention must be focused as much on how this temporary state of affairs has been invented as on its manifest virtues. So we look to the modeller. How has he done it?

Socially the history of computing in the humanities has involved a long struggle to establish computing practitioners and non-technical scholars as equals in research, 'not as a matter of courtesy', historian Jaroslav Pelikan wrote 19 years ago in *The Idea of the University: A Reexamination*, 'much less as a matter of condescension, but as a matter of justice and of accuracy'. He argued that the future of universities turns on the kind of social contract which Harold has done so much to negotiate. Thus Pelikan:

> The integrity of the idea of the university as a community of research lies to a considerable extent in the development of mechanisms for ... collaboration ... [I]f the university is to attract and hold for its teaching mission those who are engaged in ... pioneering research work, as it must, it needs to become more imaginative about devising new systems and new standards for its faculties. (1992: 62, 64)

Behold CCH/DDH at King's. But again, collaboration (if the term is to be other than a euphemism of social control from above) must occur on level ground. It must be work (*labor*) done together (*co*, from *cum*, 'with') in every sense. The technically focused researcher must work *with* not *for* the non-technically focused scholar, must serve the research co-authorially. Of course equality in research, where this is possible, brings with it equal demands on *both* sides, and so a host of questions about how both are to scale the steep learning-curve that faces each. This in turn raises questions about how scholars are trained, and so about the institutional relationship between the sciences and humanities.

By tradition, or by more than just tradition, humanists work normally alone. This makes them especially vulnerable to forgetting the social dimension of knowledge (though hero-worship in techno-scientific circles shows the same tendency to attribute everything to a solitary researcher, such as Vannevar Bush or Albert Einstein). To borrow Ludwik Fleck's insight and terminology, the many voices and resources of the 'thought-collective' within which an individual works remain mostly tacit and unrecognized, though fundamental (1979/1935). Actual collaboration makes this collective partially explicit and so can illumine the common problem by giving other voices a chance to speak, to argue. Opposition, William Blake wrote, is true friendship.

The collaborative emphasis of DDH demands that we ask not merely the question I raised earlier – 'how did he do it?' – but also, as Harold would surely insist, the collective one, 'how did *they* do it?' Much of the historical evidence needed to answer it has unfortunately vanished, because it was never recorded. The demands of establishing the department and proving its worth through successful completion of many collaborative projects, with little certainty that one day the day-to-day work would become historically interesting, left no time for gathering this evidence. No doubt at the time some of what was happening seemed better to forget than to remember! (The opportunity remains for suitable doctoral students of the sociology of knowledge and in related fields to be participant observers, and so have the chance to find out what is actually happening at this crucial moment in our history.) Lacking this evidence I cannot be certain, but my guess is that with this evidence we would have a portrait of collaboration as a spectrum of work-styles varying in time as well as with the project, from solitude at one extreme to collective reasoning at the other. On the one hand, the intense struggle to realize something heretofore unrealized, demanding all one's intellectual resources, justifies and demands a researcher's turn away from the group to solitude, summoning and dismissing interlocutors as they prove useful, or not, to whatever formal expression he or she is developing. The immediate pleasures as well as difficulties of articulating it obscure, must obscure at least for a time, the world of others' words, deeds, artefacts and expectations. On the other hand, even in the least dependent modes of work the goal is to catch someone's attention, to interest him or her in what has been made, to provoke a response, even if the maker does not know who this will be, when or where. The fundamental truth remains: our work is for communication. This is often best done as a trial with close and trusted colleagues; a good collaboration provides a formal, reliable means.

Those who come to the meeting of minds and hands from the technical side, as Harold has, are at this point especially apt to feel the fragility of collaboration's goodness (to borrow from Martha Nussbaum), if not also the peril that everywhere threatens it in these severely anti-intellectual times. They, along with the rest of us who have thrown our lot into the 'methodological commons', as Harold and I have called it, may well be inclined to chafe against the very slowly and unevenly shifting institutional barriers that in specific instances make the possibility of genuine, fully realized collaboration seem distant. But hope for better is not foolish. In 1987, when a small group of us formed the *salon des refusés* out of which *Humanist* emerged, those exclusionary barriers seemed an utterly insurmountable Berlin Wall. What indeed must the situation have seemed to Jeremiah when his words were burned to ashes by his king? For the preservation of his book 'in reasonably good shape', our debt isn't to superior muscle but to millennia of human devotion to an idea, or perhaps better, to a question whose answer keeps changing. To compare great things with small (and so gain inspiration and humility at one go), our gaze is likewise directed to the questioning for which all the work, collaborative or otherwise, is directed. How is it to be done?

We have always known (and have struggled against realizing) that as Heraclitus is reputed to have said, *ta pánta rheî*, 'all things change', and have always been changing.[1] But those of us whose professional lives orbit computing know the rapidity of this change and the instability of our intellectual objects especially well. We are of course driven with Descartes 'to cast aside the shifting earth and sand in order to find rock or clay' (1998/1637: 16), but must notice eventually that the shifting never ceases, that there is no final axiomatic bedrock, that it's turtles all the way down. 'Summoned before the Law, wisdom can no better represent itself than in the step by which it moves away from it' (Heller-Roazen, 2006: 442). We use the algorithm, strictest of the Law's forms, to govern our move toward the Something Else of the humanities, which have always defined themselves by what they were not – not the *literae divinae* of the theologians, not the nomothetic theorizing of the scientists, not the double-entry bookkeeping of the accountants. I am fond of quoting the pioneering computer scientist Alan Perlis' 74th epigram: 'Is it possible that software is not like anything else, that it is meant to be discarded: that the whole point is always to see it as a soap-bubble?' (1982). Or as the great historian of computing Michael S. Mahoney used to insist, the scheme that Alan Turing gave us is for devising indefinitely many computings, limited only by the human imagination (2005), most definitely *not* to settle forever on one form we declare final.

Data and Machine

The anthropologist and digital humanist Morgan Tamplin (Trent, Canada) taught me to think about the changes wrought with the machine by meditating on the

---

1 The attribution to Heraclitus is traditional, but those words are not to be found in his writings; they come from Simplicius' commentary on Aristotle's *Physica* (1313.11); cf. Plato, *Cratylus* 401d, 402a; Peters (1971): 178.

act of seeing an object of study 'as data'. This act involves not just filtering perception to admit only the computationally tractable elements of an object, but also choosing rather more consciously than otherwise which of them are to be digitized. Here collaboration becomes essential, whatever the project: either external, between technical and non-technical researchers, or internal, between two halves of a bicameral intelligence. The problem is not just preserving both the filtered-out and the filtered-in elements for consideration side-by-side, but more that the play of interpretation, ideally drawn out and refined with the aid of digital tools and methods, alters what we take these elements to be. Seeing 'as data' is inflected by the question, what *is* the data, or even, what is *data*? Such questions may be pursued theoretically apart from particular circumstances,[2] but my point here is that true collaboration instantiates the hermeneutic circular struggle, and that in the struggle the technical, data-minded intelligence plays half the game.

In this context the technically focused researcher is no longer a 'rude mechanical' (as I was once dubbed in my hearing, with reference to *A Midsummer Night's Dream*, by someone who really should have known better), but is nevertheless a mechanic – of a sort. It's the sort that is the revelatory rub.

In his 1968 Turing Award Lecture, the engineer-mathematician Richard Hamming celebrated the fact that the largest professional organization for computer scientists was then and is still known as the Association for Computing Machinery (1969: 5). He argued that to lose sight of the machine was to cut the ground out from under computer science. The constraints that physical implementation imposes on logico-mathematical algorithms hooks computer science into the real world of finite resources and permits discovery by experiment, but there is more to computing machinery than that, as important and exciting as that can be.

A clue to its world-altering importance is the degree to which computing has evoked fear – historically well attested, loudly in popular media during the first few decades, somewhat more quietly in the professional literature but there nonetheless.[3] Socially the upset caused by this new machinery resonated with the earlier disturbances to working life brought about by automation, to which in its early years the computer gave, and was seen to be giving, highly publicized reach and economic advantage. But public reaction to computing was not simply to its roles in business and industry (nor to its role in warfare – but that is another story). Juxtaposing two nearly simultaneous events – the release of Charlie Chaplin's *Modern Times* and the publication of Alan Turing's 'On Computable Numbers', both in 1936 – not merely suggests a relation indicating, as Robin Gandy says, 'something in the air, which different people catch' (1995: 51), but a crucial

---

2   See, especially, recent work by Jerome McGann, for example, 2004. See also Armstrong (1986), which discusses Wayne Booth's attempt to deal with the question by use of Stephen Pepper's distinction of *danda* from *data.*

3   It is still with us, as the fact of the 2009 Asilomar meeting of the American Association for Artificial Intelligence and the reactions to it demonstrate. See Markoff (2009); Horwitz and Selman (2009) .

difference. The upset caused by computing was of a wholly different order than the perceived threats to employment, the workplace and daily life. This upset is comparable, not so much to the Industrial Revolution, Taylorian principles and Fordism, as to that which Sigmund Freud called the insults 'flung at the human mania of greatness' by Copernicus in the sixteenth, Darwin in the nineteenth and Freud himself in the twentieth centuries (1920: 246–7). Each, Freud wrote, shows that we have little idea of who or what we are – hence the compelling need to rethink the human.[4]

The idea of the human as machine – something constructed and therefore constructible – has a long pre-history; it is implicit in 'Darwin's dangerous idea', as philosopher Daniel Dennett (1995) and biologists Jacques Monod (1972/1970) and Ernst Mayr (1997) have shown. But Turing's machine and the allied work which has followed is even more interesting than merely yet another blow to vanity. Commenting on Minsky's impish remark that 'The brain ... happens to be a meat machine', Pamela McCorduck remarks, in her delightful book *Machines Who Think*: 'The problem, I suppose, is our own associations with the notion of mechanism, or machine' (1979: 70f). We tend immediately to summon notions of behaviouristic absolutism, as in the work of Pavlov and Skinner. But Minsky points out that the mistake we make in this association is to apply a pre-computational notion of machine to ourselves. A new idea of 'machine' is needed. The outlines of this idea seem reasonably clear from Turing's scheme, but since this machine acts on the world, its meaning is a matter still largely to be determined from argument *and* engineering *and* experiment. Hence the pivotal role of the digital humanities: to help figure out this new 'machine' in its encounters with the study of human cultural artefacts, and to figure out what these artefacts now mean in an intellectual world permanently altered by its presence. Its potential to model and so additionally to affect our idea of the human was realized early, for example, in a paper by the philosophical neurophysiologist Warren McCulloch and the logician Walter Pitts (1989/1943), whose work informed John von Neumann's sketch of machine architecture (1993/1945; cf. McCulloch, 1989/1961), whose implementation has continued to provide the wherewithal to think about the brain. Computer to brain to computer to brain, a feed-back and feed-forward cycle to be continued.

The rootedness of technical researchers in the machine becomes an increasingly more important condition of scholarship as the accumulating effects of computing on the humanities and greater social licence to be openly digital encourage scholars to get involved. As Harold has outlined on several occasions, a *metanoia* lies at the heart of the interaction among technical and non-technical collaborators (cf. McCarty, 2005: 121–9). A crucial part of the mind-change occurs through the non-technical scholar becoming grounded in digital methods, as a result of which he or she is able to understand in detail what the translation of a research question into digital language means. This grounding renders the non-technical

---

4   National Humanities Center project, <onthehuman.org/>.

scholar fit to participate in the design of whatever tool or resource is the object of the exercise. Participation often changes the initial research questions, as several of our colleagues at King's have testified. Without this grounding, without the collaboration which provides it, scholars labour under a severe difficulty, of which the theoretically inclined are especially unlikely to be aware.

The Horizon

The computer is a product of many disciplines but chiefly those in the mathematical, physical, biomedical, psychological and social sciences. (If you are surprised at the presence-at-birth of any but mathematics, engineering and physics, look carefully at the composition of the hugely influential Macy Conferences.) Historically, the computer came to the humanities from outside and was received as a foreigner, in 'fear and trembling' (Nold, 1975), as well as with curiosity. In its reception by the humanities over the last six decades – coincident with both Harold's and my own lifespans – we can see, among other things, the opening up of an opportunity for scholars to treat their objects of concern as if these objects were natural, like rocks, rather than cultural, like sculpture, and by doing so, to embed analogies of scientific research within the humanities and learn from them (McCarty, 2009/2007). It provides great help with constructing what G.E.R. Lloyd has called 'bridgeheads of intelligibility' between the humanities and the sciences (Lloyd, 2010: 210). Actualizing such construction institutionally, across very distinct schools as well as departments, is in its very early stages. But the significance of what Harold has done reaches to it. This reaching could, if we attend to the potential thus revealed, continue into the receding horizon for as far as we can imagine going.

The contributions which follow comprise a proper *Festschrift* because they are manifestations of influence and respect from colleagues and co-workers. They are unified by their common concern with the new discipline to which the department that Harold created and shepherded into its full academic existence has given a home. They are expressions of gratitude. Well done, my friend.

References

Armstrong, Paul B., 'The Multiple Existence of a Literary Work', *Journal of Aesthetics and Art Criticism* 44.4 (1986): 321–9.

Daston, Lorraine, 'Human Nature is a Garden', in a special issue on History and Human Nature, ed. Brad Inwood and Willard McCarty, *Interdisciplinary Science Reviews* 35.3–4 (2010): 215–30.

Dennett, Daniel C., *Darwin's Dangerous Idea: Evolution and the Meanings of Life* (London: Allen Lane, The Penguin Press, 1995).

Descartes, René, *Discourse on Method and Meditations on First Philosophy*, trans. Donald A. Cress, 4th edn (Indianapolis: Hackett Publishing, 1998/1637).

Eliade, Mircea, *From the Stone Age to the Eleusinian Mysteries*, vol. 1 of *A History of Religious Ideas*, trans. Willard R. Trask. (Chicago: University of Chicago Press, 1978).

Fleck, Ludwik, *Genesis and Development of a Scientific Fact*, ed. Thaddeus J. Trenn and Robert K. Merton, trans. Fred Bradley and Thaddeus J. Trenn, Foreword by Thomas S. Kuhn (Chicago: University of Chicago Press, 1979/1935).

Freud, Sigmund, 'Traumatic Fixation – the Unconscious', in *A General Introduction to Psychoanalysis*, trans. G. Stanley Hall (New York: Boni and Liveright, 1920): 236–47.

Frye, Northrop, *The Great Code: The Bible and Literature* (New York: Harcourt Brace Jovanovich, 1982).

Galison, Peter, 'Specific Theory', *Critical Inquiry* 30 (2004): 379–83.

Gandy, Robin, 'The Confluence of Ideas in 1936', in Rolf Herken (ed.), *The Universal Turing Machine: A Half-Century Survey*, 2nd edn (Wien: Springer Verlag, 1995): 51–102.

Hamming, Richard W., 'One Man's View of Computer Science', 1968 ACM Turing Award Lecture, *Journal of the Association for Computing Machinery* 16.1 (1969): 3–12.

Heller-Roazen, Daniel, 'Philosophy Before the Law: Averroës's *Decisive Treatise*', *Critical Inquiry* 32 (2006).

Horwitz, Eric and Bart Selman, 'Interim Report from the Panel Chairs', AAAI Presidential Panel on Long-Term AI Futures, American Association for Artificial Intelligence (2009), available at: <http://www.aaai.org/Organization/presidential-panel.php> (accessed 4 December 2011).

Lloyd, G.E.R., 'History and Human Nature: Cross-Cultural Universals and Cultural Relativities', in a special issue on History and Human Nature, ed. Brad Inwood and Willard McCarty, *Interdisciplinary Science Reviews* 35.3–4 (2010): 201–14.

Mahoney, Michael S., 'The Histories of Computing(s)', *Interdisciplinary Science Reviews* 30.2 (2005): 119–35.

Markoff, John, 'Scientists Worry Machines May Outsmart Man', *New York Times* (26 July 2009).

Mayr, Ernst, *This is Biology: The Science of the Living World* (Cambridge, MA: Belknap Press, 1997).

McCarty, Willard, *Humanities Computing* (Basingstoke: Palgrave, 2005).

McCarty, Willard, 'Being Reborn: The Humanities, Computing and Styles of Scientific Reasoning', *New Technology in Medieval and Renaissance Studies* 1 (2009/2007): 1–23.

McCorduck, Pamela, *Machines Who Think: A Personal Inquiry into the History and Prospects of Artificial Intelligence* (San Francisco, CA: W.H. Freeman and Company, 1979).

McCulloch, Warren S., 'What Is a Number, that a Man May Know It, and a Man, that He May Know a Number?', Ninth Alfred Korzybski Memorial Lecture, *General Semantics Bulletin* 26–27 (1961): 7–18; reprinted in Warren S. McCulloch, *Embodiments of Mind* (Cambridge, MA: MIT Press, 1989).

McCulloch, Warren S. and Walter H. Pitts, 'A Logical Calculus of the Ideas Immanent in Nervous Activity', *Bulletin of Mathematical Biophysics* 5 (1943): 115–33; reprinted in Warren S. McCulloch, *Embodiments of Mind* (Cambridge, MA: MIT Press, 1989).

McGann, Jerome, 'Marking Texts of Many Dimensions', in Susan Schreibman, Ray Siemens and John Unsworth (eds), *A Companion to Digital Humanities* (Oxford: Blackwell, 2004), available at: <http://www.digitalhumanities.org/companion/> (accessed 4 December 2011).

Minsky, Marvin, 'Matter, Mind and Models' (1996), available at: <http://groups.csail.mit.edu/medg/people/doyle/gallery/minsky/mmm.html> (accessed 4 December 2011).

Monod, Jacques, *Chance and Necessity: An Essay on the Natural Philosophy of Modern Biology*, trans. Austryn Wainhouse (London: Collins, 1972/1970).

Nold, Ellen W., 'Fear and Trembling: The Humanist Approaches the Computer', *College Composition and Communication* 26.3 (1975): 269–73.

Pelikan, Jaroslav, *The Idea of the University: A Reexamination* (New Haven: Yale University Press, 1992).

Perlis, Alan, 'Epigrams' (1982), available at: <http://www.cs.yale.edu/quotes.html> (accessed 4 December 2011).

Peters, F.E., *Greek Philosophical Terms: A Historical Lexicon* (London: Hodder & Stoughton, 1971).

Tillyard, E.M.W., *The Muse Unchained: An Intimate Account of the Revolution in English Studies at Cambridge* (London: Bowes & Bowes, 1958).

Von Neumann, John, 'First Draft of a Report on the EDVAC', Contract No. W-670-ORD-4926, US Army Ordnance Department and the University of Pennsylvania (Philadelphia, PA: Moore School of Electrical Engineering, University of Pennsylvania, 1945); reprinted in *IEEE Annals of the History of Computing* 15.4 (1993): 27–43, available at: <http://web.mit.edu/STS.035/www/PDFs/edvac.pdf> (accessed 4 December 2011).

Chapter 2

No Job for Techies: Technical Contributions to Research in the Digital Humanities

John Bradley[1]

One of the remarkable things about the Department of Digital Humanities (DDH; formerly the Centre for Computing in the Humanities [CCH]) at King's College London (KCL) is the degree to which technical development work is recognized both as an important element in what DDH does, and as a contribution to scholarly practice. This is not a universal situation in the digital humanities. Instead, most institutions view the kind of technical contributions which DDH makes as a kind of support work – perhaps, in extreme cases, as similar to what is done to the academic's car by his garage mechanics. From this position arises, I believe, the application of the diminutive term 'techie' by some to describe those individuals doing this kind of work. Indeed, I have upon occasion been called 'techie' in my presence: not by any of our close academic collaborators (indeed, one told me he was horrified when he heard it!), but by humanities scholars who don't know and understand the work we do.

So, is there a problem with this that goes beyond some personal hurt feelings? I think the issue is rather larger than that, and connects with the role of technology in the whole programme of the digital humanities, and from the collaborative relationship between scholars and those with technical expertise. Furthermore, I believe that innovation in the digital humanities often arises out of the pooled talents of a range of experts, and in the best environment where this happens there is recognition and support for the interlinked actions of many players.

Of course, the issue is certainly one that arises in the UK, but there have been studies of the digital humanities undertaken in North America which, while on one hand offering much insight into how the digital humanities could re-invigorate humanities scholarship, are also infused with the perspective of the particular academic culture that operates in North America. One of the central issues, it seems to me, is that captured by the terms 'faculty' and 'staff' – widely used in North America to distinguish types of university employees. This operates as an unstated underlying assumption in reports on the potential for digital humanities, such as Diane Zorich's 2008 report *A Survey of Digital Humanities Centers in the United States* (prepared for the Council on Library and Information Resources), or William Mitchell, Alan S. Inouye and Marjory S. Blumenthal's 2003 report:

---

1   Paper given at DH2009, July 2009, University of Maryland.

Beyond Productivity: Information Technology, Innovation, and Creativity. The assumption is that, although digital humanities research will, of necessity, be a partnership between someone who knows the materials of study and someone who knows the technology, it will be a significantly unequal one: the academic is the visionary, and all the vision comes from him/her. The technical person simply has the job of implementing the academic's vision.

Jennifer Edmond, in her 2005 article 'The Role of the Professional Intermediary in Expanding the Humanities Computing Base', recognizes that this division between scholar and technician is inadequate, and proposes the introduction of a *technical professional* between the humanist scholar and programmer, to fill the technical gap between the two poles that she outlines. She points out that few individual humanities scholars will have the 'inclination and time to master the skills' (2005: 370) needed to work effectively in the formal systems of computing. The goal, then, of allowing humanists to exploit the power of computing technology is not so much to train them up to 'technical mastery', but to develop an 'effective form of collaboration between scholars and technical professionals' (2005: 371). She observes that the collaboration is not just 'delegation', and points out that to achieve this one needs to 'set right' the cultural mismatch between the technical professional and the scholar.

Our experience at DDH deviates from this kind of scholar/technician collaboration (even when the technician is viewed as a professional in Edmond's analysis), and instead shows the need to recognize the importance of the contribution of both academics and technical specialists in digital humanities projects, because both significantly enrich the results that come from the shared endeavour. Of course, the best academic staff *are* a powerhouse of new ideas, but driving digital humanities innovation *solely* through the ideas of a humanities scholar misses out on other important sources for innovation and insight.

DDH and the Kinds of Research

Among centres for the digital humanities, DDH uniquely fosters an environment within which academics and technical specialists collaborate and which is a source of empowerment for both.

It is almost certainly not clear to most readers how unusual DDH is. DDH is constituted as a full academic department under KCL's School of Arts and Humanities, with the same academic status and responsibilities as, say, the Department of History – indeed the recent change of name to the Department of Digital Humanities (DDH) from the Centre for Computing in the Humanities was done to make this much clearer. As an academic department, then, DDH has a teaching mandate which it carries out by offering a selection of undergraduate courses, running three MA programmes (two of them jointly with other departments and schools), and offering a PhD in Digital Humanities whose students are normally supervised in collaboration with other departments.

DDH also has a research mandate, just as any academic department would have, but what makes it relevant to this paper is that the staff that work within it – including me – represent a range of people and posts that would go outside of what in North America would be called 'faculty'.

Indeed, DDH, although a large department by KCL's standards, has proportionally fewer academic/teaching staff than other departments here at King's, and a large number of other staff who work as a part of DDH's research endeavour in non-teaching positions. Furthermore, DDH works hard to maintain a research culture that recognizes the contribution of non-teaching staff to its research goals, and works to maintain some space for non-teaching staff to work on their own research.

Part of the way that this works is through the recognition of more than one kind of activity as research. There is the traditional type: for example, John Lavignino's substantial and extended contribution as one of the two general editors to the recently published Thomas Middleton edition, and Willard McCarty's remarkable book *Humanities Computing*. Both of these are exemplary models of humanities scholarship. Even my project *Pliny* (2009) – certainly not conventional humanities scholarship, but perhaps more closely aligned with Information Studies – can be seen as containing elements of traditional personal research. It is, however, in the work that arises from DDH's collaborative involvement with humanities scholars from many departments both within KCL and outside it where perhaps the most striking differences arise.

Collaborative Scholarly Projects

DDH has been involved in about 40 projects funded by a range of funders including the AHRC (Arts and Humanities Research Council), the British Academy, the Mellon Foundation and the Leverhulme Trust. These are all multi-year projects, and represent a formal and extended collaboration between members of DDH and humanities specialists in a range of disciplines. From the writing of the project proposal to its completion, the technical side of the project is given significant billing – starting with the identification of a technical director, and ending with the recognition that DDH staff can claim some ownership of the intellectual property created by a project, and can therefore produce or co-produce publications on various aspects of it. Indeed, often the proposal is submitted with a member of DDH technical staff identified as a co-investigator.

A slide I have in my possession, from a presentation which Harold Short, founding director of CCH, now DDH, gave at UNC Chapel Hill in 2007, gives his view on the nature of the collaborative research that our project work represents. Of course the humanities researcher brings his/her specialist knowledge of the source materials, and the perspective of his/her discipline. Furthermore, these days, it is useful if they can also bring a sense of how users from outside their disciplines, including non-specialists, could make use of the resource we are building together. We also hope that they will come to work with us with a willingness to explore the potentials for digital representation in the humanities. From the DDH side, the humanities computing specialists bring, directly or indirectly, years of experience of working with a range of technologies and materials from a range of disciplines, an understanding of the nature of humanities research and its priorities, a commitment to use open standards and open source, and an open mind to be attuned to the concerns of the researcher, and the complexities and subtleties of the materials.

Personally, my main interest in and contribution to these collaborations is modelling, and in general modelling is an important intellectual contribution which we make to our many projects. However, there are other areas where our contribution is also significant. As is common elsewhere in the digital humanities community, many of our collaborative projects are text-based, and document analysis is a prominent part of our work on them – a task that is, I suspect, already well understood within the community, given the wide-ranging commitment to the Text Encoding Initiative (TEI). A key message from TEI's founders, Michael Sperberg-McQueen and Lou Burnard, is that document analysis and mark-up is an intellectual task and decisions about it carry with them an intellectual responsibility – see Sperberg-McQueen (1991) for an example of this view.

More recently (and perhaps because of the arrival of XSLT to the notice of our community), there has become a clearer separation between the underlying models of the data itself from its presentation, and a recognition that the presentation of this material can be in itself a significant intellectual activity. Furthermore, current developments in the World Wide Web (WWW), including the various Web 2.0 initiatives and also the rich presentation potential of JavaScript and CSS, has meant that highly sophisticated representation of the materials and their underlying structure is possible on the WWW. Best practice for web presentation, then, comes out of the blending of the understanding of the materials with which one is working with an understanding of how to exploit the technology to emphasize what is important. Our interest in web presentation, thus, is not only in traditional web-designer issues such as 'ease of use', or 'conformance to browser standards', but also in exploring the potential of the browser to expose fundamental intellectual concepts that our projects represent. An example of one of our projects where the focus has been on the issues involved in presentation has been the *Online Chopin Variorum Edition* (OCVE, 2006, 2010). Some of the thinking about this that has gone into OCVE can be found in Bradley and Vetch (2007).

DDH Contribution: Formal Data Modelling

Database technology has, undeservedly, often received bad press from the digital humanities community. However, the relational model provides an extraordinarily powerful way to represent aspects of objects of study on the computer, and express and exploit relationships between them. Furthermore, this modelling approach, although dating back to the 1970s, continues to be very active today in computing as a whole, and has significantly influenced many aspects of ontology modelling approaches such as those found today in the Resource Description Framework (RDF) and its related technologies. Although this kind of formal data modelling approach is an important component in projects that range in their subject matter from linguistics to art history, I will focus in the following discussion on our involvement in the formal modelling of prosopography.

DDH's approach to structured prosopography has, over many years, exploited relational database technology to represent scholarly research. DDH is involved in a number of prosopography projects, including five multi-year projects: *Prosopography of Anglo-Saxon England* (PASE, 2007, 2010); *Prosopography of the Byzantine World* (PBW, 2006); *Clergy of the Church of England* (CCEd, 2008); and *Paradox of Medieval Scotland* (PoMS, 2010) and its continuation *The Breaking of Britain* (BoB 2011). We are also involved with prosopographies with two of our PhD students: one on the Late Antique ecclesiastical history of Scholasticus, and the other on the high officials of the Portuguese court under the reign of John III. These are all projects that have as their central technology the relational database, and which take a similar approach to structured prosopography.

The kinds of sources for these prosopographies range from saints' lives to legal or administrative documents, and it may seem hard to see much commonality between the different sources upon which a useful database structure could be created. All these prosopographies, however, share a common structural core that we call *factoid prosopography*. They grew out of work that began at KCL back in the 1990s during the construction of the *Prosopography of the Byzantine Empire* (PBE), and developed from a partnership between a technical specialist, Gordon Gallacher, and a Byzantinist, Dion Smythe, who were both staff at KCL at the time.

The Factoid Prosopography model does not attempt so much to model the *texts* upon which a prosopography is built; instead it represents some aspect of the *mental process* that goes on in the mind of the prosopographer as s/he is constructing the prosopography. The central idea is the *factoid*: a reference to a snippet of text that says something about one or more persons. The factoid links the *thing that is said* in the text to the *persons* it is said about and the *spot in the source* where the thing is said. You can see a simplified schematic of a factoid in Figure 2.1. There the factoid also connects geographical *places* that are connected with the event that the factoid represents.

This simplified diagram cannot tell the whole story, of course. *What is said* by a factoid, for example, is also further structured (although not shown here), and it represents the kinds of information about people that often seem to be the preoccupation of prosopography.

The factoid has remained the central concept in the factoid model, but the model as a whole has undergone significant re-thinking three times, and revisions by us over the years, from the early model that formed the bases for factoids in the *Prosopography of the Byzantine Empire* in the 1990s, to today's significantly more versatile one, has formed the basis for most of our more recent factoid-driven prosopographies, while retaining central concepts present in the earlier models. The

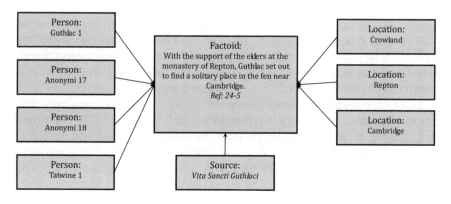

Figure 2.1   A factoid linking persons, places and a source to an historical event

revisions have represented new thinking about how the factoid model can better map the issues that the prosopographer deals with to the formal system that the model represents.

Modelling of this kind forms one of the central intellectual contributions of all of our structured database-driven projects. The ownership of the model is of necessity intertwined. Clearly, the model must reflect the understandings of our colleagues from the older disciplines. However, the modelling process is a highly formal one and, in our experience, the researcher is unlikely to come up with a model that adequately represents his or her needs without the extensive engagement of the formal training and experience of our analysts. Indeed, on two separate occasions and from partners in two different projects, our partners from the older disciplines have told us that they believed that the resulting model of the material has ideas both from the discipline and technical side that are intertwined in such a way that it is not possible to separate them.

Furthermore, approaches to modelling like that shown in our structured prosopography represent both an important intellectual contribution to our projects, but have in their own right an intellectual history. We have presented our factoid approach at several conferences (including once at the Leeds Medieval Conference, and twice at ACH/ALLC conferences, and at a European Science Foundation workshop on prosopography), and have published papers on the idea and its implications (Bradley and Short, 2002 and 2005). There is, in fact, a parallel research process going on here. The resulting digital object is the product of the joint work of us and our partners. Thus, research outputs such as papers are generated on one hand by our partners that put the work in their context, and on the other by analysts at DDH, who present our contribution in the context of the digital humanities.

For this to work at all, this modelling activity must be collaborative: combining the insights and experience of the materials of study from our discipline experts with the ability to express these things in the formal language of digital modelling that our digital humanities specialists offer. The resulting model informs the subsequent thinking of both partners. For the digital humanities specialist, it provides a way to develop a deeper and more sophisticated understanding of the business of formal modelling of humanities materials. The humanities scholar also benefits. Although the resulting model will hopefully represent significant aspects of his or her interpretation of the materials, we are often told that its formality and clarity will help to clarify the scholar's thinking, and may raise new and interesting challenges that had been hitherto overlooked.

McCarty draws our attention to a role for the computer model in humanities scholarship, and points out that '[i]n a loose sense models are not new to scholarship. To render a cultural artefact intellectually tractable, we must ignore some aspects of it and highlight others according to our abilities, interests, and purposes' (2008: 254). He goes on to point out that, whereas traditional scholarship expressed its effects primarily in a shift in language, a digital model gives its user 'the ability to manipulate something directly without reference to the author' and that 'rapid *manipulation* is what separates modelling from writing'. (2008: 254)

Parallels in the Field of Software Development

The significance of modelling as a collaborative task, involving the joint input of two quite different kinds of specialities, is already recognized within what we might call a sister field: the field of software development, where many methodologies, although developed to support software development from the perspective of the developer, emphasize the need to involve the system's eventual user in the design process as an equal participant. See this quotation on 'participatory design' by prominent researchers in human–computer interaction: 'Users are … active collaborators in the design process, rather than passive participants whose involvement is entirely governed by the designer' (Dix et al., 2004: 466).

Dix et al. are writing from the perspective of the system designer, and it is interesting to note the implied power relationship between the developer and the user. Here the developer has traditionally had the power over the design of the software, and Dix et al. are arguing that there is a need for the designer to share power with the eventual users. The established power relationship which Dix et al. are arguing against here is the opposite to that between the technical person and the scholar that is often in place in digital humanities projects, but even then, the joint nature of the work between the user and designer, and the need for more recognition of the intellectual contribution of both, and the more equal nature of their relationship, is evident in Dix et al.'s text.

The Scandinavian school of computer systems design has developed a design methodology that they call 'cooperative design'. Their work begins from the premise that, according to Sisse Finken (1998): 'Computer system development is difficult, not primarily because of the complexity of technical problems, but because of the social interaction involved when users and designers learn to create programs and express ideas together.' Finken subsequently notes that co-operative design emphasizes a process that must be central and continual throughout the work, and that needs to centre on the preservation of what he calls 'egalitarity' (1998: 6) between the designer and the person for whom the design is being done. In Finken's article, the issue is one of power and status, and involves sorting out how to manage its distribution so that, between the user and the developer, one does not dominate the contribution of the other. Indeed, he claims to base some part of his work on Foucault's understanding of the role of power in scientific discourse.

One way that designers, in his view, can get status for their work is by framing it in the context of doing research – and he maps aspects of what we might think of as scientific research onto the designer's work: first, testing and assessing methods and techniques; then reporting the results by writing about them, and thereby addressing a community of colleagues who do similar research and who have an interest in the principles and theories (the 'scientific side') of system design. Indeed, Finken calls this community of designers an 'academic community' (1998: 8). Note that by taking on the interpretation of the designer's work in this way, he is pointing out parallels with other academic communities – and in this way is working towards appropriating some of their power and status to the community of designers.

McCarty (2008) has proposed a similar argument for a somewhat different purpose. He presents an argument for humanities computing as a discipline (here, in fact, an 'interdiscipline' [2008: 257]) in its own right and discusses the role of collaborative work in the field. As a part of this argument, he refers to its 'collegial' nature and notes that we must simultaneously serve our discipline-specific partners while establishing ourselves as 'our own masters'. In his view, institutional structures that support humanities computing, such as DDH, 'should reflect the nature of the practice as it has emerged in the last few decades' (2008: 259). Establishing our own place in this way requires the taking on by a humanities computing academic department of status generated by activities which are recognized by the academic community as a peer activity. Thus, one finds DDH using the status language of 'academic department', 'professors' and 'scholarly research' to establish its own place in the hierarchy of academia. We will return to the question of power and turf shortly.

The nature of humanities computing as interdisciplinary is also explored by McCarty and Short, where we find their 'Clouds of Knowing' schematic map, which is described as being:

> ... divided into three zones. At the centre of the map, as at the core of the field, is a large, uncertainly bounded area we call the 'Methodological Commons': an abstraction for the computational methods that the various disciplines of application share. Above the Commons, in the rectangular boxes, are multidisciplinary groups with which humanities computing directly interacts. Beneath the Commons are ranged broad areas of learning that crucially bear upon our understanding of

the field, with some indication within each of the subject-areas of importance to humanities computing. (McCarty and Short, 2002)

Thus, McCarty and Short's thinking about humanities computing/digital humanities draws on a strong sense of its interdisciplinary nature. Humanities computing – by being a kind of 'methodological commons' – brings the experiences and understandings from many disciplines to bear upon the scholarly interests of the humanities as a whole. As they observe, 'what these Clouds are intended to denote is not, say, comprehensive mastery of philosophy et al., rather working knowledge of specific areas as they apply to our practice' (McCarty and Short, 2002).

But Is This Work Research?

'But sure,' I hear some of you say as you read this, 'I can see that DDH's project work clearly can provide a way of working that would *support* research by humanists – but to what extent *is* it research in and of itself?' To a large extent, this depends upon to what degree one is prepared to acknowledge that the technical work carried out within humanities computing departments such as DDH has its own independent research interest – coupled to research in the humanities, but also parallel to it and in some significant degree independent of the research which it also supports.

This is one of the points where we divert from Jennifer Edmond's 2005 article mentioned earlier. In our view, Edmond does not really recognize that the technical work has any independent research output from the humanities research which it supports. She talks in terms of investment in support for humanities scholarship done by humanities scholars – indeed, the title of her paper, referring to the professional intermediary and her placing of this individual in a 'value chain' (2005: 372–3) that connects the researcher to the technology, makes it clear that in her view the intermediary (although a highly skilled professional) is primarily filling the job of making humanities researchers more effective in their use of the technology to support their research interests than they would otherwise be. She does acknowledge that the intermediary 'should not be perceived as a technician so much as a productive dialogue partner and facilitator' (2005: 374), and she also acknowledges that the intermediary needs to do work similar to research in some ways, including reading journals, attending conferences and networking with key leaders (2005: 376) – although interestingly the creation of any independent research *output* is not included as one of her intermediary's activities. In the end, however, the intermediary's main role is to provide assistance and advice to the scholar (2005: 378). She hints at the weakness of this person's position within an academically driven institution by recognizing that her position does not fit any academic 'development pathways', and points out that institutions should find appropriate alternative opportunities to support their development. In my view, it is exactly this kind of position, with its lack of academic status within a university, which is likely to cause it to become unsustainable in the long term.

So what happens if we try to appropriate the word 'research' rather than 'support' to DDH's kind of collaborative work, and recognize that it has its own research agenda? The definition of what is research is not one which I can speak about from any kind of theoretical basis. Furthermore, what constitutes research varies between different fields: think of the difference between the humanities and the sciences, for example.

However, DDH work has, without question, at least some of the characteristics of research, in particular in terms of research outputs. For example, DDH staff publish about their work in academic journals. The publications are based on issues that have arisen out of the work done across a range of projects, and is not tied to any one of them in particular. What we write about is meant to be new thinking about the issues that we raise, and indeed we have found that the reviewers of the journals in which we publish think so too.

The 2008 Research Assessment Exercise (RAE) provides some degree of independent evidence that this work qualifies as academic research. As the RAE website itself says: 'The primary purpose of the RAE 2008 was to produce quality profiles for each submission of research activity made by institutions.' It is used by major funding agencies in the UK 'to determine their grant for research to the institutions which they fund'. It was a peer review process, with each department submitting evidence of its research to a panel of academic peers who assessed it and rated its quality in international terms.

DDH (with our sister organization at King's: the Centre for e-Research [CeRch]), was submitted by King's to the 2008 RAE as an academic research department for the first time. There was no digital humanities panel in RAE 2008, but we were submitted with 30 or so other UK departments to the panel which assessed information studies.

A large number of DDH staff (not only people who one thinks of in the normal way as academics) were submitted as researchers, and one of the RAE measures of quality was an assessment of the four pieces of research output from each staff member submitted. DDH staff's research outputs were a combination of traditional research products (writings in journals, books, and so on), but also the co-created digital resources that DDH developed in collaboration with partners from the older disciplines such as the *Clergy of the Church of England* (CCEd, 2008), or the *Prosopography of Anglo-Saxon England* (PASE, 2007). Indeed, these same digital resources were often also submitted separately by our discipline collaborators to their panel as a part of their submission.

The results showed that the quality of work by DDH and CeRch stood up very well as research as far as our peer review panel was concerned. Thirty-five per cent of our submitted research outputs were awarded the highest possible ranking (4*) as 'world-leading' (best in our group), and a further 30 per cent of the remaining was classified as 3*: 'internationally excellent in terms of originality'. Overall, our results were either first or an equal second with all the 21 departments that submitted to our panel. Furthermore, our results compared favourably with the RAE results from across the entire School of Humanities at KCL, which was ranked, overall, as among the very best in the UK. This result, I should reiterate, was from a submission that contained many contributions from people not elsewhere normally recognized as academics.

Power, Turf and Collegiality

If the staff model at DDH, which blends a mix of specialists who are not normally considered academics with people with conventional academic titles, has achieved the success which I believe it has, we can ask if this model is reproducible elsewhere. It seems to me that one of the problems, particularly in North America perhaps, is one of turf, and has at its foundation the distinction between faculty and staff which forms the basis of North American academia.

Indeed, in North America there are three ranks in the status of professional staff, with their different levels of authority and status: top are the tenured faculty, second are the untenured faculty – working like crazy to become tenured themselves – and at the bottom are the other professional, technical folk, who are viewed as a kind of 'support staff' for ventures that are run by the faculty. Furthermore, I believe there is a great deal of vested interest in keeping things this way, and prioritizing the accomplishment of the faculty even at the expense of other professional staff.

For whatever reason (and I don't think the reasons are entirely principled in ways that are necessarily sympathetic to the needs of academia), the situation in the UK is different. First there is no tenure, and academic staff cannot, then, be divided between tenured and non-tenured. Furthermore, although there are clear paths through the academic ranks for the teaching staff, there are also (albeit less clear) paths for research staff too. In general, posts in the teaching stream are called reader or lecturer, and in the research stream they are called research fellows. In both teaching and research streams, the top ranking post is professor, and in the UK this term is generally reserved for very senior academic staff who are seen as having made a significant contribution to their field or institution. Furthermore, not all academic staff, not even all professors, have PhDs, although this is, of course, the norm. Indeed, I know of two professors at King's who do not in fact have PhDs, although they are both recognized as intellectual leaders in their respective fields. As a result of all this, the identity of staff at a place like DDH is not so straightforward, and people cannot quite so easily be put in one category or another.

An important aspect of what happens at DDH is in the promotion of collegiality between DDH staff and our partners from the older humanities disciplines in our projects. McCarty (2008) notes the importance of collegiality as a way of establishing a research place for the work we do when he notes: '… the support of research simply must become a collegial, collaborative activity, which is to say, not "support" as it has been known.' He notes later in the same article that: 'The major centres built to support Humanities Computing […] have vanished, replaced in prominence and influence by those for which collaborative collegiality obtains.' DDH exemplifies exactly this approach to collegiality between the digital humanities and established humanities disciplines, and promotes the view that the language that DDH 'supports' scholarship for the rest of our school only tells a part of the story.

Furthermore, and I think perhaps not evident especially to a North American audience, the collegiality as practised by DDH is not only between faculty at DDH and faculty within other departments – say, computing science – at King's and elsewhere. It also extends to include a collegial way of working between those whom North Americans would recognize as 'faculty' and those they would not. In this sense, then, McCarty's distinction between 'centres of support' and 'centres of collegiality' does not quite tell the whole story to North Americans about what happens at DDH. Collegiality at DDH goes beyond interaction between full academic staff in our department and academics in other departments, but is also encouraged and supported for professional technical specialists, who are recognized as intellectual workers in their own right.

Indeed, I like to think that I am an example of this kind of a role for professional staff within DDH. For years, much of my work within DDH/CCH has been closer to what in the computing world would be developer rather than academic, and was centred on project development work. It involved, across a substantial range of projects, a long-term and close collaboration between me as well as others in DDH/CCH and colleagues from the older disciplines, who bring their historical or literary or whatever perspective to the projects. Indeed, although these projects which we are involved in have a significant technical component to them, at the bottom of it all one finds scholarly goals for them that can be recognized in the humanities. A more extended statement of this can be found in Bradley (2009).

The development work – the application of the technology to humanities materials – is challenging, and requires intensive interchange of ideas in both directions. We within DDH grow in our understanding of the challenges involved in applying technology to a range of different humanities issues, and from this comes some part of our research agenda, and our legitimacy as colleagues rather than support staff to our partners from the older disciplines.

Conclusions

In conclusion, the way that DDH has operated has included a significant effort to recognize the intellectual contribution from all kinds of participants – both those who in North America would be considered academic and non-academic. This has been made possible by recognizing some significant part of the work, which at first glance might appear to be essentially technical, as research within the digital humanities agenda – research carried on in parallel with that of our partners from the older humanities disciplines. Our results from the RAE show, I think convincingly, that this can be done, and the technical work we do, particularly when supported by our own publications, can be done in a way that makes it entirely legitimate as academic output. To achieve this, the language and the thinking model that supports it needs to be thought of in terms of 'egalitarity' between the technical work and the discipline work, rather than purely as 'service'.

This is facilitated by allowing the technically oriented staff to develop their own appropriate professional expertise, so that this expertise and understanding can develop outside of the constraints of only a single project. Thus, this kind of staff need more than term appointments that are tied to funding for particular projects, and they need, in spite of the difficulties which this represents, to be supported when they take time to work on their own research agenda, and to produce their own research output.

I know that operating an academic unit in this way – particularly in North America perhaps – is not a straightforward re-alignment of thinking, particularly where the present model there, as tied up as it is with issues of academic turf and authority, makes it difficult to acknowledge a different kind of professional work as, at least in some ways, equal to scholarly work. I take heart in a series of messages written by Wendell Piez in *Humanist* way back in 2005 that specifically addresses the differences between development and scholarly research, but also points out how they need to work together with a sense of collaboration, contribution and equality:

> The Developer role is a different thing from the role of the scholar, making its own demands and constituting a very special kind of contribution, [and] Humanities Computing [HC] will have to adapt itself increasingly to more of a collaborative model. That there can be a very effective and powerful 'core collaboration' between a scholar and another person [...] has actually been recognized for some time within HC. The danger of this kind of arrangement goes a bit beyond ordinary collaborations, because the skills required to do the development work [...] are far afield and remote from what Humanists are commonly called on to do [...]. [S]uch a collaboration works well when prejudices and misconceptions about the unknown are set aside, challenging the ego but opening the mind ... another reason those of us who have been 'bit by the bug' of such work like it so much. (Piez, 2005)

That arrangements such as those which I have described here may challenge prejudices and misconceptions within academia seems to me to be beyond doubt. However, that it is worth doing can be seen clearly in what has been achieved at DDH.

Acknowledgements

Much of what I have written here has developed out of my own experience of CCH, now DDH, but also from discussions with Willard McCarty, Tamara Lopez, Gabriel Bodard and Paul Spence. I must also acknowledge the contribution of this volume's editors, whose feedback has had a very positive effect on the text you are reading. In the end, how CCH operated, and DDH now operates, is due to the vision of Harold Short who, as director of CCH over many years, has been constant in his view and his actions that the technical work in our joint projects is worthy of recognition of a kind similar to how scholarly work is valued within academia. For this, I personally owe him a debt of gratitude, as do others at DDH. Of course, whatever is written here is my responsibility.

References

BoB, *The Breaking of Britain: Cross Border Society and Scottish Independence 1216–1314* (2011), available at: <http://www.breakingofbritain.ac.uk/> (accessed 13 April 2011).

Bradley, J.D., 'What the Developer Saw: An Outsider's View of Annotation, Interpretation and Scholarship', in Ray Siemens and Gary Shawver (eds), *New Paths for Computing Humanists: A Volume Celebrating and Recognizing Ian Lancashire*, Digital Studies/Le champ numérique (ISSN 1918-3666) 1.1 (13 May 2009), available at: <http://www.digitalstudies.org/ojs/index.php/digital_studies/article/view/143/202> (accessed 5 April 2010).

Bradley, J.D. and H. Short, 'Using Formal Structures to Create Complex Relationships: The Prosopography of the Byzantine Empire – A Case Study', in K.S.B. Keats-Rohan (ed.), *Resourcing Sources Prosopographica et Geneologica*, vol. 7 (Oxford. Unit for Prosopographical Research, Linacre College, 2002).

Bradley, J.D. and H. Short, 'Texts into Databases: The Evolving Field of New-style Prosopography', *Literary and Linguistic Computing* 20 (Suppl. 1) (2005): 3–24.

Bradley, J.D. and P. Vetch, 'Supporting Annotation as a Scholarly Tool: Experiences from the Online Chopin Variorum Edition', *Literary and Linguistic Computing* 22.2 (2007): 225–42.

CCEd, *Clergy of the Church of England* (2008), available at: <http://www.theclergydatabase.org.uk> (accessed 5 April 2010).

Dix, F., J. Finlay, G. Abowd and R. Beale, *Human–Computer Interaction* (Harlow, England: Pearson Prentice Hall, 2004).

Edmond, J., 'The Role of the Professional Intermediary in Expanding the Humanities Computing Base', *Literary and Linguistic Computing* 20.3 (2005): 367–80.

Elliott, T. et al., *EpiDoc: Epigraphic Documents in TEI XML* (2006–08), available at: <http://epidoc.sourceforge.net/> (accessed 5 April 2010).

Fine Rolls, *Henry III Fine Rolls Project: A Window into English History, 1216–1272* (2007), available at: <www.finerollshenry3.org.uk/home.html> (accessed 5 April 2010).

Finken, S., *Truth Is a Thing of This World: A Foucaultian Analysis of the Discursive Construction and Constitution of Cooperative Design* (1998), available at: <http://citeseer.ist.psu.edu/679102.html> (accessed 5 April 2010).

Langscape, *Langscape: The Language of Landscape; Reading the Anglo-Saxon Countryside* (2008), available at: <http://www.langscape.org.uk/index.html> (accessed April 2010).

McCarty, W., *New Splashings in an Old Pond: The Cohesibility of Humanities Computing* (2002), available at: <http://computerphilologie.uni-muenchen.de/jg02/mccarty.html> (accessed 5 April 2010).

McCarty, W., 'What's Going On?' *Literary and Linguistic Computing* 23.3 (2008): 253–62.

McCarty, W. and H. Short, *Mapping the Field* (2002), available at: <http://www.allc.org/content/pubs/map.html> (accessed April 2010).

Mitchell, W., A.S. Inouye and M.S. Blumenthal, *Beyond Productivity: Information Technology, Innovation, and Creativity* (Washington, DC: The National Academies Press, 2003).

OCVE, *Online Chopin Varioruum Edition* (2006, 2010), available at: <http://www.ocve.org.uk/> (accessed 5 April 2010).

PASE, *Prosopography of Anglo-Saxon England* (2007, 2010), available at: <http://www.pase.ac.uk/> (accessed 5 April 2010).

PBW, *Prosopography of the Byzantine World* (2006), available at: <http://www.pbw.kcl.ac.uk/> (accessed April 2010).

Piez, W., *A Response to Thread 'beyond being dubious and gloomy'*, *Humanist* 18.760 (3 May 2005).

Pliny, *Pliny: A Note Manager* (2009), available at: <http://pliny.DDH.kcl.ac.uk/> (accessed 5 April 2010).

PoMS, *Paradox of Medieval Scotland 1093–1286: Social Relationships and Identities before the Wars of Independence* (2010), available at: <http://www.poms.ac.uk/> (accessed April 2010).

RAE, *RAE 2008: Research Assessment Exercise* (2008), available at: <http://www.rae.ac.uk/> (accessed 5 April 2010).

Short, H., 'Digital Humanities: Prospects for Collaboration', presentation given at Institute for the Arts & Humanities, UNC Chapel Hill (6 November 2007).

Sperberg-McQueen, C.M., 'Text in the Electronic Age: Textual Study and Text Encoding, with Examples from Medieval Texts', *Literary and Linguistic Computing* 6.1 (1991): 46–61.

Zorich, D.M., *A Survey of Digital Humanities Centers in the United States* (Washington, DC: Council on Library and Information Resources, 2008), available at: <http://www.clir.org/pubs/abstract/pub143abst.html> (accessed 5 April 2010).

Chapter 3

A Collaboration about a Collaboration: The Authorship of *King Henry VI, Part Three*

Hugh Craig and John Burrows

Not one of the plays included in Heminge and Condell's First Folio, *Mr William Shakespeares Comedies, Histories, & Tragedies* (1623) has ever been successfully 'de-attributed' in its entirety from that author's dramatic corpus. But the consensus of modern scholars is that several of the plays are to some extent collaborative. Among these, no other has presented scholars interested in attribution with such intractable problems as the one there entitled *The third Part of Henry the Sixt, with the death of the Duke of Yorke*. The problems are relieved for some scholars but exacerbated for others by the existence of another version (or perhaps another play) published in Octavo in 1595 as *The True Tragedie of Richard Duke of Yorke, and the death of good King Henry the Sixt ...* . We shall take the Folio text as the basis of our inquiry because its inclusion there justifies an initial hypothesis that Shakespeare had a part in its authorship.[1]

In attempting a fresh investigation, in a volume honouring the work of Harold Short, we follow his admirable example in collaborative scholarship and draw such advantage as we can from our many years of working with each other. We even considered representing the actual evolution of the present article by couching it as a dialogue, but hardly knew which words to put in whose mouth. We certainly did not care to take Plato as a model. Which of us would dare assume the role of Socrates? Which of us would endure the role of those hapless interlocutors who are now and then allowed a 'Pray, do continue', a 'Please explain', or even a mildly presumptuous 'Well said!'?

Like many history plays of the period, the play itself, *3 Henry VI*, is loosely knit. In this last phase of the Wars of the Roses, battle scenes are surrounded by bouts of 'flyting' and of political diatribe. There is a long scene set in the French court (where they speak better English than some of their forebears in *Henry V*). There are reflective soliloquies like those of *Richard II* and Machiavellian ones like those of *Richard III*. Here, too, as in *Richard III*, Margaret of Anjou delivers notable (and not unjustifiable) invectives against both foe and friend. While much of this is reminiscent of Shakespeare, it does not often declare itself as uniquely

---

1 The other plays in the same trio, *1 Henry VI* and *2 Henry VI*, are also widely accepted as collaborative. For recent evidence that Shakespeare and Marlowe each had a share in the composition of *1 Henry VI*, see Craig (2009).

his. There are no Hotspurs or Glendowers and no voice at all of Eastcheap. There is no consistent imaginative vigour in the presentation of the secondary characters (several of whom reappear as ghosts on the eve of Bosworth Field in *Richard III*, urging the king to 'Despair and die!') The Shakespearean note is strongest, perhaps, towards the end of *3 Henry VI*. Richard of Gloucester, as represented in the closing scenes, might simply leave the stage and re-enter as king in the funeral procession and dark wooing that open *Richard III*.

Two other striking scenes concern the widow of that funeral, the object of that wooing. In Act III, Scene ii Edward, lately possessed of the crown, importunes a reluctant Lady Anne Grey; in Act IV, Scene i, he presents her as his bride. Both scenes include brisk exchanges involving Anne, Edward, his brothers and his chief allies. The ingenuous Clarence expresses opposition. Gloucester holds his peace and bides his time.

But the most memorable scenes of all lie in a sombre piece of theatrical bravura, emblematic of all civil war. In a sequence towards the end of Act II, King Henry, despised by his foes and rejected by his friends, broods over the battlefield, an ineffectual dove of peace. He watches a single combat between Clifford and Gloucester, the old butcher and the young. He sees a son discover that he has killed his father and a father that he has killed his son. And then a band of leading Yorkists decapitate Clifford's corpse, pass the head about and taunt it for its unaccustomed silence.

Although the belief, once widely held, that *3 Henry VI* is entirely Shakespeare's work has had less currency in more recent years, it was still supported by Andrew S. Cairncross in 1964.[2] The scholarly consensus nowadays is that it is probably a collaborative work. Even there, however, it is a long time since anyone showed the confidence with which John Dover Wilson assigns the different scenes of the play as originals or light retouchings or thorough revisions.[3] An historical summary of the case is offered in the Introduction of the most recent Arden edition of the play.[4] The editors, John D. Cox and Eric Rasmussen, turn at last, with perceptible relief, to Roland Barthes' doctrine that questions of authorship are a bourgeois caprice and not really worth attention. But, before surrendering, they report that, besides Shakespeare, the candidates who have found most scholarly support are Robert Greene, Christopher Marlowe and George Peele. We added Thomas Kyd to the group because Brian Vickers has recently argued that Kyd collaborated more than once with the young Shakespeare and has associated Kyd with *1 Henry VI*.[5] (As we proceeded with our analyses, George Chapman and Anthony Munday came briefly into view, but did not justify inclusion.) We shall set off, then, with five recognized candidates in view, but proceed for a time in such a way as to leave their various contemporaries on an equal footing with them.

---

2   Cairncross (1964): xliii.
3   Wilson (1952): 127–206 *passim*.
4   Cox and Rasmussen (2001): 44–9, 104–5.
5   Vickers (2008).

Our tasks, as we see them, are two: to determine whether the methods of computational stylistics give evidence of Shakespeare's presence; and to consider whether other dramatists can be shown as having a hand in the play.

As the basis for comparison with *3 Henry VI*, we took a set of 54 plays from Craig's collection of digital texts. We believe they comprise all of the surviving well-authenticated single-author English plays of the period between 1580 and 1599. The full set is listed in Table 3.1. It does not include translations like Kyd's *Cornelia*, closet dramas like Fulke Greville's *Mustapha*, or recognized collaborations like *Titus Andronicus*. (This last, however, along with some plays written just after 1600, will be used for corroborative purposes.) Of the 54 plays, 31 are by the candidates we have named. Sixteen of these are Shakespeare's, five Marlowe's, five Peele's, four Greene's and one is Kyd's. The remaining 23 plays are distributed among ten other dramatists. Eight are by Lyly, three each by Jonson and Wilson, and two each by Chapman and Dekker. Haughton, Lodge, Munday, Nashe and Porter have one apiece. In our opening analyses, we shall treat these 54 as separate plays whose authorship is known, but not as members of separate authorial groups. All told, our 16 Shakespeare plays amounted to 338,193 words. The 15 plays by Greene, Kyd, Marlowe and Peele amounted to 230,736. And the other 23 plays amounted to 412,124.

For the first series of tests, we chose the Delta procedure[6] and used it to compare a succession of target texts, each of them a whole play, with the 54 plays just mentioned. Our own experience and that of other scholars over a period of almost a decade confirms the original suggestion that Delta is at its best in winnowing a large group of texts, identifying those that show least difference from a given target text and effectively excluding those that differ more. Its further virtue is that, when all the Delta scores are unusually high, there is reason to suspect some kind of mismatch. This may stem from a marked difference, as of genre, between the target text and the rest, or it may imply that the true author of the current target text is not to be found among those with whose work it is being compared. A particular caveat must always be kept in mind: while Delta has mostly been used on authorial problems, with a high rate of success, it is inherently a ranking procedure. To begin, as we shall, by comparing the target text with other individual texts is to allow *any* strong affinities, authorial or not, to reveal themselves. But to make the best use of Delta as a test of authorship, the target text should be compared with authorial groups of texts. That will be undertaken at a later point in our argument. It should also be noted that small differences in Delta scores can sometimes yield false rankings. For that reason, it is rarely advisable to use Delta alone.

------

6 Burrows (2003). This article represents the Roberto Busa Award Lecture, delivered in New York in June 2001. See also Burrows (2002). For two assessments of the method, see Hoover (2004) and Argamon (2008). While well disposed towards the method, both Hoover and Argamon offer valuable criticisms and suggest possible changes. For a part-precursor, see Forsyth, Holmes and Tse (1999): 393.

Table 3.1 List of plays

'Genre' and 'Date' as in Harbage and Schoenbaum, *Annals of English Drama 975-1700* (Philadelphia, 1964)

Sets: 1, *Henry VI Part 3*; 2, fifty-four single author well-attributed plays dated 1580-1599; 3, test plays

Author	Title	Genre	Date	Copytext	Date of copytext	Set
Chapman, George	*Blind Beggar of Alexandria*	Comedy	1596	STC4965	1598	2
Chapman, George	*Bussy d'Ambois*	Foreign History	1604	STC4966	1607	3
Chapman, George	*Humorous Day's Mirth*	Comedy	1597	STC4987	1599	2
Chapman, George	*May-Day*	Comedy	1602	STC4980	1611	3
Dekker, Thomas	*If This Be Not a Good Play, the Devil Is in It*	Comedy	1611	STC6507	1612	3
Dekker, Thomas	*Old Fortunatus*	Comedy	1599	STC6517	1600	2
Dekker, Thomas	*Shoemaker's Holiday*	Comedy	1599	STC6523	1600	2
Greene, Robert	*Alphonsus*	Heroical romance	1587	STC12233	1599	2
Greene, Robert	*Friar Bacon and Friar Bungay*	Comedy	1589	STC 12267	1594	2
Greene, Robert	*James IV*	History	1590	STC12308	1598	2
Greene, Robert	*Orlando Furioso*	Romantic Comedy	1591	STC12265	1594	2
Haughton, William	*Englishmen for My Money*	Comedy	1598	STC12931	1616	2
Jonson, Ben	*Case is Altered*	Comedy	1597	STC14757	1609	2
Jonson, Ben	*Cynthia's Revels*	Comedy	1601	STC14773	1601	3
Jonson, Ben	*Every Man in his Humour*	Comedy	1598	STC14766	1601	2
Jonson, Ben	*Every Man out of his Humour*	Comedy	1599	STC14767	1600	2
Jonson, Ben	*Sejanus his Fall*	Tragedy	1603	STC14782	1605	3
Kyd, Thomas	*Spanish Tragedy*	Tragedy	1587	STC15086	1592	2
Lodge, Thomas	*Wounds of Civil War*	Classical History	1588	STC16678	1594	2
Lyly, John	*Campaspe*	Classical legend (Comedy)	1584	STC17048a	1584	2
Lyly, John	*Endimion*	Classical legend (Comedy)	1588	STC17050	1591	2

Author	Title	Genre		STC		
Lyly, John	Gallathea	Classical legend (Comedy)	1585	STC17080	1592	2
Lyly, John	Love's Metamorphosis	Pastoral	1590	STC17082	1601	2
Lyly, John	Midas	Comedy	1589	STC17083	1592	2
Lyly, John	Mother Bombie	Comedy	1589	STC17084	1594	2
Lyly, John	Sappho and Phao	Classical legend (Comedy)	1584	STC17086	1584	2
Lyly, John	Woman in the Moon	Comedy	1593	STC17090	1597	2
Marlowe, Christopher	Edward II	History	1592	STC17437	1594	2
Marlowe, Christopher	Jew of Malta	Tragedy	1589	STC17412	1633	2
Marlowe, Christopher	Massacre at Paris	Foreign History	1593	STC17423	1594	2
Marlowe, Christopher	Tamburlaine the Great Part 1	heroical romance	1587	STC17425	1590	2
Marlowe, Christopher	Tamburlaine the Great Part 2	Heroical romance	1588	STC17425	1590	2
Munday, Anthony	John a Kent and John a Cumber	Pseudo-history	1589	Malone Soc. Reprint	1923	2
Nashe, Thomas	Summer's Last Will	Comedy	1592	STC18376	1600	2
Peele, George	Arraignment of Paris	Classical legend (Pastoral)	1581	STC15930	1584	2
Peele, George	Battle of Alcazar	Foreign History	1589	STC19531	1594	2
Peele, George	Edward I	History	1591	STC19535	1593	2
Peele, George	King David and Fair Bethsabe	Biblical history	1587	STC19540	1594	2
Peele, George	Old Wives Tale	Romance	1590	STC19545	1595	2
Porter, Henry	Two Angry Women of Abington Part 1	Comedy	1588	STC20121.5	1599	2
Shakespeare, William	As You Like It	Comedy	1599	STC22273	1623	2
Shakespeare, William	Comedy of Errors	Comedy	1592	STC22273	1623	2
Shakespeare, William	Hamlet	Tragedy	1601	STC22276	1604	3
Shakespeare, William	Henry IV Part 1	History	1597	STC22280	1598	2
Shakespeare, William	Henry IV Part 2	History	1597	STC22288	1600	2
Shakespeare, William	Henry V	History	1599	STC22273	1623	2
Shakespeare, William	Julius Caesar	Tragedy	1599	STC22273	1623	2

Table 3.1 List of plays (continued)

Shakespeare, William	King John	History	1591	STC22273	1623	2
Shakespeare, William	Love's Labours Lost	Comedy	1595	STC22294	1598	2
Shakespeare, William	Merchant of Venice	Comedy	1596	STC22296	1600	2
Shakespeare, William	Midsummer Night's Dream	Comedy	1595	STC22302	1600	2
Shakespeare, William	Much Ado about Nothing	Comedy	1598	STC22304	1600	2
Shakespeare, William	Richard II	History	1595	STC22307	1597	2
Shakespeare, William	Richard III	History	1593	STC22314	1597	2
Shakespeare, William	Romeo and Juliet	Tragedy	1595	STC22323	1599	2
Shakespeare, William	Taming of the Shrew	Comedy	1594	STC22273	1623	2
Shakespeare, William	Twelfth Night	Comedy	1600	STC22273	1623	3
Shakespeare, William	Two Gentlemen of Verona	Comedy	1593	STC22273	1623	2
Shakespeare, William and Peele, George	Titus Andronicus	Tragedy	1594	STC22328	1594	3
Unknown	Henry VI Part 3	History	1591	STC22273	1623	1
Unknown	Henry VI Part 3	History	1591	STC21006	1595	1
Wilson, Robert	Cobbler's Prophecy	Comedy	1590	STC25781	1594	2
Wilson, Robert	Three Ladies of London	Moral	1581	STC25784	1584	2
Wilson, Robert	Three Lords and Three Ladies of London	Moral	1588	STC25783	1590	2

For each of a number of specimens (in this case the 54 plays specified), its Delta score for the current target text rests upon the behaviour of a set of variables (a chosen set of words). How did we establish the list of word-variables used in the Delta tests that follow? The texts in Craig's main corpus are based on old-spelling early printed versions. They are edited to the extent that all instances of a predetermined set of 201 words, covering all the common function words, have been standardized, so that precise counts of these words can be made. Some function words that have identical forms for distinct grammatical functions have been tagged to separate them: *that* as a conjunction can be counted separately from *that* as a demonstrative and *that* as a relative, and so on. Forms that are contracted and separated in the original texts are regularized so that *I'm* counts as one instance of *I* and one of *am*, while *him selfe* counts as one instance of *himself*. To arrive at our final list of 150 function words, we counted all instances of the 201 function words in the 54 texts, ranked them in order of total instances across the corpus, and chose the top 150.[7]

Delta operates upon each specimen-text in turn. The standardized frequency of each listed word is compared with its mean-frequency in the whole set (or its mean-frequency in some other suitable set) and a z-score is calculated. The corresponding entries for the target text are treated in the same way. Absolute differences between the z-scores for the target text and those for each specimen-text are determined. The mean of its absolute differences from the target text is the Delta score for that specimen.[8] Provided the number of specimens suffices, as it does in the present case, the full range of Delta scores for a given target text can be transformed into z-scores. These 'Delta z-scores', which we shall employ at a later stage of our argument, allow well-matched comparisons of the results for different target texts.

Of the Delta scores for a given set of specimens, the lowest will be those that differ least from the target text. When the specimens are authorial sets, each embracing several texts, the true author of the target text is almost always among

---

7   The list is as follows: a, about, again, against, all, am, an, and, another, any, are, art[verb], as, at, be, because, been, before, being, both, but, by[preposition], can, cannot, could, did, do, done, dost, doth, down, ere, even, ever, every, for[conjunction], for[preposition], from, had, hast, hath, have, he, hence, her[adjective], her[personal pronoun], here, him, himself, his, how, I, if, in[adverb], in[preposition], is, it, like[preposition], many, may, me, might, mine, more, most, much, must, my, myself, never, no[adjective], no[exclamation], none, nor, not, nothing, now, o, of, off, on[adverb], on[preposition], one, only, or, other, our, out, own, shall, shalt, she, should, since, so[adverb of degree], so[adverb of manner or conjunction], some, still, such, than, that[conjunction], that[demonstrative], that[relative], the, thee, their, them, then, there, these, they, thine, this, those, thou, though, through, thus, thy, till, to[infinitive], to[preposition], too, unto, up[adverb], upon[preposition], us, very, was, we, well, were, what, when, where, which[relative], while, who[interrogative], who[relative], whom, whose, why, will[verb], with, within, without, ye, yet, you, your.

8   A formal definition and a more complete account of the procedure can be seen in Burrows (2002).

Table 3.2 Lowest eight Delta scores for each of eight plays

3 Henry VI Folio		3 Henry VI Octavo		Hamlet		Twelfth Night	
Spanish Tragedy	0.652	Spanish Tragedy	0.681	2 Henry IV	0.675	As You Like It	0.622
Richard II	0.680	Richard II	0.693	1 Henry IV	0.747	Merchant of V.	0.653
Edward II	0.693	Richard III	0.699	Love's Labours	0.749	Much Ado	0.721
Richard III	0.747	Edward II	0.719	Henry V	0.751	Taming of Shrew	0.732
Edward I	0.754	Edward I	0.725	Richard II	0.771	Case is Altered	0.741
Friar Bacon	0.769	King John	0.750	Julius Caesar	0.771	Two Gentlemen of V.	0.776
King John	0.784	Friar Bacon	0.788	Richard III	0.772	Every Man out	0.779
Blind Beggar	0.828	2 Henry IV	0.832	Merchant of V.	0.783	2 Henry IV	0.791

Dekker, If This Be Not ...		Chapman, May Day		Chapman, Bussy		Jonson, Sejanus	
Old Fortunatus	0.815	Much Ado	0.769	Henry V	0.834	Henry V	0.912
Shoemaker	0.955	As You Like It	0.780	2 Henry IV	0.960	Richard II	0.989
Romeo and Juliet	0.967	Blind Beggar	0.783	Midsummer Night's D.	0.966	Julius Caesar	1.042
1 Henry IV	0.978	Every Man out	0.799	Richard II	0.978	2 Henry IV	1.056
Jew of Malta	0.981	Taming of Shrew	0.804	As You Like It	0.978	Three Lords and L.	1.057
Cobbler's Prophecy	0.998	Every Man	0.806	Old Fortunatus	0.985	Richard III	1.072
2 Henry IV	1.000	Merchant of V.	0.811	Merchant of V.	0.995	Summer's Last Will	1.073
Richard II	1.019	Humorous Day	0.837	Blind Beggar	0.995	Tamburlaine Pt. 1	1.075

the sets with the lowest Delta scores. An inference about its authorship is legitimate and usually holds good when other tests are brought into play.

But in such cases as the one under consideration, it is best to begin with single texts as specimens. Where Shakespeare has 16 plays and Kyd only one, it is unreasonable to match their 'authorial means'. Where, in some dramatists much more than others, the change of style from one genre to another is pronounced, the concept of stable authorial signatures must be approached with caution. The scores set out in Table 3.2 would not guarantee, if guarantee were needed, that Shakespeare wrote *Hamlet* or *Twelfth Night*. They do show, however, that both of those plays have strong affinities for others in Shakespeare's repertoire – and that, in a comparison with plays by many other dramatists, those affinities are elicited by the Delta procedure.

Of the 54 specimens in our set, plays by Shakespeare rank first to eighth when *Hamlet* is the target text. Of the other great tragedies, only *Julius Caesar* appears: being written after 1600, the others are not among our 54. The top eight Delta scores for *Hamlet* all lie below 0.8, as do the top eight for *Twelfth Night*. But, among the plays that show most affinity for *Twelfth Night* are two of Ben Jonson's comedies. Although the outcome for *Hamlet* and *Twelfth Night*, both written shortly after our boundary of 1600, speaks so plainly of Shakespeare's authorship, genre seems to be another factor in the scores for *Twelfth Night*.

Before addressing ourselves to the scores for other plays set out in Table 3.2, the possible influence of yet another factor should be entertained. (The following comments draw upon the more detailed work described below in the Appendix.) In a field where Shakespeare has 16 entries out of 54 and Kyd only one, a statistical bias towards Shakespeare might very well damage the results. Now if the behaviour of the plays were free of such influences as authorship and genre, any specified 16 of 54 would yield only two or three of the first eight – not all eight as in *Hamlet* or even six as in *Twelfth Night*. Nor, at the other extreme, would Kyd's *Spanish Tragedy* ever be likely to achieve first place, as it does for both versions of *3 Henry VI*. These few examples, perhaps, are enough to show that Delta scores are no mere chance effects. The answer we seek lies deeper.

We should next consider that, almost irrespective of the target text being tested, the 16 entries for plays by Shakespeare usually yield more than their share of the lowest Delta scores and far fewer than their share of the highest. The work described in our Appendix suggests that this is not a statistical artefact, the product of a prejudiced analysis. The diversity, one from another, of Shakespeare's 16 early plays may offer part of an answer. Whatever the target text, it seems, something in Shakespeare is likely to show an affinity for it. But a study of many instances also suggests that, in such basic stylistic features as are reflected in the frequency patterning of very common words, plays by Shakespeare must somehow be typical of their times. All this notwithstanding, the very lowest Delta scores of a given set usually include texts by its true author, a truth that holds good even when he is only sparsely represented. And when that is not true, it is seldom difficult to see why.

A clear impression of all this can be gained from the lower part of Table 3.2 where four other plays dating from soon after 1600 are taken as target texts and compared with the main set of 54 plays dating from 1580 to 1599. By the turn of the century, all of our main candidates except Shakespeare had died. The early dramatists who were still active included George Chapman, Thomas Dekker and Ben Jonson. When the target text is Dekker's *If This Be Not a Good Play* ..., the only Dekker specimens in the 54 rank first and second. But the pattern of success observed so far weakens when the target text is Chapman's *May-Day*: in that case, his *The Blind Beggar of Alexandria* ranks third and his *Humorous Day's Mirth* only eighth. When Chapman's *Bussy d'Ambois* becomes the target text, his *Blind Beggar* ranks eighth and his *Humorous Day's Mirth* has so little in common with the high heroics of *Bussy* that it ranks only 26th out of 54. Here, too, the lowest of the Delta scores is higher than what we have been seeing, suggesting that none of the 54 plays has much affinity for the target text. That is also true of Ben Jonson's *Sejanus*, which finds no near match among the three Jonson comedies included in our set. For Jonson's *Cynthia's Revels*, however (in scores not shown in Table 3.2), the three Jonson comedies rank first, seventh and tenth. Jonson's other Roman tragedy, *Catiline* (1611), might well show an affinity for *Sejanus*. But that comparison lies beyond our present ambit. *Bussy d'Ambois* and *Sejanus*, at all events, are sufficient reminder that the Delta procedure is genre sensitive as well as author sensitive, and that, valuable as they are, its unsupported results should not be taken either as conclusive or as purely authorial.

How can it be, to pause for a moment, that the frequency patterns of the very common words reflect differences of genre? Two examples, each broad in its collateral effects, may serve. Whether in its declamatory or its reflective mode, its self-assertion or its self-scrutiny, tragedy characteristically yields much higher frequencies of *I/my* than are usual in comedy, where brisk dialogic interplay brings *thou/you* into prominence. By the same token, the long speeches of much tragedy rely on a more complex syntax, with a corresponding increase in the incidence of the major connectives.

Meanwhile Table 3.2 also shows, as noted above, that in both versions of *3 Henry VI* Kyd defies the apparent odds against him and *The Spanish Tragedy* leads the whole field. More broadly, the plays yielding the first eight scores for each version are in close consonance with the other set of eight and the scores themselves are low. Beyond that again, only one play in the first eight for either version is the work of a dramatist from outside our list of five candidates. The exception is Chapman's *Blind Beggar*, which ranks eighth for the Folio version. Plays by Shakespeare occur more often than chance would suggest. Plays by Kyd, Marlowe, Peele and Greene complete the group. We are not yet justified in declaring that any part of *3 Henry VI* is the work of any of these dramatists. But the play shows more affinity for works of theirs than for those of their contemporaries. As has been increasingly the case in recent times, computational stylistics yields results in keeping with the consensus of traditional scholarship.

So far, so good. But the loose consensus here is only to the effect that *3 Henry VI* is probably collaborative and that some dramatists lead the likely field. Different scholars advocate different candidates from among those mentioned and hold different opinions about various parts of the play. We must therefore move beyond treating *3 Henry VI* as an entity and consider how best to break it into parts.

Neither of the original texts was divided into acts and scenes, but these divisions do offer themselves as the record of editors' judgements about breaks in the action and thus as possible points where one collaborator might hand over to another. Although scene-breaks are usually the less arbitrary, scenes differ too much in length to offer an immediate point of departure for work like ours. In the Folio text, the scenes range down from the 2,211 words of I.i to the 104 of II.iv and the 191 of V.iii. We chose first, accordingly, to test each version act by act. The Delta procedure remained appropriate for the purpose and there was no reason to abandon the word-list we have been using.

These shorter specimens yielded rather higher Delta scores, as might be expected, with minima now approaching 1.00. The results for the five acts of our post-1600 test-plays were less clear cut than those yielded when they were treated as whole plays. But, except for *Sejanus* and *Bussy d'Ambois*, they still showed convincing affinities for their true authors. As for *3 Henry VI*, the results for both versions, as displayed in Table 3.3, still remained consistent with each other. In both versions, Acts I and IV, especially the latter, were markedly non-Shakespearean, but elsewhere his plays ranked among the leaders. Thus, in Act IV, the five leaders for the Folio text included none of Shakespeare's plays while the Octavo yielded only one. In Act II, on the other hand, plays by Shakespeare occupied the first three places for the Folio text and four of the first five for the Octavo. Of the other leading scores, all except two of the top five for any act of either version came from plays by the same group of candidates as before. The exceptions, both in the Folio, were Chapman's *Blind Beggar*, which ranked fifth for Act III, and Munday's *John a Kent and John a Cumber*, which ranked fourth for Act IV. We kept these plays under scrutiny but later work gave them no further support.

The results for *Titus Andronicus*, set out at the foot of Table 3.3, bear on a case much like that of *3 Henry VI*. Of the plays from the earlier part of Shakespeare's career, before the advent of John Fletcher, *Titus Andronicus* is the most firmly accepted as collaborative. Not only is it generally regarded as the work of Shakespeare and Peele, but there is substantial agreement about the authorship of particular scenes.[9] As a first step, consider the effect of proceeding act by act, as shown in Table 3.3. Peele's *Edward I* ranks first for Acts I, II and IV. In Acts III and V, it ranks fourth and second respectively. And in Act I, it is accompanied by two other plays by Peele, *The Battle of Alcazar* and *The Arraignment of Paris*. Of Shakespeare's plays, *Richard III* ranks among the first five in every act. Only in

---

9   See Vickers (2002): 148–243 and Table 3.11.

Table 3.3   Lowest Delta scores for the five acts of three plays

3 Henry VI Folio

Act I		Act II		Act III		Act IV		Act V	
Edward II	0.955	Richard II	0.933	Span. Tragedy	1.011	Edward II	0.982	Edward I	0.981
Span. Tragedy	0.973	Richard III	1.006	Richard III	1.057	Span. Tragedy	1.052	Span. Tragedy	1.028
Richard II	0.977	King John	1.015	Friar Bacon	1.085	Mas'cre at Paris	1.105	Richard II	1.034
Edward I	0.981	Edward I	1.033	Edward II	1.090	John a Kent	1.125	Edward II	1.034
Friar Bacon	1.009	Span. Tragedy	1.046	Blind Beggar	1.110	Friar Bacon	1.146	Richard III	1.038

3 Henry VI Octavo

Act I		Act II		Act III		Act IV		Act V	
Edward II	0.983	Richard II	1.015	Richard III	1.161	Edward II	1.097	Span. Tragedy	1.086
Edward I	0.99	King John	1.055	Span. Tragedy	1.182	Mas'cre at Paris	1.112	Richard III	1.088
Span. Tragedy	1	Span. Tragedy	1.071	Friar Bacon	1.217	Edward I	1.114	Richard II	1.115
Richard II	1.031	Richard III	1.073	Edward II	1.231	Henry V	1.155	Edward I	1.122
Friar Bacon	1.044	Henry V	1.092	Edward I	1.237	Friar Bacon	1.171	Edward II	1.129

Titus Andronicus

Act I		Act II		Act III		Act IV		Act V	
Edward I	1.067	Edward I	0.974	Romeo & Juliet	1.317	Edward I	0.909	Richard III	0.913
Battle of Alcazar	1.103	M. N. Dream	1.005	Old Fortunatus	1.354	Richard III	0.939	Edward I	1.012
Span. Tragedy	1.184	Romeo & Juliet	1.022	Richard III	1.383	Taming of Shrew	0.943	Cobbler's Proph.	1.035
Arraignment	1.185	Richard III	1.045	Edward I	1.389	Jew of Malta	0.949	1 Henry IV	1.042
Richard III	1.205	Taming of Shrew	1.045	Richard II	1.40	Edward II	0.966	Jew of Malta	1.05

Act I is it unaccompanied by other plays of his. But two plays by Marlowe also figure here while Kyd, Dekker and Wilson make one appearance each. Our tests, in short, definitely support the case for Shakespeare and Peele, despite the fact that, according to the consensus view at least, the two dramatists did not divide their work precisely by acts.

Taking stock of all our results so far, we find no real support for any dramatist but those named as candidates. We consider that Act IV of *3 Henry VI* shows least affinity for Shakespeare. The results for the other acts are indeterminate enough to suggest that they may be of mixed authorship.

If the play did have more than one author, there is no reason to assume that they apportioned their task act by act. We must stoically assume, however, that they did not apportion it in segments of equal length for the benefit of number-crunchers then unborn and unimaginable. The arbitrariness of proceeding in that way is greatly mitigated by the use of 'rolling segments'. These are sets, still of equal length, in which each successive segment abandons the opening of its predecessor and replaces it by advancing a further step into the text. In the present case, we took the first 2,000 words of the target text as our opening segment; words numbering from 201–2200 as the second, 401–2400 as the third; and so on for the 108 such segments that make up the Folio text of *3 Henry VI*, with the last segment of all absorbing the residual words. Though the boundaries are still arbitrary, the slow advance through the text allows close study of the changes that occur and admits something of a scene by scene impression.

A table of the results in 108 columns, each 54 rows deep, is not lightly to be undertaken by a reader. The corresponding line-graph is a much tangled skein. It is time to take yet another step forward. We have treated so far 54 plays of known authorship but have allowed each of them to speak for itself. By proceeding in that way, we have avoided any premature conclusions and allowed the influence of genre to be observed. We have also paid respect – too much respect, perhaps – to a shibboleth that had its hour of glory towards the end of the last century. Nobody who encounters a work of literature is obliged to take the slightest interest in its authorship. But nobody who has the least respect for the published evidence can maintain that the author's 'stylistic signature' is not a genuine (though sometimes elusive) presence in literary works. To deny that literary works bear evidence of their authorship is to fly in the face of common sense, educated opinion and the scholarship of many centuries. This body of established belief is supported by the outcome of much computational work in recent times. We have each written more extensively about the alleged 'death of the author' and we are aware that, by treating the very processes of rational inquiry as just another bourgeois figment, Foucault surpasses Barthes and arms himself against rational rejoinder. Encouraged by the long history of our species, whether as *homo sapiens* or even as *homo rationis capax*, we can be content to match assertion against assertion and allow the more rational to prevail. Like any other human beings, authors not only unite with but also mark themselves off from their fellows in everything they do. And the different ways in which

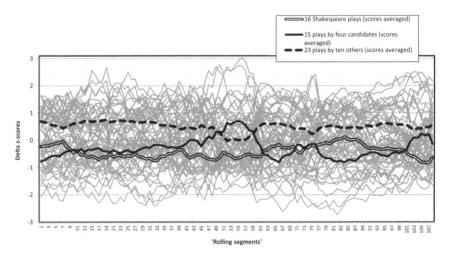

Figure 3.1   *3 Henry VI* (Folio)

humans each use language is among the more personally revealing things that they do.[10]

Figure 3.1 is the first step in our study of authorial groups of plays. The dense grey web of entry-lines in its background registers the full intricacy of the information afforded when, taking *3 Henry VI* as target text, the successive Delta z-scores for all 54 plays are traced through 108 rolling segments. In the online version of this graph, it is possible to highlight the entry-line for any of the plays and consider its changing levels of affinity for the target text.[11] It comes as no surprise, by now, that *Richard II, Richard III, Edward I, Edward II* and *The Spanish Tragedy* are prominent among the inhabitants of the lower regions of the graph. The fanciful plays of Lyly are among those that lie towards the upper extremity, utterly remote from *3 Henry VI* and, indeed, from the mainstream of the Elizabethan public theatre.

The three heavy black entry-lines trace the successive Delta z-scores for the three authorial groups to which we have assigned the 54 plays: 16 by Shakespeare, 15 by the other four recognized candidates, and 23 by ten other dramatists. (The three groups, *as groups*, did not contribute to the calculation of the means and standard deviations. Those were derived from the original range of 54 plays and then used to assess the behaviour of the groups.)

Of the three, the entry-line for the 'other dramatists' is almost always the most remote from the base of the graph, denoting an overall lack of affinity for *3 Henry VI*. (The only exception, about halfway across the graph, occurs when the entry-line for the 'four candidates' briefly rises above it.) In the lower part of the graph,

---

10   See Burrows (1995/1999). And see Craig (2010).

11   A sufficiently enthusiastic reader will find an e-version of this graph at <www. newcastle.edu.au/school/hss/research/groups/cllc/publications.html>.

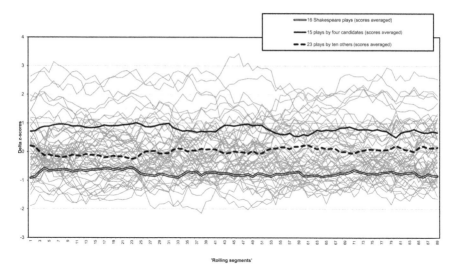

Figure 3.2 *Twelfth Night*

a markedly different picture can be seen. As each in turn shows more affinity for *3 Henry VI*, the other two entry-lines cut back and forth across each other. The first few segments, for example, are non-Shakespearean while the last few are Shakespearean.

By way of contrast, Figure 3.2, in which *Twelfth Night* is the target text, represents a typical outcome for a single-author play. The entry-lines for the three authorial groups run more smoothly across the graph with the true author's entry-line well below the other two. In this case, the entry-line for 'Others' takes the middle station. That is because those 23 plays include much more comedy than do the 15 plays of Greene, Kyd, Marlowe and Peele.

Table 3.4 sums up this information and adds corresponding results for two other target texts. Among the mean-scores, all the negatives and none of the positives attach to authorial groups with a genuine claim to the text in question. Among the standard deviations, by far the lowest attach to the bonds linking the Shakespeare group with *Hamlet* and with *Twelfth Night*. By the same token, the ranges of Delta z-scores for *Hamlet* and *Twelfth Night* are narrow and strongly negative. The affinity of both plays for Shakespeare is clear and consistent. In both cases, the behaviour of the other two groups is appropriate to the given target text. If the authorship of *Hamlet* and *Twelfth Night* were in question, results like these would justify a firm authorial inference and suggest the likely outcome of corroborative tests.

In both of the putative collaborations, however, a different picture can be seen. The group of 'other dramatists' is now the one that stands apart. When *3 Henry VI* and *Titus Andronicus* are the target texts, the group of four candidates and that of Peele's plays, respectively, behave much more like the Shakespeare group. And yet the high standard deviations in these cases signify a high degree of volatility, a reflection of the way the entry-lines criss-cross in Figure 3.1 (and as they do in a

Table 3.4   Summary of Delta z-scores for four target texts

	Divergence		Range	
	Mean	St. Dev.	Min.	Max.
Target text	*3 Henry VI* (108 segments)			
16 Shakespeare plays	-0.419	0.228	-0.831	0.121
15 plays by four candidates	-0.286	0.357	-0.811	0.709
23 plays by others	0.503	0.173	-0.025	0.747
Target text	*Hamlet* (136 segments)			
16 Shakespeare plays	-0.840	0.098	-1.021	-0.582
15 plays by four candidates	0.373	0.310	-0.442	0.867
23 plays by others	0.346	0.201	-0.071	0.793
Target text	*Twelfth Night* (89 segments)			
16 Shakespeare plays	-0.743	0.087	-0.915	-0.546
15 plays by four candidates	0.799	0.121	0.505	1.009
23 plays by others	0.015	0.122	-0.247	0.234
Target text	*Titus Andronicus* (87 segments)			
16 Shakespeare plays	-0.565	0.210	-0.982	-0.058
5 Peele plays	-0.063	0.599	-1.473	0.725
33 plays by others	0.308	0.051	0.201	0.461

corresponding graph for *Titus Andronicus*). See, by contrast, the graph for *Twelfth Night*, where (as in a corresponding graph for *Hamlet*) the Shakespeare entry-line runs across the lower part of the page, while the other two run well above it.

Now Figure 3.1 suggests, as noted earlier, that the opening segments of *3 Henry VI* are not Shakespeare's but that the closing ones may well be his. His hand also seems evident around the middle of the play but a strong non-Shakespearean phase soon follows. The need to translate such broad observations into a more precise analysis obliges us to offer more detailed evidence than we have done so far. It also entails the introduction of a second statistical test to verify what the Delta procedure suggests. And it will require patient scrutiny from those who are willing to accompany us on the path forward.

Our second statistical test deals in an entirely different frequency stratum of the English vocabulary from that of the very frequent function words. Whereas those are words that everybody uses all the time, we now turn our attention to such words as are used in one authorial group of texts – used there even once – but not used at all in another comparable group. IotaPlus,[12] as this second test is becoming known, rests upon an assumption about relative degrees of likelihood – that an author who uses a given word even once in a batch of his or her work is somewhat more likely to use it in a fresh text than are authors in whose sample-batches it

12   Burrows (2007).

does not occur at all. Only 'somewhat', we say, because the first author may never revert to some of the words of the sample-batch and because the other authors may turn to words not used in their sample-batches. But experience is giving increasing weight to the assumption and the IotaPlus test is yielding extremely accurate results.

Table 3.5 brings the results of the Delta procedure together with those of IotaPlus for each of the 108 rolling segments of *3 Henry VI*. It compares the two outcomes for each segment and arrives at a combined verdict as to its likely authorship. Column A lists the sequence of segments. Columns B and C show how each advances further into the text than does its immediate predecessor, abandoning 200 words and embracing a fresh 200. Column D shows the Delta z-score for each segment, registering its affinity for the Shakespeare group of 16 plays. (These same data supply the Shakespeare entry-line shown in Figure 3.1.) Column E shows how these scores rank against each other from one to 108.

Column F assigns the 108 segments, by rank, to four quartile groups of 27 members, ranging down from the most 'Shakespearean' to the least. The 'Delta verdicts' of Column G mark members of the first and fourth quartiles as S1 and NS1 respectively. It will be seen that, in conformity with Figure 3.1, Column G opens with a series of NS1 entries and closes, at the foot of its second page, with a series of S1s. By using quartiles in this way, we have accepted the assumptions, clearly supported by Figure 3.1, that over a quarter of the play shows an affinity for Shakespeare and that over a quarter shows a definite disaffinity. To set the shares as low as a quarter apiece is, indeed, to work conservatively and establish a basis for further investigation of the segments not marked as either S1 or NS1.

The results of the IotaPlus test begin in Column H, a simple record of 'hits' as distinct from 'occurrences'. Occurrences show how many times the listed words appear – a total of what linguists call 'word tokens'. To count up all the instances of each listed word yields weaker data because it gives too much weight to little flurries in which an unusual word can suddenly occur several times or many. By treating of 'word-types', we reduce each word's count of occurrences, one or many, to a single 'hit'. It should, however, be noted that this more robust measure requires that, as here, the segments of text be closely similar in length. The early rows of Column H show rather low numbers of 'hits', whereas those of the last few segments are distinctly higher. In this case, of course, the higher score is the more 'Shakespearean' and the pattern matches that of the Delta results but in the inverse. Overall, the scores range down from 40 in Segment 23 to only 12 in Segments 2, 93 and 95. The mean is 22.34 and the standard deviation a moderate 7.14.

Column I translates this raw count of 'hits' into a percentage rate in order to allow for the residual words in Segment 108. Column J converts them into z-scores, which are ranked in descending order in Column K. Four quartiles are established as before and the 108 segments are assigned to their respective quartiles in Column L. This enables us, as before, to label members of the first quartile as S1 and those of the fourth as NS1 and so to form a record of IotaPlus verdicts.

Table 3.5 Assigning likely authorship of segments

Delta and IotaPlus results for 108 'rolling segments'

	A Rolling segment	B From	C To	D Delta 16Shak zscore	E Delta 16Shak rank/108	F Delta 16Shak quartile /108	G Delta 16Shak verdict	H Iota 16Shak count	I Iota 16Shak as %	J Iota 16Shak zscore	K Iota 16Shak rank/108	L Iota 16Shak quartile /108	M Iota 16Shak verdict	N Delta/Iota sum of quartiles /108	O Delta/Iota combined quartiles verdict
	1	1	2000	−0.22	87	4	NS1	16	0.80	−0.84	81	3		7	**NS2**
	2	201	2200	−0.21	88	4	NS1	12	0.60	−1.41	106	4	NS1	8	**NS1**
	3	401	2400	−0.20	89	4	NS1	14	0.70	−1.12	95	4	NS1	8	**NS1**
	4	601	2600	−0.14	93	4	NS1	14	0.70	−1.12	96	4	NS1	8	**NS1**
	5	801	2800	−0.12	97	4	NS1	13	0.65	−1.26	100	4	NS1	8	**NS1**
	6	1001	3000	−0.08	99	4	NS1	15	0.75	−0.98	87	4	NS1	8	**NS1**
	7	1201	3200	−0.04	100	4	NS1	16	0.80	−0.84	82	4	NS1	8	**NS2**
	8	1401	3400	−0.23	82	4	NS1	19	0.95	−0.41	62	3	NS1	7	**NS2**
	9	1601	3600	−0.31	72	3		20	1.00	−0.26	53	2		5	
	10	1801	3800	−0.45	56	3		25	1.25	0.45	29	2		5	
	11	2001	4000	−0.36	62	3		25	1.25	0.45	30	2		5	
	12	2201	4200	−0.54	43	2		26	1.30	0.59	25	1	S1	3	**S2**
	13	2401	4400	−0.53	45	2		28	1.40	0.88	20	1	S1	3	**S2**
	14	2601	4600	−0.63	21	1	S1	28	1.40	0.88	21	1	S1	2	**S1**

15	2801	4800	-0.57	37	2		31	1.55	1.31	13	1	S1	3	S2
16	3001	5000	-0.64	16	1	S1	34	1.70	1.73	8	1	S1	2	S1
17	3201	5200	-0.70	9	1	S1	39	1.95	2.45	3	1	S1	2	S1
18	3401	5400	-0.61	25	1	S1	37	1.85	2.16	4	1	S1	2	S1
19	3601	5600	-0.64	17	1	S1	36	1.80	2.02	5	1	S1	2	S1
20	3801	5800	-0.50	51	2		34	1.70	1.73	9	1	S1	3	S2
21	4001	6000	-0.62	23	1	S1	34	1.70	1.73	10	1	S1	2	S1
22	4201	6200	-0.55	41	2		34	1.70	1.73	11	1	S1	3	S2
23	4401	6400	-0.55	40	2		35	1.75	1.88	7	1	S1	3	S2
24	4601	6600	-0.60	28	2		40	2.00	2.59	1	1	S1	3	S2
25	4801	6800	-0.57	38	2		40	2.00	2.59	2	1	S1	3	S2
26	5001	7000	-0.58	35	2		36	1.80	2.02	6	1	S1	3	S2
27	5201	7200	-0.50	50	2		31	1.55	1.31	14	1	S1	3	S2
28	5401	7400	-0.59	32	2		31	1.55	1.31	15	1	S1	3	S2
29	5601	7600	-0.62	22	1	S1	30	1.50	1.16	18	1	S1	2	S1
30	5801	7800	-0.68	11	1	S1	31	1.55	1.31	16	1	S1	2	S1
31	6001	8000	-0.66	13	1	S1	31	1.55	1.31	17	1	S1	2	S1
32	6201	8200	-0.74	4	1	S1	32	1.60	1.45	12	1	S1	2	S1
33	6401	8400	-0.73	6	1	S1	29	1.45	1.02	19	1	S1	2	S1
34	6601	8600	-0.59	31	2		24	1.20	0.31	33	2		4	
35	6801	8800	-0.59	34	2		23	1.15	0.16	38	2		4	
36	7001	9000	-0.49	52	2		23	1.15	0.16	39	2		4	
37	7201	9200	-0.49	53	2		23	1.15	0.16	40	2		4	
38	7401	9400	-0.44	58	3		22	1.10	0.02	44	2		5	
39	7601	9600	-0.34	69	3		24	1.20	0.31	34	2		5	

Table 3.5 continued

A Rolling segment	B From	C To	D Delta 16Shak zscore	E Delta 16Shak rank/108	F Delta 16Shak quartile /108	G Delta 16Shak verdict	H Iota 16Shak count	I Iota 16Shak as %	J Iota 16Shak zscore	K Iota 16Shak rank/108	L Iota 16Shak quartile /108	M Iota 16Shak verdict	N Delta/Iota sum of quartiles /108	O Delta/Iota combined quartiles verdict
40	7801	9800	-0.36	63	3		21	1.05	-0.12	48	2		5	
41	8001	10000	-0.54	42	2		19	0.95	-0.41	63	3		5	
42	8201	10200	-0.65	15	1	S1	17	0.85	-0.69	76	3		4	
43	8401	10400	-0.59	30	2		17	0.85	-0.69	77	3		5	
44	8601	10600	-0.52	46	2		19	0.95	-0.41	64	3		5	
45	8801	10800	-0.52	48	2	S1	20	1.00	-0.26	54	2		4	
46	9001	11000	-0.63	20	1	S1	19	0.95	-0.41	65	3		4	
47	9201	11200	-0.69	10	1	S1	18	0.90	-0.55	68	3		4	
48	9401	11400	-0.72	7	1	S1	18	0.90	-0.55	69	3		4	
49	9601	11600	-0.73	5	1	S1	18	0.90	-0.55	70	3		4	
50	9801	11800	-0.63	19	1	S1	20	1.00	-0.26	55	3		4	
51	10001	12000	-0.44	57	3		24	1.20	0.31	35	2		5	
52	10201	12200	65, 66	47	2		25	1.25	0.45	31	2		4	
53	10401	12400	-0.57	39	2		23	1.15	0.16	41	2		4	
54	10601	12600	-0.68	12	1	S1	23	1.15	0.16	42	2		3	S2

55	10801	12800	-0.66	14	1	S1	21	1.05	-0.12	49	2		3	S2
56	11001	13000	-0.61	26	1	S1	23	1.15	0.16	43	2		3	S2
57	11201	13200	-0.53	44	2		24	1.20	0.31	36	2		4	
58	11401	13400	-0.51	49	2		25	1.25	0.45	32	2		4	
59	11601	13600	-0.59	33	2		21	1.05	-0.12	50	2		4	
60	11801	13800	-0.59	29	2		20	1.00	-0.26	56	3		5	
61	12001	14000	-0.60	27	1	S1	16	0.80	-0.84	83	4	NS1	5	NS2
62	12201	14200	-0.38	60	3		15	0.75	-0.98	88	4	NS1	7	
63	12401	14400	-0.35	65	3		17	0.85	-0.69	78	3		6	
64	12601	14600	-0.23	84	4	NS1	16	0.80	-0.84	84	4	NS1	8	NS1
65	12801	14800	-0.23	83	4	NS1	17	0.85	-0.69	79	3		7	NS2
66	13001	15000	-0.16	91	4	NS1	18	0.90	-0.55	71	3		7	NS2
67	13201	15200	-0.27	80	3		18	0.90	-0.55	72	3		6	
68	13401	15400	-0.28	78	3		19	0.95	-0.41	66	3		6	
69	13601	15600	-0.29	76	3		21	1.05	-0.12	51	2		5	
70	13801	15800	-0.22	85	4	NS1	20	1.00	-0.26	57	3		7	NS2
71	14001	16000	-0.42	59	3		20	1.00	-0.26	58	3		6	
72	14201	16200	-0.46	55	3		20	1.00	-0.26	59	3		6	
73	14401	16400	-0.28	77	3		22	1.10	0.02	45	2		5	
74	14601	16600	-0.27	79	3		20	1.00	-0.26	60	3		6	
75	14801	16800	-0.17	90	4	NS1	22	1.10	0.02	46	2		6	
76	15001	17000	-0.22	86	4	NS1	20	1.00	-0.26	61	3		7	NS2
77	15201	17200	-0.16	92	4	NS1	18	0.90	-0.55	73	3		7	NS2
78	15401	17400	-0.13	96	4	NS1	15	0.75	-0.98	89	4	NS1	8	NS1
79	15601	17600	-0.09	98	4	NS1	14	0.70	-1.12	97	4	NS1	8	NS1

Table 3.5 continued

A Rolling segment	B From	C To	D Delta 16Shak zscore	E Delta 16Shak rank/108	F Delta 16Shak quartile /108	G Delta 16Shak verdict	H Iota 16Shak count	I Iota 16Shak as %	J Iota 16Shak zscore	K Iota 16Shak rank/108	L Iota 16Shak quartile /108	M Iota 16Shak verdict	N Delta/Iota sum of quartiles /108	O Delta/Iota combined quartiles verdict
80	15801	17800	-0.14	94	4	NS1	14	0.70	-1.12	98	4	NS1	8	NS1
81	16001	18000	-0.02	102	4	NS1	15	0.75	-0.98	90	4	NS1	8	NS1
82	16201	18200	0.03	105	4	NS1	15	0.75	-0.98	91	4	NS1	8	NS1
83	16401	18400	0.05	107	4	NS1	13	0.65	-1.26	101	4	NS1	8	NS1
84	16601	18600	0.12	108	4	NS1	13	0.65	-1.26	102	4	NS1	8	NS1
85	16801	18800	0.03	106	4	NS1	15	0.75	-0.98	92	4	NS1	8	NS1
86	17001	19000	0.01	103	4	NS1	16	0.80	-0.84	85	4	NS1	8	NS1
87	17201	19200	0.03	104	4	NS1	17	0.85	-0.69	80	3	NS1	7	NS2
88	17401	19400	-0.03	101	4	NS1	18	0.90	-0.55	74	3		7	NS2
89	17601	19600	-0.14	95	4	NS1	18	0.90	-0.55	75	3		7	NS2
90	17801	19800	-0.25	81	3		15	0.75	-0.98	93	4	NS1	7	NS2
91	18001	20000	-0.30	73	3		13	0.65	-1.26	103	4	NS1	7	NS2
92	18201	20200	-0.29	75	3		14	0.70	-1.12	99	4	NS1	7	NS2
93	18401	20400	-0.32	71	3		12	0.60	-1.41	107	4	NS1	7	NS2

94	18601	20600	-0.34	68	3		13	0.65	-1.26	104	4	NS1	7	NS2
95	18801	20800	-0.32	70	3		12	0.60	-1.41	108	4	NS1	7	NS2
96	19001	21000	-0.30	74	3		13	0.65	-1.26	105	4	NS1	7	NS2
97	19201	21200	-0.34	66	3		15	0.75	-0.98	94	4	NS1	7	NS2
98	19401	21400	-0.36	64	3		16	0.80	-0.84	86	4	NS1	7	NS2
99	19601	21600	-0.34	67	3		19	0.95	-0.41	67	3		6	
100	19801	21800	-0.37	61	3		21	1.05	-0.12	52	2		5	
101	20001	22000	-0.46	54	2		26	1.30	0.59	26	1	S1	3	S2
102	20201	22200	-0.58	36	2		22	1.10	0.02	47	2		4	
103	20401	22400	-0.61	24	1	S1	24	1.20	0.31	37	2	S1	3	S2
104	20601	22600	-0.70	8	1	S1	27	1.35	0.74	22	1	S1	2	S1
105	20801	22800	-0.82	2	1	S1	27	1.35	0.74	23	1	S1	2	S1
106	21001	23000	-0.82	3	1	S1	27	1.35	0.74	24	1	S1	2	S1
107	21201	23200	-0.83	1	1	S1	26	1.30	0.59	27	1	S1	2	S1
108	21401	23483	-0.64	18	1	S1	27	1.30	0.58	28	2		3	S2

Table 3.6 Relationship between segments and scenes

Rolling segment	From	To	Quartiles verdict (from Table 3.5)	Scenes within range	Contributions from successive scenes	Scene	Words	From	To
1	1	2000	**NS1**	I.i	2000	I.i	2211	1	2211
2	201	2200	**NS1**	I.i	2000				
3	401	2400	**NS1**	I.i-ii	1800+200	i.ii	603	2212	2814
4	601	2600	**NS1**	I.i-ii	1600+400				
5	801	2800	**NS1**	I.i-ii	1400+600				
6	1001	3000	**NS1**	I.i-iii	1200+600+200	I.iii	405	2815	3219
7	1201	3200	**NS2**	I.i-iii	1000+600+400				
8	1401	3400	**NS2**	I.i-iv	800+600+400+200	I.iv	1478	3220	4697
9	1601	3600		I.i-iv	600+600+400+400				
10	1801	3800		I.i-iv	400+600+400+600				
11	2001	4000		I.i-iv	200+600+400+800				
12	2201	4200		I.ii-iv	600+400+1000				
13	2401	4400	**S2**	I.ii-iv	400+400+1200				
14	2601	4600	**S1**	i.ii-iv	200+400+1400				
15	2801	4800	**S2**	I.iii-iv II.i	400+1500+100	II.i	1681	4698	6378
16	3001	5000	**S1**	I.iii-iv II.i	200+1500+300				

17	3201	5200	**S1**	I.iv-II.i	1500+500				
18	3401	5400	**S1**	I.iv-II.i	1300+700				
19	3601	5600	**S1**	I.iv-II.i	1100+900				
20	3801	5800	**S2**	I.iv-II.i	900+1100				
21	4001	6000	**S1**	I.iv-II.i	700+1300				
22	4201	6200	**S2**	I.iv-II.i	500+1500				
23	4401	6400	**S2**	I.iv-II.i	300+1700				
24	4601	6600	**S2**	I.iv II.i-ii	100+1700+200	II.ii	1421	6379	7799
25	4801	6800	**S2**	II.i-ii	1600+400				
26	5001	7000	**S2**	II.i-ii	1400+600				
27	5201	7200	**S2**	II.i-ii	1200+800				
28	5401	7400	**S2**	II.i-ii	1000+1000				
29	5601	7600	**S1**	II.i-ii	800+1200				
30	5801	7800	**S1**	II.i-ii	600+1400				
31	6001	8000	**S1**	II.i-iii	400+1400+200	II.iii	460	7800	8259
32	6201	8200	**S1**	II.i-iii	200+1400+400				
33	6401	8400	**S1**	II.ii-iv	1400+500+100	II.iv	104	8260	8363
34	6601	8600		II.ii-v	1200+500+100+200	II.v	1122	8364	9485
35	6801	8800		II.ii-v	1000+500+100+400				
36	7001	9000		II.ii-v	800+500+100+600				
37	7201	9200		II.ii-v	600+500+100+800				
38	7401	9400		II.ii-v	400+500+100+1000				
39	7601	9600		II.ii-v	200+500+100+1200				
40	7801	9800		II.iii-vi	500+100+1200+200	II.vi	886	9486	10371
41	8001	10000		II.iii-vi	300+100+1200+400				

Table 3.6 continued

A	B	C	D	E	F	G	H	I	J
Rolling segment	From	To	Quartiles verdict (from Table 5)	Scenes within range	Contributions from successive scenes	Scene	Words	From	To
42	8201	10200		II.iii-vi	100+100+1200+600				
43	8401	10400		II.iii-vi	1200+800				
44	8601	10600		II.v-vi III.i	1000+900+100	III.i	866	10372	11237
45	8801	10800		II.v-vi III.i	800+900+300				
46	9001	11000		II.v-vi III.i	600+900+500				
47	9201	11200		II.v-vi III.i	400+900+700				
48	9401	11400		II.v-vi III.i	200+900+900				
49	9601	11600		II.vi III.i-ii	900+900+200	III.ii	1638	11238	12875
50	9801	11800		II.vi III.i-ii	700+900+400				
51	10001	12000		II.vi III.i-ii	500+900+600				
52	10201	12200		II.vi III.i-ii	300+900+800				
53	10401	12400		II.vi III.i-ii	100+900+1000				
54	10601	12600	**S2**	II.vi-III.i-ii	800+1200				
55	10801	12800		II.vi-III.i-ii	600+1400				
56	11001	13000	**S2**	II.vi-III.i-ii	400+1600				

57	11201	13200		III.i-iii	200+1600+200	III.iii	2109	12876	14984
58	11401	13400		III.ii-iii	1600+400				
59	11601	13600		III.ii-iii	1400+600				
60	11801	13800		III.ii-iii	1200+800				
61	12001	14000		III.ii-iii	1000+1000				
62	12201	14200	NS2	III.ii-iii	800+1200				
63	12401	14400		III.ii-iii	600+1400				
64	12601	14600	NS1	III.ii-iii	400+1600				
65	12801	14800	NS2	III.ii-iii	200+1800				
66	13001	15000	NS2	III.iii	2000				
67	13201	15200		III.iii-IV.i	1900+100	IV.i	1195	14985	16179
68	13401	15400		III.iii-IV.i	1700+300				
69	13601	15600		III.iii-IV.i	1500+500				
70	13801	15800	NS2	III.iii-IV.i	1300+700				
71	14001	16000		III.iii-IV.i	1100+900				
72	14201	16200		III.iii-IV.i	900+1100				
73	14401	16400		III.iii-IV.ii	700+1200+100	IV.ii	223	16180	16402
74	14601	16600		III.iii-IV.iii	500+1200+200+100	IV.iii	493	16403	16895
75	14801	16800		III.iii-IV.iii	300+1200+200+300				
76	15001	17000	NS2	III.iii-IV.iii	100+1200+200+500				
77	15201	17200	NS2	IV.i-iv	1100+200+500+200	IV.iv	282	16896	17177
78	15401	17400	NS1	IV.i-v	900+200+500+300+100	IV.v	234	17178	17411
79	15601	17600	NS1	IV.i-vi	700+200+500+300+200+100	IV.vi	790	17412	18201
80	15801	17800	NS1	IV.i-vi	500+200+500+300+200+300				

Table 3.6 continued

A	B	C	D	E	F	G	H	I	J
Rolling segment	From	To	Quartiles verdict (from Table 5)	Contributions from successive scenes	Contributions from successive scenes	Scene	Words	From	To
81	16001	18000	NS1	IV.i-vi	300+200+500+300+200+500				
82	16201	18200	NS1	IV.i-vi	100+200+500+300+200+700				
83	16401	18400	NS1	IV.ii-IV.vii	100+500+300+200+800+100	IV.vii	724	18202	18925
84	16601	18600	NS1	IV.iii-IV.vii	400+300+200+800+300				
85	16801	18800	NS1	IV.iii-IV.vii	200+300+200+800+500				
86	17001	19000	NS1	IV.iv-IV.vii	300+200+800+700				
87	17201	19200	NS2	IV.iv-IV.viii	100+200+800+700+200	IV.viii	491	18926	19416
88	17401	19400	NS2	IV.v-IV.viii	100+800+700+400				
89	17601	19600	NS2	IV.vi-V.i	700+700+500+100	V.i	912	19417	20328
90	17801	19800	NS2	IV.vi-V.i	500+700+500+300				
91	18001	20000	NS2	IV.vi-V.i	300+700+500+500				
92	18201	20200	NS2	IV.vi-V.i	100+700+500+700				
93	18401	20400	NS2	IV.vii-V.i	600+500+900				
94	18601	20600	NS2	IV.vii-V.ii	400+500+900+200	V.ii	424	20329	20752
95	18801	20800	NS2	IV.vii-V.ii	200+500+900+400				

96	19001	21000	NS2	IV.viii-V.iii	500+900+400+200	V.iii	191	20753	20943
97	19201	21200	NS2	IV.viii-V.iv	300+900+400+200+200	V.iv	677	20944	21620
98	19401	21400	NS2	IV.viii-V.iv	100+900+400+200+400				
99	19601	21600		V.i-V.iv	800+400+200+600				
100	19801	21800		V.i-V.v	600+400+200+700+100	V.v	736	21621	22356
101	20001	22000	S2	V.i-V.v	400+400+200+700+300				
102	20201	22200		V.i-V.v	200+400+200+700+500				
103	20401	22400	S2	V.ii-V.v	400+200+700+700				
104	20601	22600	S1	V.iii-V.vi	200+200+700+700+200	V.vi	761	22357	23117
105	20801	22800	S1	V.iii-V.vi	200+700+700+400				
106	21001	23000	S1	V.iv-V.vi	700+700+600				
107	21201	23200	S1	V.iv-V.vi	500+700+800				
108	21401	23483	S1	V.iv-V.vii	300+700+800+366	V.vii	366	23118	23483

The two columns of quartile scores, from Columns F and L, are then added together in Column N so as to produce the combined verdicts of Column O. A combined score of 2, meaning that the segment ranks in the first quartile on both texts, is now marked S1, while one that scores 3, by ranking in a first and a second quartile, is marked S2. A score of 8, signifying two entries in the fourth quartile, is marked NS1 while a score of 7 is marked NS2. All other segments remain unassigned. The robustness of these combined verdicts is indicated by the strong coefficients that derive from correlating any of the matched pairs of columns for Delta and Iota in Table 3.5. For the two sets of z-scores or of rankings or of quartiles, the coefficients reach out beyond 0.68, with such associated probabilities for 108 cases as p <0.0001. The likelihood is that the outcome is a chance-effect, that is to say, is less than one in 10,000. In a literary perspective, moreover, it is reassuring to see that, in general, the authorship holds firm, one way or the other, for sizeable phases of the play. Our statistical results point to a plausible (though not a necessary) manner in which the contributors may be supposed to have approached their task. In making this broad suggestion, we remain aware that parts of the text may have been revised by others than their first author and that particular speeches may have been interpolated here and there.

Table 3.6, in its turn, enables us to study the relationship between the 108 rolling segments and the successive scenes embraced, partly or entirely, by each of them. Columns A to C, listing the segments, are taken directly from Table 3.5. Column D, our set of combined quartile verdicts, replicates Column O of Table 3.5. Columns G–J list the successive scenes, give the word-length of each one, and mark the point at which each of them enters and then departs from the sequence of spoken words comprising *3 Henry VI*.

The main work of Table 3.6 is carried out in Columns E and F. Column E shows which scenes make part of each successive segment. And, counting only to the nearest hundred, Column F shows how many words each of its scenes contributes to a given segment. Since Act I Scene i runs to 2,211 words, it occupies the whole of Segments 1 and 2: the former comprises its first 2,000, the latter the 2,000 running on from Word No. 201. Segment 3 includes its last 1,800, supplemented by the first 200 of Act I Scene ii. With their relative contributions changing step by step, these two scenes occupy Segments 3–5. Act I Scene iii makes its entry in Segment 6, Act I Scene iv in Segment 8, and so on. But it is not until Segment 12 that Act I Scene i ceases to play any part. There are moments when the entry-points shown in Columns B and I go out of alignment. That is because we create transient surfeits and deficits by rounding to the nearest hundred.

A comparison between Columns D and E gives good reason to believe that Act I Scene i and Act I Scene ii are non-Shakespearean. Not until Act I Scene iii and Act I Scene iv begin to gather force in Segment 9 does the opening sequence of NS results give way to segments less easily assigned. From Segment 12, however, with Act I Scene i finally out of play and the later scenes of Act I beginning to have an influence, we enter upon a Shakespearean phase which runs on into Act II and which is at its strongest in the 'S1' entries of Segments 16–18 where Act I Scene iv is dominant.

After a long sequence of unassigned segments embracing the latter part of Act II, more clear-cut results begin to emerge. The S entries associated with Act III Scene i and Act III Scene ii give way to a broad band of NS entries running from Act III Scene iii to early Act V. The closing scenes of all, however, show a strong return to S.

Our next step was to declare our hand about some scenes in order to establish a basis for further inquiry into others. We sought to err on the side of caution in choosing our two 'pools' of scenes. Pool A, made up of scenes with strong Shakespearean results, comprised seven scenes from Acts III and V. The non-Shakespearean Pool B comprised eight scenes from Acts I and IV. This left a residue of 13 scenes for further investigation.

We approached this new task in two ways. We began by adding each unassigned scene, in turn, to both pools and observing the effects in a new Delta analysis. (After each was considered, it was removed and a fresh start was made with the next.) This approach led us to accept Act II Scene ii as Shakespearean and four other scenes (II.iii, III.iii, IV.vii, and V.ii) as non-Shakespearean. The scenes still offering indeterminate results included the shortest two of all, but they amounted, all told, to about a quarter of the play.

Our second approach was to introduce a third statistical test, one dealing in words not previously used in this study. In its original form, the Zeta test has been most useful in cases, like the present one, where only two possibilities arise.[13] Craig has since refined the procedure (says Burrows) in a powerful 'Zeta variant'. In both forms, Zeta addresses word-types that occur with some consistency in one sample-batch but not in another comparable batch. It follows that neither the common function words that occur freely in both batches, nor the words that occur but seldom in either, will qualify for analysis. In the original Zeta, Burrows varied the strictness of his stipulations in an attempt to reconcile the need for a sizeable list of words with the need to maintain a strong enough contrast between the two samples. Once a word-list was established, it was used to examine whatever test-specimens were at issue.

Craig took a simpler and more robust path. He, too, began with all the word-types of the first sample. He then excluded all proper nouns, titular adjectives and all words already used in the current battery of tests. (In the present case, these include forms like 'King Henry', the 150 function-words used for Delta, and all the words used in IotaPlus.) He broke each sample-batch into successive segments of 2,000 words, applied his culled word-list, and registered the hits and misses in each segment. He calculated, for each word-type, the proportion of hits in Batch A and that of misses in Batch B. These were expressed, in each case, as decimal fractions ranging up to a maximum of 1.00. For each word-type in turn, these two decimal fractions were added to yield a Zeta Index. He ranked these in descending

---

13   See Burrows (2007).

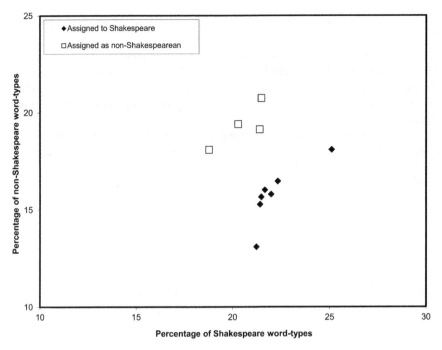

Figure 3.3   *3 Henry VI* (Folio): 'Zeta variant' scores for eleven 2,000-word segments

order, selected the top 500 as his word-list and applied it to the test-specimens. The process was then reversed and Batch B became the base. To allow Zeta full freedom, we chose to include all 38 of our non-Shakespeare plays in one batch and not to focus on Greene, Kyd, Marlowe and Peele.

For the Zeta test whose outcome is represented in Figure 3.3, *3 Henry VI* is separated into two blocks of text. One, amounting to 14,439 words, comprises the 16 scenes we finally assigned to Shakespeare. The other, amounting to 9,044 words, comprises the twelve scenes we assigned as non-Shakespeare. Each block is arranged in its natural sequence and each is broken into successive segments (not rolling segments) of 2,000 words, seven Shakespearean and four not. The horizontal axis bears on the Zeta word-list derived from Shakespeare's 16 early plays. It shows what percentage of those word-types occurs in each of the eleven segments. The entries for the seven blocks embracing scenes assigned to Shakespeare tend a little further to the right than the other four. The vertical axis bears on the Zeta word-list derived from our set of 38 early plays by other dramatists. It shows what percentage of those word-types occurs in each of the eleven segments. One of the seven Shakespeare entries lies at the lower edge of the non-Shakespeare cluster but far to the right of that cluster. The other six entries for segments embracing scenes assigned to Shakespeare lie decidedly lower than the non-Shakespeare cluster. It can be seen, overall, that the two clusters of

Table 3.7 **Assignation of scenes of *3 Henry VI* (Folio) to Shakespeare (S) or to the 'candidates' group (NS)**

Act	Scene	Length in words	Assignation	
I	i	2211		NS
I	ii	603		NS
I	iii	405	S	
I	iv	1478	S	
II	i	1681	S	
II	ii	1421	S	
II	iii	460		NS
II	iv	104	S	
II	v	1122	S	
II	vi	886	S	
III	i	866	S	
III	ii	1638	S	
III	iii	2109		NS
IV	i	1195	S	
IV	ii	223		NS
IV	iii	493		NS
IV	iv	282		NS
IV	v	234		NS
IV	vi	790		NS
IV	vii	724		NS
IV	viii	491		NS
V	i	912	S	
V	ii	424		NS
V	iii	191	S	
V	iv	677	S	
V	v	736	S	
V	vi	761	S	
V	vii	366	S	
Totals	Play	23483		
	S	14439		
	NS	9044		

Table 3.8   Summary of Delta z-scores for six target texts

	Divergence		Range	
	Mean	St. Dev.	Min.	Max.
Target text	*3 Henry VI* (108 segments)			
16 Shakespeare plays	-0.419	0.228	-0.831	0.121
15 plays by four candidates	-0.286	0.357	-0.811	0.709
23 plays by others	0.503	0.173	-0.025	0.747
Target text	*Hamlet* (136 segments)			
16 Shakespeare plays	-0.840	0.098	-1.021	-0.582
15 plays by four candidates	0.373	0.310	-0.442	0.867
23 plays by others	0.346	0.201	-0.071	0.793
Target text	*Twelfth Night* (89 segments)			
16 Shakespeare plays	-0.743	0.087	-0.915	-0.546
15 plays by four candidates	0.799	0.121	0.505	1.009
23 plays by others	0.015	0.122	-0.247	0.234
Target text	*Titus Andronicus* (76 segments)			
16 Shakespeare plays	-0.565	0.210	-0.982	-0.058
5 Peele plays	-0.063	0.509	-1.473	0.725
33 plays by others	0.308	0.051	0.201	0.461
Target text	*3 Henry VI* ('Shakespeare scenes')			
16 Shakespeare plays	-0.607	0.103	-0.836	-0.325
15 plays by four candidates	0.059	0.356	-0.446	0.765
23 plays by others	0.408	0.243	-0.095	0.738
Target text	*3 Henry VI* ('non-Shakespeare scenes')			
16 Shakespeare plays	-0.074	0.096	-0.223	0.164
15 plays by four candidates	-0.707	0.082	-0.855	-0.559
23 plays by others	0.542	0.065	0.453	0.695

entries stand clear of each other. Given the way in which the two word-lists were selected, we believe that we are justified in claiming that the clusters are separated by difference of authorship.

Table 3.7 is a simple record, scene by scene, of the decisions we made based on all the tests we have described. Those traditionalists who are still dubious about the use of computational methods in literary studies may be either consoled or irritated to find that the play's more memorable scenes fall to Shakespeare. For our part, it is enough to say that we allowed each scene to declare itself and that we did nothing to pre-empt our findings. In going so far as to make an ascription of every scene of the play, we realize that we may appear to be repeating what now seems the over-confidence of Dover Wilson in his 1952 Cambridge edition. Table 3.7 represents what is, as far as we are aware, the first attempt since his

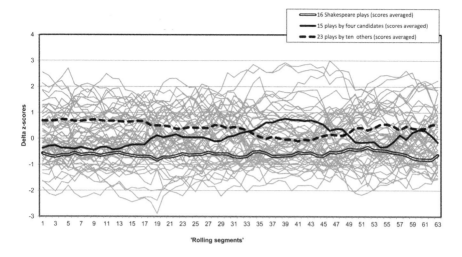

Figure 3.4 *3 Henry VI* (Folio): sixteen scenes assigned to Shakespeare

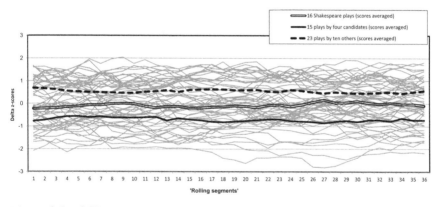

Figure 3.5 *3 Henry VI* (Folio): twelve scenes assigned as non-Shakespearean

to make a precise division of the play between Shakespeare's part and that of others. Whatever the *hubris* involved, we can claim at least that we are giving our successors the benefit of a large and static target to aim at.

Table 3.8 is an extension of Table 3.4, adding results for two new target texts. These 'texts' are, of course, the 16 scenes assigned to Shakespeare and the twelve assigned as non-Shakespearean. The respective means, standard deviations and ranges all have more in common with the homogeneity of *Hamlet* and *Twelfth Night* than with the heterogeneity of *Titus Andronicus* or of *3 Henry VI* when it is treated as a whole. A successful division of the 28 scenes of *3 Henry VI* into two such subsets would more than match our hopes. The results shown in Table 3.7 point to a worthwhile level of success.

Figures 3.4 and 3.5, which illustrate these remarks and complete our case, gain their full force when they are compared with Figures 3.1 and 3.2. In each of the new pair of graphs, the three main entry-lines distinguish Shakespearean from non-Shakespearean components of *3 Henry VI*. The familiar separation between our four candidates and the ten dramatists who wrote our 'other' 23 plays fails in one phase of Figure 3.4 but nowhere else in either graph. In that phase, as in Figure 3.2, the other dramatists lie closer to Shakespeare.

This is a suggestive irregularity, which testifies to Shakespeare's authorship of the scenes we have assigned to him. The phase in question embraces the two scenes of brisk dialogue involving Lady Anne. (They are brought side by side here because Act III, Scene iii has been assigned to the non-Shakespearean set of scenes.) Elsewhere in the 'Shakespeare' scenes, *Richard II* and *Richard III* tend to show most affinity for the segments under review. But in the segments embracing this part of the play, the nearest affinities lie with *The Taming of the Shrew* and *The Two Gentlemen of Verona* – Shakespeare still, but now in early comic mode.

The lowest of the three main entry-lines in Figures 3.4 and 3.5 is less low than that of Figure 3.2. This can also be seen in the averages offered in Table 3.8. Thoughts of possible revision of the text as we have it or of interpolated speeches here and there cannot be dismissed. But the smooth entry-lines for the assigned authorial group in Figures 3.4 and 3.5, like the low standard deviations corresponding to them in Table 3.8, testify against any heavy effects of either kind.

We are conscious that, though our results offer more than we had hoped within the present article, the task is not complete. We believe that our tests have enabled us to meet our immediate goals of establishing whether Shakespeare had any authorial role and of distinguishing which other dramatists were the most likely contributors to a collaboration. But we have not yet attempted to distinguish among the possible contributions of Greene, Kyd, Marlowe and Peele. Until that is done, the case for a possible interloper cannot be completely extinguished. Nor have we pursued the relationship between the Folio and the Octavo texts as far as it deserves.

These further tasks are daunting and may prove insurmountable. The main difficulty is that, except perhaps for Marlowe, the other candidates offer small or very mixed sets of plays. The difficulty may well be relieved by the fact that we can now focus directly on the twelve scenes that declare themselves as non-Shakespearean. As for the 16 that declare themselves Shakespearean, it is a pleasure to find that they include the most memorable parts of the play. Robert Greene is thought to have been alleging plagiarism when he turned a line from *3 Henry VI* itself to declare that Shakespeare had a 'Tygers heart wrapt in a Players hide'. Perhaps he knew a better dramatist when he saw one and could not contain his envy.

Appendix

We observed in our tests that Shakespeare plays were over-represented among the low Delta scores. Three explanations offered themselves: the word-list was biased towards words where Shakespeare was distinctive; the means and standard deviations were biased towards Shakespeare patterns of use; or, the style of Shakespeare's plays was such that their counts of common words tended to come out close to overall means.

We tested the first explanation by comparing a list of the 150 most common among the 201 function words (which was the total pool of such variables available) in the full 54-play set with a list of the 150 most common in the 38 plays written by authors other than Shakespeare. Of the 150 words, 146 were common to both lists. (The second list lost two words and acquired two others from the pool.) This difference was so small that we ruled out bias in the word-list as a factor. Membership of the list is all that matters here: mere differences of rank in the frequency-hierarchy do not govern the outcome.

We examined the second and third explanations together by running a Delta procedure with the 'target text' scores as in fact means. We were thus using Delta to measure the proximity of the plays to a given mean. The first mean we used was the mean of the full set (that is to say, the same mean used as the basis for Delta). Shakespeare plays were over-represented among the plays that lie closest to this mean. Take, for example, the ten closest plays. Given that there were 16 Shakespeare plays in the set of 54, the random expectation was $10*16/54=3.0$, but there were in fact eight Shakespeare plays in the top ten. The expectation for the ten most remote plays, those with the highest Delta scores, was again 3.0, but there were no Shakespeare plays in this group.

We then ran a Delta procedure using the means for the 38 non-Shakespeare plays as the 'target text'. There was some small variation compared to the preceding outcome but there were five Shakespeare plays in the closest ten and none in the furthest ten. Evidently the contribution of the Shakespeare plays to the 54-set means and standard deviations does not explain the tendency of Shakespeare plays to lie closer to the mean.

We also ran a Delta where the non-Shakespeare means and standard deviations were the base for the analysis and the non-Shakespeare means formed the 'target text'. In this case there were again five Shakespeare plays in the ten closest (e=3.0) and still no Shakespeare plays in the furthest ten (e=3.0). Thus, even when the target is a mean that excludes scores for Shakespeare, Shakespeare plays are generally much closer than expected to the mean. *Richard III* was the closest of all 54 plays to the non-Shakespeare mean. Not surprisingly, the Shakespeare plays are not so closely clustered towards the mean overall when the mean is a non-Shakespeare one as when the mean includes the Shakespeare plays.

We have also sometimes suspected that Marlowe plays are also biased towards the mean. The mean-to-mean results (using the full set of 54) do not support this. The expectation that a Marlowe play would come in the closest or furthest ten is 10*5/54=0.9. The actual counts were none in the closest ten and two in the furthest ten.

Shakespeare plays tend to be longer than the others (mean length: 21,137 words, compared to 16,917). It is possible that this helps explain the Shakespeare tendency to yield lower Delta scores and closer proximity to means. A good way to test this would be to use the first 5,000 or 10,000 words of each play, rather than the whole plays, for calculations of distances from the mean. We postponed this analysis to a future time when Craig and Whipp's 'Intelligent Archive', the software used here, is able to make such tests automatically. Despite this reservation, it appears that the last of our three possible explanations is best – that the style of Shakespeare's plays is such that their counts of common words tend to come out close to overall means. Osvaldo Rosso and his collaborators have examined a larger set of plays by Shakespeare and his contemporaries alongside a set of poems from the same period, and conclude that the Shakespeare works are indeed unusually close to the overall mean.[14]

References

Argamon, Shlomo, 'Interpreting Burrows's Delta: Geometric and Probabilistic Foundations', *Literary and Linguistic Computing* 23 (2008): 131–48.

Burrows, John, 'Computers and the Idea of Authorship', in Deryck Schreuder (ed.), *The Humanities and a Creative Nation: Jubilee Essays* (Canberra: Australian Academy of the Humanities, 1995): 89–108. Reprinted by invitation in Fotis Jannidis, Gerhard Lauer et al. (eds), *Rückkehr des Autors. Zur Erneuerung eines umstrittenen Begriffs* (Tübingen: Niemeyer Verlag, 1999): 133–44.

Burrows, John, 'Delta: A Measure of Stylistic Difference and a Guide to Likely Authorship', *Literary and Linguistic Computing* 17 (2002): 267–86.

Burrows, John, 'Questions of Authorship: Attribution and Beyond', *Computers and the Humanities* 37 (2003): 1–26.

Burrows, John, 'All the Way Through: Testing for Authorship in Different Frequency Strata', *Literary and Linguistic Computing* 22 (2007): 27–47.

Cairncross, Andrew S. (ed.), *The Third Part of King Henry VI*, Arden edn, second series (London: Methuen, 1964).

Cox, John D. and Eric Rasmussen (eds), *King Henry VI Part 3*, Arden edn, third series (London: Thomson, 2001).

Craig, Hugh, 'The Three Parts of *Henry VI*', in Hugh Craig and Arthur F. Kinney (eds), *Shakespeare, Computers, and the Mystery of Authorship* (Cambridge: Cambridge University Press, 2009): 40–77.

Craig, Hugh, 'Style, Statistics, and New Models of Authorship', *Early Modern Literary Studies* 15 (2009–10), paragraphs 1–42, available at: < http://purl.oclc.org/emls/15-1/craistyl.htm>.

---

14   Rosso, Craig and Moscato (2009).

Dover Wilson, John (ed.), *The Third Part of King Henry VI* (Cambridge: Cambridge University Press, 1952).

Forsyth, Richard, David Holmes and Emily Tse, 'Cicero, Sigonio, and Burrows: Investigating the Authenticity of the *Consolatio*', *Literary and Linguistic Computing* 14 (1999): 375–400.

Hoover, David, 'Testing Burrows's "Delta"', *Literary and Linguistic Computing* 19 (2004): 453–75.

Rosso, Osvaldo, Hugh Craig and Pablo Moscato, 'Shakespeare and Other English Renaissance Authors as Characterized by Information Theory Complexity Quantifiers', *Physica A* 388 (2009): 916–26.

Vickers, Brian, *Shakespeare Co-Author: A Historical Study of Five Collaborative Plays* (Oxford: Oxford University Press, 2002).

Vickers, Brian, 'Thomas Kyd: Secret Sharer' *TLS* (13 April 2008): 13–15.

Chapter 4

Collaboration and Dissent: Challenges of Collaborative Standards for Digital Humanities

Julia Flanders

Collaboration—literally a shared work—is always understood to carry with it some kind of sacrifice, a trade-off between autonomy and synergy. In our collaborative relationships, we intensify the concessions we make to the demands of the social contract, and we voluntarily submit to norms of behavior and constraints on our freedom of action in order to gain the benefits of a group undertaking: a barn-raising, a collection of essays, a successful conference. But even before we as collaborators can adopt these norms, we (in a larger sense) also have to develop them. The collaboration of conversation is predicated on the norms of language; collaboration on a scholarly edition is predicated on a set of private agreements about the editorial mission, set against the backdrop of larger disciplinary expectations concerning what editing means and how it proceeds. So we might start by observing that collaboration takes place within frames of expectation that may be private, local, professional, or broadly social. The vectors of agreement and conformance are thus not solely between the collaborators themselves, but also between the collaborators and some standards that operate beyond their own sphere of activity.

What makes collaboration between projects in the digital humanities particularly interesting—and particularly challenging—is the way that these different frames of expectation intersect. Digital humanities projects take place, strikingly, in a universe constrained by a set of technical norms that govern the informational and operational behavior of the digital environment. Because these collaborations are so often aimed at building something that works—a tool, a resource, an online collection—the collaborative activities are typically mediated through things like software tools and data standards that are quite uncompromising. For instance, XML documents must obey the rules of structural well-formedness prescribed by the XML standard; dates entered into a metadata record must follow the agreed-upon format or the sorting routines that operate on this data will not work. (Geoffrey Nunberg's 2009 critique of Google Books' metadata illustrates the consequences of failure vividly.) These technical standards mediate the collaboration by eliminating the need to create all of these conventions from scratch, and the more exacting they are (and the more exactly they are observed), the more powerful the technical outcome. High-function digital projects arise from strong adherence to the right standards.

But in addition, as these projects arise from humanities research, they also require agreement concerning disciplinary norms that shape the practices of digital representation. These include, for instance, acceptable practices of transcription, regularization and emendation; acceptable standards of authenticity and verification; the kinds of commentary and contextualization that are acceptable or required; and beliefs about the interpretive or analytical or critical goals that are at stake. These norms arise from detailed, ongoing debates concerning both the ultimate goals of scholarship and the methods and practices by which we achieve them.

A traditional humanities view of this picture might ask what these two sets of norms have to do with one another, any more than the editorial standards for a critical edition have to do with the standards guiding the machinery that binds the book. But what the field of digital humanities as a whole has revealed is precisely how tightly interwoven and mutually consequential "technical" and "disciplinary" standards often are. Our concern in this discussion is in fact a domain in which disciplinary and technical norms overlap and where we see, locked in struggle, the drive towards absolute consistency and technical processability on the one hand, and the drive towards critical independence and disciplinary debate on the other. I am referring here to the arena of standards for digital representation of research materials, and in particular the domain of scholarly markup languages. Standards of this kind are an essential precondition for the development of collaborative projects in the digital humanities, because they permit us to exchange scholarly information about research materials in a digital form.

A markup language is a method of digital representation through which we can create highly complex models of textual artifacts. The markup constitutes an information structure which formalizes, labels, and enhances the source material: it makes explicit the nature and function of each piece of information, and through that explicitness makes it possible for non-human processes (such as computers) to "understand" and make use of the resulting digital object in ways that take advantage of its self-knowledge about its own structure and content. A manuscript letter marked in this way can carry with it the knowledge of which words have been deleted or replaced by the author, and a software system can use that knowledge (for instance, to generate a final edited version of the text). A collection of such manuscripts, if marked consistently, can yield a systematic analysis of their authors' revision practices.

Text markup of this kind, as practiced in the digital humanities world, sits at the juncture of humanities scholarship—textually nuanced, exploratory, and introspective—and digital technology, with its emphasis on formalism, consistency, and upward scalability. As a result its norms carry a double weight: they must achieve some kind of technically actionable uniformity, but they must also express useful scholarly concepts and differentiations. They draw their functional precision and power from the domain of technical norms, and also their capacity to broker collaborative exchange at a practical level. But they draw their relevance and intellectual usefulness from the domain of disciplinary norms, which as we have seen are fundamentally and on principle resistant to standardization, and in fact might be said to thrive like yeast in a state of fermentation (though without drowning in their own byproducts).

Debates about how to balance these competing concerns in the markup community—and particularly in the community of the Text Encoding Initiative (TEI)—are lively and sustained. The goals of standardization and facilitated interchange were articulated by the planners of the TEI at the earliest stages of their discussion in the Poughkeepsie Planning Conference of 1987, as documented in the first of the so-called "Poughkeepsie Principles": "Poughkeepsie Principle 1: The guidelines are intended to provide a standard format for data interchange in humanities research" (TEI, 1988). These goals have remained strongly in view during the succeeding years, during which the TEI Guidelines have undergone sustained development and use, and have become one of the most deeply researched features of the digital humanities landscape. At the same time, the challenges of maintaining the double force noted above—the power of both strong formalism and expressive nuance—have become much more vividly apparent. For some developers, the attempt to maintain expressiveness simply undermines the goal of interchange and places the entire enterprise at risk. Characteristic of this view is the following quote from a 1997 posting by Mark Olsen to the *Humanist* discussion list, in which he is complaining about the laxity and permissiveness of the TEI Guidelines as a technical standard, a few years after the first public release of those guidelines:

> The real test of an INTERCHANGE format, however, is … that the format can be automatically converted TO and FROM any number of systems with a minimum of effort. My principal objection to TEI is that it is by far the most difficult representation to convert into something else, because of its expressive power. The more tightly constrained a specification, the easier it is to write converters. It is a BALANCING act, which I do not believe the TEI community has—because of its make-up and structure—really tried to perform. (Olsen, 1997; emphasis in original)

This position has also been strongly argued in subsequent debates about the nature and value of what is termed "TEI conformance": that is, the formal methods by which adherence to the TEI Guidelines can be assessed. The rationale for the current definition of conformance, in which conforming documents must be a strict subset of the unmodified TEI,[1] focuses on several practical goals involving the exchange of data:

---

1   That is, they must use only elements and element structures that are defined in the unmodified TEI; any conforming TEI-encoded document must be valid against

- interchange or integration of documents amongst different researchers or users;
- software specifications for TEI-aware processing tools;
- agreements for the deposit of texts in, and distribution of texts from, archives;
- specifying the form of documents to be produced by or for a given project. (TEI Consortium, 2011: 23.3)

The countering position, equally strongly felt and argued, is that one can only achieve such strong standardization and uniformity by eliminating a degree of depth and nuance that is essential to the intellectual quality of the enterprise. Michael Sperberg-McQueen, one of the original editors of the TEI Guidelines, responded to an earlier version of Mark Olsen's plea above by offering him an extremely reduced and simplified subset of the TEI and:

> ... demonstrating, by a reductio ad absurdum, how reducing a tag set to this size ... forces one to omit too much material which can be useful in the encoding of virtually any text, and which is absolutely essential for dealing rationally with some texts. (Sperberg-McQueen, 1995)

Sperberg-McQueen's point about textual complexity is even more true when we consider the role that markup plays in representing not just texts but our views about texts: our methodological assumptions, our editorial decisions, our critical debates. The prospects for representing these in a simple and uniform manner are generally acknowledged on both sides of the debate to be extremely poor. Clearly these arguments would not apply to projects whose goals for text representation are quite simple (for instance, digital library projects where the transcription serves only to provide searchable full text to accompany a page image). But for projects in which the TEI functions as a representation of scholarly work, the accommodation of nuanced intellectual expression is clearly crucial.

In debates about this issue, it is usually assumed (as Mark Olsen assumes) that a strongly enforced uniformity will facilitate collaboration, and conversely that heterogeneity and dissent will militate against it. Our instinct may thus be, in the context of digital standards, to treat disciplinary debate as the opponent: something that needs to be eliminated or ignored in order for collaboration to proceed. I would like instead to suggest otherwise: that in fact the humanities dimension of digital humanities work makes this elimination impossible and also undesirable. But it will help if we can first establish a more nuanced and carefully structured view of the precise role of dissent within our collaborative ecology.

---

the unmodified TEI schema or be transformable into a valid document with no loss of information.

Collaboration and Dissent

One place where collaboration has been examined from a philosophical and political (rather than a business-efficiency) perspective is in theories of collaborative learning, and John Trimbur, in a 1989 essay entitled "Consensus and Difference in Collaborative Learning," provides a particularly thoughtful and critical analysis of some key points: he is considering the dynamics of consensus within learning environments but also making a larger point about the way that social negotiations take place. Trimbur marks consensus as central to collaboration, but for him, a crucial element of the discursive practice of consensus is dissent: not just the need to democratically acknowledge a minority view, but the need to base consensus on "collective explanations of how people differ" (1989: 610). This "dissensus" is a representation of fractures within the discourse: an acknowledgement of the existence of the periphery, the discourses out of power:

> We will need, that is, to look at collaborative learning not merely as a process of consensus-making but more important[ly] as a process of identifying differences and locating these differences in relation to each other. The consensus that we ask students to reach in the collaborative classroom will be based not so much on collective agreements as on collective explanations of how people differ, where their differences come from, and whether they can live and work together with these differences. (Trimbur, 1989: 610).

Dissensus thus functions as a way of establishing a critical relationship between the consensus and the dissenting voices. In other words, dissent occupies an informationally important and illuminating position in the universe: "not as the goal of the conversation but rather as a critical measure to help students identify the structures of power." With this understanding of the role of dissent, Trimbur argues, we can finally see consensus not as a rational, realizable goal (akin to finding out that we really all do want the same thing) but rather as a recognition of the "inexhaustibility of difference" and a will to "organize the conditions in which we live and work accordingly" (1989: 615).

This argument offers a very interesting perspective on standards development, and one that understandably does not get much play in that domain. However, the digital humanities is in a position to attend to the fact that standards do arise from and represent power structures; they represent the functional homogenization that is one outcome of "community": the consent to being homogenized. And as a community-driven standard arising from the digital humanities, the TEI is rare (but perhaps also characteristic) in taking seriously the legitimacy of dissenting views while also seeking a technically functional outcome. It needs such views to exist—indeed, it relies on their existence as the driving force behind its own onward progress—but it wants them to exist *in relation to the community at large*, as part of the discourse rather than apart from it.

We can now usefully circle back to comment on the word "standard" in the context of Trimbur's observations, especially since in an important sense the TEI is not in fact a standard according to a strict definition of the term. The sphere in which strict definitions operate with relevance to the digital humanities is that of governmental and para-governmental standards (such as the American National Standards Institute), international non-governmental organizations (such as the International Organization for Standardization), and industrial standards bodies (such as the World Wide Web Consortium). Standards promulgated by such bodies have the force, if not always of law, at least of definitional hegemony: a standard for measuring photographic film speed or tuning frequencies sets the parameters within which all activities will effectively operate.

Standards by their nature thus impose a uniformity that, in effect, creates consensus by fiat. Once they are in place, we obey them because we value the consensus they represent (and the cohesion and practical efficiency they enable) more than our own individual right to do things differently. Furthermore, within the domain of digital humanities, adherence to (open) standards is framed as a kind of good citizenship, the necessary precondition for a free interchange of data. The world without standards is a world of chaos—a post-Babel cacophony of conflicting and mutually unintelligible voices. But it is also a world of plurality, and the transition from that plurality to the uniformity of the standard is worth noting as an important change of state. The website of the British Standards Institution (BSI) includes this succinct statement on the nature of consensus standards, which tellingly places its emphasis on this exact point:

> All formal standards are developed with a period of public enquiry and full consultation. They incorporate the views and expertise of a very wide range of interests from consumers, academia, special interest groups, government, business and industry. As a result, standards represent a consensus on current best practice. (BSI, 2010)

The deftness with which we move from that "wide range of interests" (which has a double force: both a variety of differing interests and a representative set of interests) to the "consensus on current best practice" elides what must necessarily have happened: the elimination or bypassing by one means or another of that original plurality of views.

In fact, hard-headedly, standards present us with a balance or trade-off: they represent an operation of power, which may have been exercised with more or less attention to minority opinions, and may place more or less constraint on our meaningful freedom of action, and may provide more or less practical benefit to us and to society. Different standards bodies and different standards sit at different points along these three axes. It is hard to feel very put out about not being consulted about the standard for measuring the twist of single-ply yarn, but many of us may feel a greater stake in the ISO standard for representing the sex of humans, in which the permitted values are 0 (not known), 1 (male), 2 (female), and 9 (not specified) (ISO, 2004). But even the best arrangement of these factors—the most open process, the least constraint, the greatest practical benefit—in the end does represent as "consensus" an end-product about which there actually has been, and may still be, disagreement. There is no need to standardize what no one differs on.

Collaboration and the TEI

The TEI occupies a distinctive position within this landscape—first of all, because it does not claim the status of a standard for its guidelines. They "make recommendations" about methods of representing textual sources in digital form, but these recommendations have their force solely within the sphere of activity of the TEI itself: in order to claim to be using the TEI Guidelines, you have to use the TEI Guidelines. This internal regulation of the TEI community positions the TEI as a standards body *for that community of usage*, and for this reason the TEI is often described as a "community standard," both in its own self-description and by others. But this terminology deserves some scrutiny because, even thus qualified, it aligns the TEI's guiding enterprise with goals of uniformity and consensus that, as we have seen above, have proven problematic from the outset. In order to understand how this "community standard" operates *as a standard* within the TEI community and hence as a collaborative tool, we need to understand the role that dissensus, in Trimbur's sense, may play in its formation and use.

Encoding standards like the TEI are foundationally collaborative technologies: they presume the need and the desire to co-ordinate shared work, to generalize individual insight to a community, and to support the extension, critique, and re-use of ideas and techniques. But how, concretely, does the TEI figure in a typical digital humanities project? A simple example would be a pair of scholars who are working together on a digital edition of a very long manuscript that must be transcribed and annotated: for instance, the Almanacks of Mary Moody Emerson—a 1,000-page manuscript currently being edited and encoded by Sandra Petrulionis and Noelle Baker, in collaboration with the Women Writers Project (WWP) at Brown University. If they divide up the manuscript, each taking a section, their agreement on a shared encoding system such as the TEI makes it possible for them to work together while also working separately: the encoding standard diminishes the need for day-to-day consultation on details of digital representation. When they combine their work, it should form a consistent whole, and when at last they hand it to the WWP for publication, it should fit in with the other materials in our collection that have also been prepared in this way.

In this typical kind of collaboration, the parties to the shared effort know of each other, and their intention to work together is explicit; in effect, a collaborative vector is established between them that operates in real time, mediated by their use of the encoding standard. As a more complex example, however, take a project like the Electronic Archive of Greek and Latin Epigraphy, which is a federation of epigraphic databases: online collections of ancient inscriptions on stone, metal, clay, and other durable surfaces. Scholars in several different countries want to be able to contribute to such collections, knowing that in doing so they are contributing to a single, vast, comprehensive resource, rather than to one of many that are small, isolated, and partial. In order to accomplish this goal, they need a common standard for transcription and editing, and in fact this group is now using the TEI as the basis for their digitization efforts: the TEI-based epigraphic transcription standard is known as EpiDoc. In this collaboration, although the scholars involved know that they are contributing to a shared resource, they do not necessarily feel themselves to be working at all times directly *with* all of the other scholars: the model is more of a hub and spokes, rather than a direct person-to-person network.

This kind of indirect collaboration leads us in turn to a third case which has particular importance for the digital humanities. Imagine the same hub-and-spokes model, but now let us think of the spokes as extending not only into space but into time as well. The recent rise of interest in humanities data curation demonstrates how crucial these longitudinal collaborative vectors can be. Digital resources that we create today do not exhaust their value in the first few years of use; on the contrary, unlike research in the sciences, which has a fairly deterministic half-life, humanities research materials have a horizon of usefulness that is much more complex, unpredictable, and prolonged. The British Women Romantic Poets (BWRP) project is a substantial collection of Romantic-era poetry by women, created at the University of California, Davis in the late 1990s; it has been available on the web in its original form for years.[2] But in addition, this project contributed texts from their collection to the WWP's online collection, Women Writers Online, and the BWRP collection is now also included in NINES, the large federated collection of resources for the study of nineteenth-century literature.[3] The WWP and NINES are taking advantage of the intelligibility of the BWRP data—its use of standards like the TEI—to do things with these materials that were not specifically envisioned by their creators. But the intelligibility of the data in itself—the intention that it be re-used—constitutes an important collaborative gesture. The "collaboration" here is real and important, and yet takes place across time and without direct interaction.

This kind of indirect collaboration is at present rare—and indeed, there is a strong anecdotal "literature" attesting to the difficulties in accomplishing it—but it exercises a powerful mythic influence on the ways in which we think about how we create digital humanities resources and why. As *digital* humanists, we are committed to encoding our data in a standard way so that it can be shared, so that it will remain comprehensible: in fulfillment of an implicit contract with unknown scholars of the future who need to know what we know and understand what we have done. But at the same time, as we have already seen, as digital *humanists,*

---

2   See: <http://digital.lib.ucdavis.edu/projects/bwrp/>.

3   NINES is the Networked Infrastructure for Nineteenth-Century Electronic Scholarship: <http://www.nines.org>.

we know that a crucially important dimension of that representation is precisely the disciplinary norms that we adopt, and these we know to be founded on debate rather than on straightforward agreement. We can assume, in other words, that our future collaborators will disagree with us on some fundamental point, while nonetheless wishing to make use of what we have done. So the question then is: what needs to be expressed in order for this kind of longitudinal collaboration—one in which the first collaborator has to play their full hand before the other even comes into the game—to work? Is there any conduit through which such a negotiation can take place?

There is, but it takes a complex form. What is needed in this case is not simply a common language for data representation, but more importantly, a common mechanism for *negotiating about data representation*. And that, I would like to argue, is exactly what the TEI properly provides: not a perfect language for collaboration, but a—let us call it functional—mechanism for negotiating about language: in fact, a mechanism for negotiating dissent.

TEI Customization

In order to give some concreteness to this assertion, we need to take a brief excursus into the details of the TEI customization mechanism, which is the form given to this negotiation process. The TEI encoding language is not a single, unitary thing: it is a vast landscape of possibility that covers domains as remote as manuscript description, dictionaries, drama, oral history, and linguistic corpora. The TEI community as a whole needs to be able to represent all of these things, but any individual project needs just a selection: manuscripts and drama, say, or verse and scholarly editing. So the TEI language is represented at the most basic level as a set of possibilities: a single source file (called the "ODD")[4] that represents the entire landscape of the TEI in potential terms.

To represent our own, more selective view of that landscape, we need another piece of information, a separate file which is called an ODD customization. The ODD customization file represents the world of an individual user or project: the set of choices through which the individual adapts the TEI schema to local usage. These choices may simply be selections from among the various parts of the TEI (elements to encode manuscripts, elements for scholarly editing, elements for representing dictionaries or drama or verse). They may also take the form of added constraint: for instance, a project may wish to limit the vocabulary used to describe poetic genres. But they may also be extensions: added elements for things that the TEI cannot yet represent, or changes to TEI elements to reflect local needs.

From these two files (the main TEI ODD and the ODD customization), with appropriate processing, one can then generate a schema that expresses the

---

4 The origin of this terminology is whimsical: because the ODD file represents both the schema itself and the documentation of the schema, "one document does-it-all."

TEI landscape as viewed through the lens of the individual application. And by comparing any two (or more) customization files, one can also in principle gain an understanding of how two projects differ in their representation of data. There are thus several potential vectors of difference or dissent that can be expressed here: between the individual researcher or project and the TEI community as a whole (expressed through actual changes and extensions to the unmodified TEI language), and also between different individual researchers or projects.

To give a concrete example, let us take the Women Writers Project again: a long-standing TEI project with a somewhat idiosyncratic set of texts, experimental views on text encoding, and a strong collaborative instinct. The WWP's TEI customization captures a number of important things:

- the specific sections of the TEI that the project actually uses (for instance, the TEI module for names and dates, the module for linking);
- the controlled vocabularies used in classifying things like verse structures;
- the changes which the project has made to individual textual structures, to accommodate the idiosyncrasies of the WWP's texts or of their thinking about them.

So in this case, the customization immediately serves two important functions: first, to express and document the rationale behind the WWP's encoding practice; and second, to express in formal terms the relationship between that practice and the TEI Guidelines themselves.

Imagine, though, that in a few decades, after the project has run its course and its data is part of the Brown University repository, another group of researchers (perhaps working on women's writing in French) wants to use this data, in combination with their own, to compare ideas of genre across languages. In the wild, this project is utterly hopeless. But if both groups are using the TEI, the process is eased: the peculiarities of each project's encoding are expressed as points of dissent from the TEI itself: in other words, from a known quantity. In areas where the WWP does not disagree with the TEI, it uses the standard terms and structural concepts. The second project, coming later, is able to use the standard TEI markup present in the existing project data unmodified; from the WWP's ODD file they can also see explicitly where this encoding dissented from the TEI consensus, and assess how these points of difference accord with their own methods (and modify the WWP data if necessary). They can also bring in data from other TEI projects on the same basis: because all of the dissent has been organized into a set of vectors all pointing in towards the same hub (instead of being expressed combinatorially), the challenge of harmonizing the data and discerning the points of essential agreement and disagreement is significantly diminished (though, of course, not eliminated).

What is taking place here is a form of negotiation that manages in a subtle and bizarre way to be bi-directional, even though it takes place across the passage of time. Each project, through its TEI customization, places its data in an explicit relation to the standard, with any reservations or qualifications clearly expressed: thereby deliberately putting the data "up for collaboration." What is distinctive about the TEI customization mechanism is that it formalizes dissent in this way, in relation to the standard, and allows its vector to be traversed in two directions. The same path that leads away from the unmodified TEI standard towards the individual application (from generality to specificity) can also be followed back to the center again. This traversal can be effected both by human beings and by computer processes. Information concerning what has been changed and why can be expressed in human-readable form and may serve as a valuable support in understanding the methodological choices that underlie a project's encoding practice.

Similarly, the ODD customization file can serve as the basis for automated analysis of difference and similarity of encoding methods. By analyzing a set of customization files, for example, we could identify all projects from a large set that use the same set of TEI modules or remove the same set of elements. We could generate a list representing the greatest common set of values for a given vocabulary (such as poetic genres) across a group of projects, and also identify the values that are unique to each project, or identify the range of new elements created by each project, together with their closest TEI equivalents.

Interoperability and Collaboration

Considered as a whole, the customizable approach taken by the TEI permits the standard to function (both socially and technically) as an agreement at many levels—on the intention to treat data as a sharable and preservable resource, on the value of shared data standards, on the descriptive utility of this particular approach to modeling humanities texts, and on the impossibility of creating a single descriptive model that will satisfy all needs.

This last point may seem like a significant or even fatal concession, and it may be appropriate to consider here whether collaboration, in the absence of a single descriptive model, is really possible at all. Would it not enhance the collaborative effect in the examples given earlier, for instance, if, instead of the elaborate articulations of the customization mechanism, we had a simple and uniform standard for exchanging data in an unambiguous manner? Is this not in fact the mission with which the TEI was initially begun? Martin Mueller put the case for the value of uniformity in a presentation at the 2008 TEI conference:

> To compare is to look for significant difference, but without comparability difference cannot be identified in the first place ... consistent encodings across many texts in a heterogeneous document space have a greater scholarly pay-off than finely grained encodings in closely defined but not necessarily compatible environments. (Mueller, 2008)

From this perspective, in which the goal of interoperability is given primacy, the heterogeneity of different encoding approaches looks simply like grit in the works.

The challenge here is to understand the relationship—and the difference—between interoperation and collaboration. Interoperation is a functional property of data and tools: a measure of how seamlessly a new data set will perform within a system not explicitly designed for it. If I have written a stylesheet that expects a certain kind of TEI data, and your data flows through it without producing error messages or an unprocessable residuum, then your data is interoperable with my stylesheet.

Or is it? What if our measure of seamlessness here is not the unimpeded working of the tool, but the meaningfulness of the output? Take as an example a stylesheet that is designed to generate an index of first lines in poetry. It looks for the first "verse line" child of each "poem", extracts it, and sorts the resulting list. Imagine now that my collection of poems includes some with epigraphs or introductory notes following the poem title. If the schema for poetry does not include separate markup elements for these features and I cannot alter it, I may be compelled to represent them as part of the poem itself, using the element designated for verse lines. The stylesheet, none the wiser, obediently identifies these and extracts them as "first lines" without complaint, and the resulting index contains a mix of first lines and things that are not first lines but cannot be distinguished from them. From the standpoint of interoperability, the error is hard to detect. The data itself is structurally indistinguishable from what the system anticipates; the problem is simply that the data is lying.

This problem is not a belated discovery, but a deep tension that has inhabited the design of the TEI from the start. Let us now recall, from earlier on, Poughkeepsie Principle 1: "The guidelines are intended to provide a standard format for data interchange in humanities research." This seems like an unambiguous statement about the primacy of interchange and its dependency on concepts of standardization. But in the "Design Principles for Text Encoding Guidelines" which comment and expand on these principles, the editors of the TEI Guidelines note concerning this point: "For interchange, it must be possible to translate from any existing scheme for text encoding into the TEI scheme without loss of information. All distinctions present in the original encoding must be preserved" (TEI, 1988). Meaningful interchange and interoperability thus require us to attend not only to the structural uniformity of our data, but to its semantic uniformity as well:[5] in other words, the distinctions being preserved in one encoding must be mapped onto the distinctions that are relevant in another encoding. The brief admonition that "all distinctions present in the original encoding must be preserved" is in fact a statement in support of the distinctiveness of that "original encoding" and the legitimacy of its distinctions: the role of the interchange format is to permit

---

5 I am indebted to my colleague Syd Bauman for discussions that have helped me clarify this point. His article "Interchange vs. Interoperability" (Bauman 2011) appeared too late to be discussed in detail here but is essential reading.

translation, not to efface difference. As Sperberg-McQueen's admonition to Olsen insists, uniformity comes only at the cost of eliminating what is "absolutely essential for dealing rationally with some texts." Fifteen years after that exchange, with digital editing now an important application of the TEI, we might expand this point to read "… and for dealing articulately with some editorial problems." The uniformity that cannot be assumed in our primary sources is equally rare in our scholarly methods. To collaborate effectively under these circumstances is thus a matter not of enforcing an artificial uniformity through which vital distinctions are elided, but rather of supporting the real and accurate exchange of the data in which we have a strong stake. The fundamental question, in other words, is whether we really want to hear what our collaborators really have to say.

This is not an argument for diversity for its own sake. In a strong collaborative ecology, the corollary of respecting each other's differences is respecting the commonalities that draw us into joint work in the first place. Structurally speaking, the TEI customization mechanism is as well suited to creating schemas that reflect a well-honed, tightly constrained expression of those commonalities as it is to expressing individual divergences from the consensus. But while a well-constructed schema can represent and support a consensus of this kind, it cannot create it. A standard like the TEI, in other words, is not the appropriate mechanism for *producing* a successful collaborative agreement except in cases where the quality of the data (its semantic nuance or its methodological rigor) is of no consequence. It is, rather, an extraordinarily effective mechanism for *representing* such an agreement once it has been made by the collaborating parties.

This point complicates what is commonly assumed about data standards in the digital humanities: that they support collaboration unproblematically, and that the better we standardize, the stronger our collaborations will be. Representational systems like the TEI operate in a domain where our descriptions, in their complexity and their consequentiality, reach towards the condition of human language and thought. This complexity is a strength and a measure of the intellectual potential of these representations, not a weakness. The challenge—as with human language—is to achieve mutual intelligibility while still being able to say what is worth saying. Collaboration, too, walks this precarious line between egoism and altruism, between private insight and public communication, between local nuance and common ground. In this respect, the TEI is not simply a tool for collaboration but a methodological reflection of its structure at the deepest level.

References

Allen, C., 'Guidelines for Supporting ISO Code Sets' (2007), available at: <http://ns.hr-xml.org/2_5/HR-XML-2_5/CPO/GuidelinesForISOUtilities.html> (accessed 20 May 2010).

Bauman, S. 'Interchange vs. Interoperability', Balisage: The Markup Conference, Montreal, 2–5 August 2011. In *Proceedings of Balisage: The Markup*

Conference 2011. Balisage Series on Markup Technologies, Vol. 7 (2011), available at: http://www.balisage.net/Proceedings/vol7/html/Bauman01/ BalisageVol7-Bauman01.html (accessed 17 February 2012).

British Standards Institution (BSI), 'What Are the Differences between Consensus and Commissioned Standards?' (2010), available at: <http://www.bsigroup.com/en/Standards-and-Publications/About-standards/Differences-between-Consensus-and-Commissioned-standards/> (accessed 20 May 2010).

Burnard, L. and S. Bauman (eds), 'Guidelines for Electronic Text Encoding and Interchange', TEI Consortium (2007), available at: <http://www.tei-c.org/release/doc/tei-p5-doc/en/html/index-toc.html> (accessed 20 May 2010).

ISO, 'Information Technology: Codes for the Representation of Human Sexes' (2004), available at: <http://standards.iso.org/ittf/PubliclyAvailableStandards/c036266_ISO_IEC_5218_2004(E_F).zip>. See also <http://en.wikipedia.org/wiki/ISO_5218> (accessed 20 May 2010).

Mueller, M., 'TEI-Analytics and the MONK Project', TEI Annual Conference, London, 6–8 November 2008, available at: <http://www.cch.kcl.ac.uk/cocoon/tei2008/programme/abstracts/abstract-169.html> (accessed 20 May 2010).

Nunberg, G., 'Google's Book Search: A Disaster for Scholars', *The Chronicle of Higher Education* [Online] (31 August 2009), available at: <http://chronicle.com/article/Googles-Book-Search-A/48245/> (accessed 20 May 2010).

Olsen, M., *Humanist Discussion Group* 10.895 (1997), available at: <http://www.digitalhumanities.org/humanist/Archives/Virginia/v10/0515.html> (accessed 20 May 2010).

Sperberg-McQueen, C.M., 'Preface to TEI Bare' [Online] (1995), available at: <http://www.tei-c.org/Vault/Bare/> (accessed 20 May 2010).

TEI, 'Design Principles for Text Encoding Guidelines', TEI ED P1 (1988), available at: <http://cmsmcq.com/1990/edp1.html> (accessed 20 May 2010).

TEI Consortium (eds), *TEI P5: Guidelines for Electronic Text Encoding and Interchange*, Version 2.0.1, last updated 22 December 2011, available at: <http://www.tei-c.org/Guidelines/P5/>.

Trimbur, J., 'Consensus and Difference in Collaborative Learning', *College English* 51.6 (October 1989): 602–16.

Chapter 5

Digital Humanities in the Age of the Internet: Reaching Out to Other Communities

Susan Hockey

We are now living in an age when the Internet has extended far beyond its original uses in the academic and defence communities. For many of us it is the normal way of paying the bills, arranging travel, and buying books, clothes and the other necessities of everyday life, as well as communicating with our friends and family. Since use of the Internet is the norm for access to information and for interacting with vendors of products, is there anything in particular for the digital humanities to do other than to provide the equivalent for academia? Are its centres, conferences, journals and the other paraphernalia of academic life still justified? After all, much of what we read and use now in our work is in digital form.

This chapter will attempt to explore the role and impact of digital humanities in the age of the Internet. On the assumption that using digital resources in the course of humanities research or teaching is no longer worthy of special mention, the chapter will concentrate on how research and teaching within the digital humanities community can benefit Internet users as a whole. It will examine the influence which digital humanities has had so far and discuss potential developments. Overall the argument is made that the digital humanities is likely to have a strong future, but that this future could be even more robust if it looks not just at the traditional audience of academia but beyond that into the wider society, reaching out to communities beyond academia and developing links with a broader range of organizations.

Universities were early adopters of the Internet, but perhaps in some areas the ivory tower image still lives on and the impact of digital humanities research on the wider world outside has not been highlighted as much as it might have been. The current system of peer review, tenure and promotion places the emphasis on research, and on publication in outlets which are rarely read outside academia, in language which is best understood by the immediate intended audience. In my view, in this time of financial stringency and budget cuts, the importance of research carried out within digital humanities would benefit from more emphasis beyond its immediate audience. There is scope to provide plenty of evidence of value and to stress the benefits for a wider community as well as for academia.

Within academia activities are not driven by financial goals in the way that they are in the business world. However, universities do have budgets and they have to make ends meet. In the UK much of their income comes from the public purse, that is, from the taxpayer. In the eyes of university administrators, the one thing that singles out projects that are creating digital materials and associated tools is their expense in terms of resources, especially human resources. For those who are carrying out research, digital resources obviously save enormous amounts of time and effort, but they are costly to provide and maintain. Overall, it is easy to make the argument that digital research in the humanities is more expensive than traditional library-based work. In universities it has created more expense for libraries which is measured in real cash terms, whereas it is much more difficult to put a figure on the amount of time saved by using digital resources. In any case this figure does not appear in any financial statement in university accounting procedures. In this era of economic troubles and financial hardship, it is even more appropriate to examine the impact of digital humanities research and to identify evidence of value beyond that which is immediately obvious to the academic community.

Possibilities for Collaboration

The theme of this volume is collaboration, which in digital humanities is usually considered in terms of specific joint projects within academia, where the benefits of working together are reasonably well understood and where each party can identify outcomes that satisfy the requirements of their particular discipline. But what about collaboration in the broader sense, where resources, applications and tools reach a wider community and impact on what they do? Web 2.0 technologies facilitate feedback and information sharing. For digital humanities resources this feedback may not necessarily come from academic users. It could ultimately place a different perspective on the resource and encourage the resource creators and managers to move into different directions and to forge links with organizations outside the academic world.

What are the possibilities of collaboration with partners outside academia? Computers are now widely used in schools and a means of access could be provided to humanities resources at an appropriate level, perhaps even semi-automatically by using layers in markup. This would engage pupils and perhaps encourage some to get more involved with digital humanities activities, but can resources that are created for a more advanced audience be retooled with automatic assistance to meet the needs of younger users? With the growth in numbers of the so called 'silver surfers', life-long and leisure users form an increasing proportion of Internet users. They may be researching holidays for literary, historical or archaeological interest, starting either with Google or with websites mentioned in a printed guide book. Or they may be pursuing local and family history research, using archives or local and family history resources. These people are not subject to as many time pressures as those in employment and often have the ability to investigate a range of resources on a particular topic and to send feedback without the constant need to meet deadlines. More such 'crowd-sourcing' experiments are now taking place. It remains to be seen how much quality control might be required, although this will perhaps also depend on the nature of the primary audience for the resource.

Since I retired in 2004, I have had more time to pursue travel and local and family history interests, and I have been surprised at the number of possible links with digital humanities. In particular very large numbers of people are researching their own family history and looking for references to names in specific parts of the country. In a survey of six repositories carried out in 2002–2003, the LEADERS (Linking EAD to Electronically Retrievable Sources) Project found that in the National Archives and a sample of local authority repositories, most users were personal leisure orientated and 64 per cent of them were interested in individuals or organizations rather than specific topics (Sexton et al., 2004). There are many possibilities for tool development in name and record linkage, particularly when linked to place and other geographical information. The ReACH (Researching e-Science Analysis of Census Holdings) workshops organized by Melissa Terras in 2006 investigated how the huge family history databases held by Ancestry.co.uk might benefit from digital humanities tools, and concluded that there was potential for high performance processing of large scale census data, but that significant IPR issues need to be addressed when commercial data is involved (Terras, 2006).

Partnerships with the National Archives and other public bodies do exist and can turn out to be very successful, but these are partnerships between organizations that are all in the public sector and operate within public sector financing. While they need to deliver on their promises, they are less subject to the financial constraints of the commercial world. Partnerships with commercial organizations can provide an outlet for publication of the resource, and investment in marketing and support which is not easily found in academia. However, commercial organizations are driven primarily by the need to make money. They need income with which to pay their staff and operating overheads, and they need to satisfy their shareholders who expect a return on their investment. Otherwise they will no longer exist. Because of this, the possibilities for experimentation are fewer. The emphasis is on a final product which can generate sales, and provide sufficient income to support future releases and ensure that the company continues to exist. Moreover, in some instances, the need to protect intellectual property in which the company has significant investment may also begin to stifle imaginative use of the electronic resource by third parties.

The Impact of Digital Humanities Research

The Research Excellence Framework, which is the new system for assessing the quality of research in UK Higher Education Institutions, is an added impetus for reaching out beyond the academic community. It will include an evaluation of the impact of research. It states that: 'In the Research Excellence Framework significant additional recognition will be given where high quality research has contributed to the economy, society, public policy, culture, the environment, international development or quality of life' (HEFCE, 2010). This statement is sufficiently wide-ranging to be interpreted in many different ways and for many different disciplines. But at the core is an assumption that research that has significance beyond academia will attract additional recognition in the assessment process. Here again digital humanities has a strong case to make.

Research in digital humanities has already had a significant impact beyond its immediate community of users and beyond humanities disciplines. This impact has led to what I would like to call 'indirect collaboration', that is the take-up of knowledge created within the academic world, but not specifically disseminated for the purposes of use outside academia. To examine this further, it is appropriate to consider terminology. The term 'digital humanities' might be interpreted as humanities computing, that is, the application of computing tools to research and teaching in the humanities. It might also be interpreted in a wide sense to describe all the many web sites that contain material from the humanities, for example, those used by family historians or by schools, or for self-publication. Although the term 'digital humanities' has now been widely adopted, in the long term, as we move further into a digital world, it may become less meaningful in an academic context. More advances are likely to be made in the manipulation and delivery mechanisms for resources, that is, in the computational methods and tools. For the future a return to the term 'humanities computing' might be more appropriate and this term is used here to denote tools and methodologies.

Research in humanities computing has concentrated on tools and techniques. Two areas have made a substantial impact on the wider world. Firstly, concordances, used by the founder of our discipline, Fr Roberto Busa, are an important component of language analysis, understanding and creation systems. In the early days of humanities computing our conferences included many papers on the linguistic analysis of text. Eventually those working in this area spun off into two separate groups. In the first of these, after many years of mostly ignoring work on real texts, computational linguists began to embrace the benefits of large-scale text analysis and to develop more sophisticated tools. Statistical probabilities based on word frequencies and the contexts of keywords began to be used to separate out the meanings of ambiguous words. These fed into language understanding and creation systems which are now in everyday use, an example being Google's Translate this Page function. Oddities in the language created by these systems often cause amusement, but in many instances in everyday life it does not matter if the language understanding system is not correct down to the last word, provided that it gives a reasonably accurate gist of the source text. Language understanding systems also form part of voice recognition systems used by airlines, telephone companies and the like. Here they are linked with speech recognition tools, but once some possible interpretations of the spoken words are identified, statistical probabilities based on word frequencies are used to select the appropriate word and meaning. In the long term these tools will become more accurate and they will begin to have a significant impact on the economy as they save costs. At present there appears to be little development work in the use and potential of these tools for humanities material, one major exception being current research at the Perseus Project. See, for example, Bamman and Crane (2008, 2009).

Concordance applications now appear in many other discipline areas. At the time of writing, the 2010 British General Election campaign is in full swing. The transcripts of the party leaders' television debates are being studied in great detail and journalists are basing their commentary and analysis on the number of times that certain words and phrases occur in these debates. Word clouds, such as those produced by Wordle which shows frequently occurring words in larger type, are in widespread use. For example, the party manifestos in the election campaign have been 'Wordled' by the BBC's technology correspondent, Rory Cellan-Jones (Cellan-Jones, 2010). Each week the *Sunday Independent* newspaper features a Wordle display, inviting readers to guess who is speaking or writing. Wordle may have a bigger future, as its author Jonathan Feinberg noted on his blog that he joined the team behind Google Books in March 2010 (Feinberg, 2010). The attraction of Wordle is in the display, but similar approaches have often been used in medical, legal and social research, analysing interview transcripts and the like. This is not much different from content analysis used in the social sciences, where word frequencies are linked to structured thesauri or categories of information.

In the early days, humanities computing conferences also included papers on language learning. For example, in English language teaching concordances can help learners use the correct form in phrasal verbs or understand the differences between 'may' and 'might' or 'will' and 'shall'. This second group of researchers also spun off and developed its own conferences and publications. Much language teaching is now carried out outside schools and universities and is seen as a commercial operation. The Internet has fuelled the need to learn English as well as other languages, and also provides a means of learning for people in many countries. In my own travels in Laos, Vietnam and Cambodia in March 2010, I was pleasantly surprised to find that many of the local people were teaching themselves English and other languages using concordance-based tools they had found on the Internet. Some had also bought talking dictionaries which must have been developed using language technology tools.

Humanities computing has had a significant impact on the wider world in one other major area. The XML markup scheme created by the Text Encoding Initiative forms the basis of electronic publishing systems, especially reference works and journal articles. The principles on which it was built have been adopted by XML developers in other application areas. In many ways the TEI was ahead of its time. When the project started in 1987, few publishers had systems for handling text with generic markup. While the TEI developers had already defined a basic format for text structures and were concentrating on markup for some of the more obscure aspects of scholarly texts, the rest of the world was embracing HTML as a means of delivering material over the Internet. It took some time for the limitations of HTML to be understood.

TEI researchers were actively involved in the development and promotion of XML in its early days, but within the community of users who already understood the need for XML. Without their input, it is arguable whether XML would have developed in the way it has. Now it is all pervasive behind the scenes on the Internet and in commercial applications, ranging from documentation to accounts to medical resources. As far as can be ascertained, the TEI humanities computing community was among the first to think about linking beyond the simple links provided in HTML. The TEI's work on the documentation of electronic texts was also groundbreaking as it sought to document not just the description of the source material, but also the technical aspects of the electronic representation of the source material and the changes made to it, all using the same format as the text itself.

The TEI was a major influence on the early development of the Encoded Archival Description (EAD), an XML application for archival finding aids. The structure of the EAD was modelled on that of the TEI with a header and body of the finding aid. Since then the EAD has become a standard maintained by the Library of Congress, in partnership with the Society of American Archivists, and its use has become mainstream in archival description. In the UK, it is the basic structure of the Archives Hub, a gateway to descriptions of archives in UK universities and colleges (Archives Hub, 2000–2010). In the US, the Online Archive of California 'provides free public access to detailed descriptions of primary resource collections maintained by more than 150 contributing institutions', and accepts finding aids encoded in the EAD according to its practice guidelines (California Digital Library, 2010).

Research leading to tool development continues, for example, in image interpretation where improvements in OCR can be made, and in linking across resource collections. In traditional publishing technologies, the number of images is usually restricted because of cost, particularly so with colour reproductions. On the Internet there are far fewer restrictions in the number of images that can be present, and multimedia with video and sound is normal practice. The popularity of YouTube is enough evidence in itself. The visual has come to the forefront. Pages which consist solely of text are unattractive and often bypassed. However, searching for images can realistically only be carried out by retrieving tags or descriptive text associated with the images. A human has to create this text and ensure that it contains standard keyword terms. What is really needed is technology that can examine a digital image file and identify features within the picture with little or no human intervention. Research in humanities computing leading to better tools for the analysis of digital images of artefacts and works of art would also greatly benefit the large numbers of people who share photographs over the Internet. They would be able to load their pictures on to an image archive and have search text and metadata added to the pictures automatically. There is also plenty of scope for further research in linking methodologies and in the applications of Geographical Information Systems and mapping tools. These, too, would benefit many people outside academia.

The humanities computing community has also made a significant contribution to our understanding of the issues around sustainability and maintenance of digital resources. Humanities source material lasts for a very long time and digital representations of that material need to be equally long-lived. One of the original aims of the TEI was to create an encoding scheme that would be independent of any particular computing system. The data would be separate from the software. It would thus outlive any particular program and be capable of analysis by future tools not yet developed or even envisaged. Underlying this is the idea of reusability, that data created for one purpose could be used for many others without the need to make changes to it. With XML it is easy to reuse portions of a dataset without removing the unwanted material from the data, or to treat the data as layers, not all of which are used at the same time. The work of the Arts and Humanities Data Service was very significant here. It is a pity that the funding bodies which did not renew the AHDS funding in 2008 did not appear to have sufficient understanding of what is involved in creating reusable data and the potential future savings when data can be reused rather than recreated from scratch.

Digital Humanities and Information Professionals

Outside the immediate academic world, perhaps those who work most closely with digital humanities resources are librarians, archivists and museum curators who work in the public sector. There are instances of direct collaboration between digital humanities projects and these professionals, but these are relatively few in number. The developers of digital resources could benefit from information professionals' education and experience in knowledge organization and management. Information professionals might benefit from a better understanding of what users want to do with digital resources beyond simply viewing them or carrying out simple searches. It is encouraging to note that more newly qualified information professionals are beginning to work in digital humanities. As these people develop their careers and achieve positions of more responsibility, it is likely that there will be more true joint projects with a better understanding of all perspectives on the creation and management of resources.

Publishers, too, are collaborating with digital humanities projects. They can act as the delivery and maintenance vehicle, often using the basic structures of the TEI which are adequate for delivery and simple searches. But even academic publishers need to generate income and thus ensure that the maintenance and support of these resources do not become too costly for them. They need to have sufficient subscriptions to cover their costs. This means either to publish resources which have a very wide appeal, such as the *Oxford English Dictionary*, or to charge rather more than many academic libraries might want to pay. Moreover, they find themselves in competition with resources that are free at the point of use, that is, resources that are supported or maintained within the academic community without the need to justify time spent on the maintenance. The traditional role of the publisher has been to act as a gatekeeper, but with free resources, the gatekeeper is normally Google which leaves the user to assess the quality of the resources. A better understanding of digital humanities can help to assess the quality of resources and how to choose between them.

The Impact of Teaching Digital Humanities

Teaching also has a big role to play in the future of humanities computing and in developing new collaborations beyond academia. Students arriving at university now are extremely comfortable with electronic tools and digital resources, but perhaps they have less curiosity about how these tools actually work and how they might be made to work better. In the humanities, our students can be taught how to be critical about digital resources so that they think about how the resources can be made better and how they can outlast the current generation of computing systems. Most of our students do not go on to work in academia, but will almost certainly use computers in their future employment and be more employable when equipped with critical skills.

Courses in digital humanities applications exist at various levels. In many cases the focus of an individual course is the particular interest of the faculty member who offers the course. This may, for example, be digital imaging, or corpus linguistics, or GIS systems in archaeology. Such courses are often options for undergraduates and are normally offered towards the end of an undergraduate degree. Why should students want to take these courses? Personal interest is one reason, but students are focused more and more on their future employment prospects. Anything that gives them an edge over their peers in the job market is attractive to them.

There are still very few masters courses specifically in digital humanities. In the UK at any rate, new masters programmes are starting up in many disciplines. Since many more students are doing undergraduate degrees, a masters degree is seen by many students as a way to get more qualifications and thus a route to better employment prospects. However, an institution must invest in order to start a new degree and see a way to make that degree cover its costs. If these involve recruiting additional staff, the costs become quite high. From the perspective of the student who is, after all, faced with a choice between programmes in many different areas, the masters degree must offer something that is interesting to do and something that will be of long-term benefit. We must remember that few of our students want to have an academic career and, in choosing a programme, they are looking for something which will further their own causes.

Masters programmes in digital humanities have a lot to offer these students, especially those who have a first degree in the humanities. Humanities resources can be used as an example to show students the principles and to get them to think about how these principles can apply to other data and resources. It can now be assumed that all students are very familiar with the Internet and Office tools, and with handling digital photographs. Courses can now start at a higher level without having to spend time teaching fairly elementary applications. They can provide means of learning more about technologies which are relevant for everyday Internet usage and also of developing skills in critical thinking and appraisal. A well-designed assignment enables a student to build a pilot resource and then to write an essay reflecting on the process. Both these aspects provide learning outcomes which will benefit students in their future lives.

Digital humanities masters programmes will help students acquire a better idea of time management for digital projects, even if these aspects are not specifically assessed. In their undergraduate career, they should have a gained a reasonable idea of how long it takes to research and write an essay. However, people always tend to underestimate how long it takes to complete a digital project or at least to get it to a state where it is usable by those who have not been involved in its development. Experience of actually doing it is the best way to find this out, and reflection on the whole process can provide a better understanding of the timescales involved and the whole aspects of managing a digital project.

Employment prospects for those with a masters degree in digital humanities are very good. Publishing is one possibility, either in editing or marketing. There are many opportunities in web development, not particularly in the technical aspects but in copy writing and overall design. Most websites now are driven by content management systems or in-house software linked to a database and with input from graphic designers. Digital humanities graduates who have an overall grasp of how the technology works are better equipped to develop content or to work in marketing, leaving the technology and graphic design to specialists in these areas. Overall the combination of practical and theoretical work is attractive to many employers and this kind of knowledge transfer opens up more possibilities.

Work placements, where a student spends a few weeks with a company, can also be a useful part of these courses. They are an opportunity for the university to forge links with the company, perhaps leading to future collaboration, and the programme tutors get a chance to see what their students might be doing once they complete their degree. As a result of the placement, the students may be offered permanent employment or they may decide that this is not for them and that they need to seek an alternative career. Overall, in my view, it is important to forge links with possible employers. This obviously benefits the students but it also provides possibilities for future collaboration in an era where university funding is becoming more and more insecure.

If further programmes in digital humanities are to be developed, accreditation becomes an issue. It strengthens the impact of the programme and provides a means for the host institution and potential employers to emphasize the value of the programme. Accreditation implies the existence of a professional body under which the programme is recognized. This would most likely include employers among its assessors and thus again enhance the opportunities for outreach and possible collaboration.

In the UK, accreditation for information professionals is provided by the Chartered Institute of Library and Information Professionals (CILIP). While most of their accredited courses are mainstream professional qualifications leading to librarianship and information management, some are concerned with specific applications, for example, Geographic Information Management (City University) or Health Informatics (Sheffield University). The British Computer Society also accredits programmes where there is a substantial computing component. The Society of Archivists accredits programmes in Archives and Records Management which have specialized requirements. At the time of writing, the accreditation requirements of all these professional bodies appear to include aspects which are not normally found in digital humanities work. However, programmes that have accreditation do have more opportunity to reach out to employers and other professionals in the same field.

It can be assumed that, by now, all students who come to university have grown up with computers. They are familiar with a whole range of applications and are often better equipped than their teachers in using these. It is now a better time than ever to introduce more digital humanities courses or options. Time does not have to be taken up with teaching elementary usage of software, but effort can concentrate on a curriculum which is more appropriate for university-level work. This could include more advanced tools and methods, perhaps with more emphasis on reflection and assessment of the relevance of the tools and applications. Within the timescale of a masters programme, students can gain a good overview, be critical of what they use now and think about how to develop better resources.

Towards Better Communication

In my view, with a few exceptions, the humanities computing community has not been particularly good at promoting its activities beyond academia. Conferences and journals inevitably preach to the already converted. I have argued here that the major impact of humanities computing is tool development, but it is less easy to see the impact of tool development as opposed to the visibility of resources on the Internet. It is harder to explain what is going on with tools, and it takes longer for potential users to understand why new tools might be needed and what benefit these tools might offer. Moreover, until recently, there has not been much incentive to communicate beyond academia. In fact the publication and peer review system is in many ways a disincentive, as it is designed to address a primarily inward-looking audience. In addition, granting agencies do not provide sufficient funds for marketing other than perhaps small amounts for dissemination to the academic world.

It can be argued that marketing is easier in the Internet age, but unless the site appears on the first two or three pages in Google, it is actually more difficult, unless paid-for advertising tools are used. Outside the Internet, marketing is targeted either by using specific publications or addressing specialized audiences. Putting several keywords into Google produces better search results, but this implies that the user is looking for a known item which matches those keywords. Serendipitous searches with one or two keywords produce wide-ranging results, leaving the user to sift through much unwanted information. Moreover, much information is now passed by word of mouth or, more likely, as fingers on keyboards. Misleading information can easily be circulated, and once again potential users have to exercise more of their own judgement – judgement which depends on detailed knowledge which they may not have.

The future of the Internet seems to lie with computing on the move, with mobile devices such as phones, netbooks and the new iPad. Wireless technologies will become more widely available and at higher speeds. Future users of humanities resources will expect video on demand on their handheld devices and the ability to find things with one or two taps on a touchpad screen. There will be a need to make content usable on screens which have to be smaller so that people can carry them around, or as talking devices which eliminate the need for anything other than a simple screen. Smart books, not just replicas of print books, will appear on e-book readers which will merge with other handheld devices. At home, the Internet will combine with television technology as a single means of delivering content. In my view, all these requirements present opportunities for outreach from digital humanities and collaboration with technology developers and users. New content will be based on well-marked-up text that can be reused for other purposes and linked to multimedia formats and/or language and speech analysis and creation tools. There will always be a need for professionals who have an understanding of the technology and can place a critical perspective on what it offers in the everyday world which is encompassed by the study of the humanities.

References

Archives Hub (2010), available at: <http://www.archiveshub.ac.uk/datacreation> (accessed 22 April 2010).

Bamman, D. and G. Crane, 'Building a Dynamic Lexicon from a Digital Library', *Proceedings of the 8th ACM/IEEE-CS Joint Conference on Digital Libraries, Pittsburgh PA* (2008): 11–20.

Bamman, D. and G. Crane, 'Computational Linguistics and Classical Lexicography', *Digital Humanities Quarterly* 3.1 (2009) [Online], available at: <http://www.digitalhumanities.org/dhq/vol/003/1/000033/000033.html> (accessed 22 April 2010).

California Digital Library, *Online Archive of California: Submitting EAD Collection* Guides (2010), available at: <http://www.cdlib.org/services/dsc/contribute/submitead.html> (accessed 22 April 2010).

Cellan-Jones, R., *Conservative Manifesto Wordle* (2010), available at: <http://www.flickr.com/photos/rorycellan/4517036123> (accessed 22 April 2010).

Feinberg, J., *Wordle Blog 1 April 2010* (2010), available at: <http://blog.wordle.net/> (accessed 22 April 2010).

HEFCE, *Research Assessment Framework: Impact Pilot* Exercise (2010), available at: <http://www.hefce.ac.uk/research/ref/impact//> (accessed 22 April 2010).

Sexton, A., C. Turner, G. Yeo and S. Hockey, 'Understanding Users: A Prerequisite for Developing New Technologies', *Journal of the Society of Archivists* 25.1 (2004): 33–49.

Terras M., *ReACH Researching e-Science Analysis of Census Holdings Project Report* (2006) [Online: UCL], available at: <http://www.ahessc.ac.uk/files/active/0/ReACH-report.pdf/> (accessed 21 April 2010).

Chapter 6

Collaboration in Virtual Space in Digital Humanities

Laszlo Hunyadi[1]

Introduction

The introduction of computing methodologies into the humanities has brought about significant changes both in the scope of humanities research and in the way that research is to be carried out. These new methodologies have offered the chance to ask questions that have never been asked before and to give new and more satisfying answers to questions previously asked. Importantly, interdisciplinarity as a scientific approach to the study of complex issues has gained more and more importance, and technological advances, together with the need for interdisciplinary studies, have made it increasingly essential to do research in collaboration. The development of humanities computing has been noticeably enhanced by the various emerging forms of virtual collaboration offered by the use of the internet. To name a few pioneering initiatives without trying to give a comprehensive overview, HUMBUL, which started in 1985, offered catalogued and reviewed websites relevant to the humanities at a time when today's search engines did not even exist. Nearly ten years on, the book *The Whole Internet* (Krol, 1992) could still be printed on a few hundred pages. The discussion group *Humanist* started in 1987 and is probably one of the oldest existing international online seminars still in existence and flourishing today. And of course the humanistic disciplines themselves have been enhanced by the emergence of easier and faster ways for colleagues to collaborate across the boundaries of subjects, institutions and countries.

The emergence of international organizations for humanities computing attests to the rapid growth in communities in the field: the Association for Literary and Linguistic Computing (ALLC), founded in 1973, and the Association for Computing in the Humanities (ACH), founded in 1978, initially served the communities mainly in Europe and North America, respectively, and the new publications— *Literary and Linguistic Computing* and *Computing and the Humanities*—which they established opened new forums for scholarly work in the field throughout the world. Community building and support has been continuous ever since: the

1 This article was partly supported by the joint Hungary–EU Grant No. TÁMOP 4.2.2-08/1-2008-0009.

emergence of the Alliance of Digital Humanities Organizations (ADHO) in 2007 as the umbrella organization of ALLC and ACH is a natural consequence of the growth and globalization of computing in the humanities. Other organizations are encouraged to join ADHO, and the Society for Digital Humanities/Société pour l'étude des médias interactifs (SDH-SEMI, founded in 1986 as the Consortium for Computers in the Humanities/Consortium pour ordinateurs en sciences humaines) has recently done so. ADHO hopes to promote the emergence of new, online publications in the field, such as *Digital Humanities Quarterly* (*DHQ*), which began publication in 2007.

In general, the emergence and development of interdisciplinary research in the humanities has been accompanied and/or supported by the emergence and development of various forms of collaboration in the past decades. The two seem to go hand in hand, one facilitating the other and offering new perspectives both for academic studies and research activities. What seems to be shared by many of these efforts is preference for virtual, online forms of collaboration. In what follows, we will give examples of virtual collaboration as it appears in today's practice, ranging from academic education to academic research to R&D activities. This attempts to show how digital humanities can contribute to advances in other research fields and also, vice versa, how it can benefit from traditionally "remote" disciplines.

The activities and thoughts associated with and inspired by the idea of collaborative work described in these pages are strongly influenced by the intellectual spirit I had the chance to encounter through the many years of my acquaintance with Professor Harold Short. One main message that has remained for me as a guiding light ever since is that we have to turn to our fellow colleagues with a keen interest in their work, offer and incorporate new ideas, and seek further and ever more productive forms of interdisciplinary research. The international community of digital humanities has always been a "safe haven" for me where I could experience a warmly welcoming and stimulating, but critical, intellectual environment for the development and testing of innovative ideas on the crossroads of exciting, mutually complementary as well as competing fields. It has been motivating for me to see a new discipline emerge and to understand that this new discipline will leave enough room for our original fields (linguistics in my case) while creating a "virtual cloud" of collaboration within and across individual disciplines. I can only hope to be able to contribute to handing over this spirit to the next generation.

Collaboration in Virtual Centers for "Real" Education

There is a perception in a number of universities in Europe that humanities faculties are currently facing troubled times, only partly shared by some other academic disciplines. The decrease of state funding has noticeably affected the humanities, while the number of students enrolled in many traditional majors is stagnating or even gradually falling. The cut in state funds has affected the humanities especially badly because—in contrast to the sciences—external funds are much harder to generate. Whereas in the sciences demands for technological advances obviously generate additional funds, the traditional approach of the humanities, not being technology- or even "consumer"-oriented, results in the humanities disciplines becoming less competitive in the race for funds. In addition, the decrease of enrolments is ominous: fewer students choose traditional humanities disciplines, mainly due to market pressure—they wish to have a degree which opens their way to a decent career and prestige. Regardless of sound argumentation based on well-tested traditional values, entering the competition both for funds and for students with old perceptions seems not too promising. However, studying present-day and prospective future demands may offer a solution: the introduction of computing in humanities education and research may have the effect that, similarly to the introduction of computing in several other disciplines, the use of computing methodologies might enhance traditional studies in the humanities and result both in new answers and new discoveries. This is the route some leading universities in Europe and America have chosen. They introduced computing in various aspects of the humanities, thus enhancing and further widening the scope of humanities computing for education, research and application development. One of the institutional forerunners in humanities computing was King's College London, where a new department was set up to pursue the goal of institutional development of humanities computing. The emergence of digital humanities (DH) as a new discipline, as we know it now, was the result of continuous development in many areas of humanities computing, both in education and research. The idea was gradually developed that DH as an academic offering could find its place among disciplines in the humanities and even offer a contribution to disciplines beyond the humanities as well.

When we at the University of Debrecen were first contemplating introducing humanities computing into the Faculty of Humanities, we hoped that by doing so we could give fresh momentum to humanities education and humanities research. We expected that, as a result, we could build a community that would bring about a substantial renewal of the practice of traditional humanities and create a new, more comprehensive "space" for humanities education and research. We discovered, however, that to start a new program with no history in the country at all is no easy matter. It is first necessary to establish DH as a recognized academic discipline and then get the accreditation to begin a program in a particular institution. Both requirements need an institutional background that we, at the outset, equally lacked. Normally, the traditional way of running an academic program is to associate it with a single (rarely more) academic discipline, but we soon realized that DH cannot be associated with a single "traditional" humanities discipline. Therefore our endeavor was twofold: establish a single organizational unit for DH and then a single discipline associated with it.

Initially, we were aware that there were individual academics teaching a subject that in one way or another included some applied computational methodology. There was, however, no collaboration or any other professional relationship among the individual teachers. Thus, we decided as the first step to establish a community that would later on undertake the education as well.

In order to build the institutional background necessary for any hope of success in national accreditation, we needed some traditional form of organization that would submit the proposal for accreditation, either a department or a research center. Since DH was a new discipline not belonging to the profile of any existing department or research center, we decided to establish a new, virtual Center for Digital Humanities. It needed to be virtual because it would rely on existing teaching positions; these positions would remain in their respective departments and offer an extra service to run courses in humanities computing as well.

The Center for Digital Humanities set out its program: it planned to elaborate a proposal for an MA in Digital Humanities, secure the teaching staff, and offer additional activities. The proposal was essentially based on two sources: similar DH programs elsewhere for reference, consultations, and possible co-operation; and the availability and interest of the potential teaching staff. The two specializations offered by the program would reflect two classes of broader interest: *cultural heritage preservation* and *language technology*. The disciplines that are thus represented are quite numerous, enabling students to enter the program with a BA in, among other subjects, modern and classical languages and literatures, history and ethnology. The disciplines taught in the MA program range from classical humanities and information science to music, even to related issues in architecture and the sciences.

We cannot leave this story without documenting its outcome. In the first round, our submission for recognizing DH as an independent discipline was unsuccessful. For the second submission, we had to convince the respective bodies that: (a) what we offer is not information science proper, but a humanities-oriented teaching and research scenario with a strong reliance on approaches, methodologies, and techniques of IT; and (b) what information science, especially some exams, such as ECDL, offers does not—contrary to some superficial assumptions—cover those fields that are the characteristics of DH: the integration of humanities and some other disciplines with information science from a particular, unique perspective. Based on strong arguments supported by spectacular achievements in the wider field of digital humanities, DH was finally recognized as an independent academic discipline at the masters level. Shortly after that, the University of Debrecen received national accreditation to also run the program. Following a successful series of lectures in 2010 as an introductory course, with the enrollment of more than two dozen students with a wide variety of subjects as their primary humanities background, we look forward with enthusiasm to launching the first full-fledged program in 2011. Beyond its own advancement, DH will also serve as an example in Hungary of how interdisciplinary co-operation across traditional academic boundaries can contribute to the modernization of higher education.

Virtual Space: The Academic Benefit of Professional Collaboration

Today's technology allows us to disseminate knowledge to a much wider audience than is possible in a traditional classroom setting. To reach as wide an audience as possible is especially important in the case of a new discipline such as DH.

This is what led us to make our participation at the annual European Researchers' Night, an international event, through videoconferencing. In the last three consecutive years our hub in Debrecen has connected participants from Debrecen, Budapest, Oulu and Dublin via cyberspace. As in an ordinary event, we had "plenary talks" and "round table discussions" alike. The audience from all sites could enjoy the event and be part of it by asking questions and reflecting upon any issues arising. A videostream was also broadcast to enable "unregistered" viewers to participate. The impact of these two events on the audience was quite measurable: being mostly students, they received the talks and discussions with much enthusiasm. Even some term papers originated from them as a reflection on the scientific merit of these events, suggesting that DH has found a fruitful ground to further grow and develop. The impact on students of these events is also measurable by the fact that last year's was organized and run by PhD students, suggesting that DH will have its future among the younger generation.

In addition to these European Researchers' Night events, the same technology has also been tested and utilized in further educational activities within the framework of our Culture and Technology Seminar Series. The series were jointly designed by the universities of Debrecen, Leipzig, Oulu, and King's College. Later Glasgow, Bologna, and Dublin also joined in our effort to bring the major ideas of DH closer to undergraduates in the respective universities. Students of various disciplines across the continent were connected weekly by the central idea as well as the technology. Professors from the respective universities (E. Burr, D. Buzzetti, L. Hunyadi, W. McCarty, M. Moss, L.L. Opas-Hänninen, and others) gave inspiring talks on their research, all focusing on a particular aspect of digital humanities, ranging from linguistics to literature, history, computer science and engineering. Later, as interest grew, calls for participation were also extended to PhD students. We had exciting and highly motivating presentations by graduate students from Bologna, Debrecen, and Dublin, three universities located far away from each other but connected in the virtual space by a common interest in DH. Already the fact that regular scientific meetings in such a virtual space, under the umbrella of digital humanities, was made possible shows that DH as a discipline has found its place in higher education.

The idea that culture and technology could organically meet, sharing the approach of DH, was further developed in Leipzig where the first Summer Schools in Culture and Technology were held in the summers of 2009 and 2010. There are further plans as well: based on the success of seminars run by doctoral students, we intend to offer a virtual conference for young scientists in DH, to be organized simultaneously at various university sites in Europe and broadcast to the participating institutions and possibly beyond. We hope that such a conference will become yet another means of scientific motivation for those young people who are engaged in any aspect of DH and are interested in developing collaboration without borders. This is how the inter- and multidisciplinary concept of DH equally inspires the "virtual" and the "real."

The Benefit of Professional Collaboration in Virtual Space for Research and Development

Digital humanities is, by definition, inter- and multidisciplinary. Being part of the DH community, one has a strong sense of the benefits of crossing traditional academic boundaries in order to collaborate with respective partners from other disciplines in order to "arrive home," that is, to give answers to questions often proving too complex for one's single primary discipline. We can see the benefits of such collaboration in at least three areas: (a) at the institutional, organizational level; (b) in activities of dissemination; and (c) in running individual projects. Below, I will suggest some concrete examples of these benefits.

(a) At the institutional, organizational level, we must give credit to a significant event with far-reaching consequences for the future of DH, originally initiated and gradually pursued by Harold Short and John Unsworth, backed by their respective organizations: the "merger" of ALLC and ACH under the umbrella of ADHO. Originally, ALLC and ACH used to function on a semi-geographical basis; by the establishment of ADHO (Alliance of Digital Humanities Organizations: <www.digitalhumanities.org/>) in 2005, the DH community has come of age by offering global collaboration and expandability, while at the same time preserving the "local" focuses of the constituting organizations. Going global means that, based on previous successful large-scale projects and both geographically and professionally wide scope actions, it has now become possible to institutionalize the achievements and concentrate our academic, human, and material resources to accomplish even further reaching goals. The first impact at the organizational level was the joining in 2007 of SDH-SEMI, the Canadian organization for DH, a move that simply accomplished a professionally supported natural process. Recently, this movement towards globalization is perceived more and more strongly with regard to Japan: the establishment of ADHO gave significant impetus to strengthen and further enhance the presence of DH in that country, with the possibility of establishing a regional chapter some time in the future. It is also expected that the increasingly global reach of DH through ADHO will result in further academic and organizational advances in other parts of the world as well.

(b) Activities of dissemination are very important in the development of an ever growing community, through making available new advances and sharing best practice in particular fields. Several seminars and other similar events have been initiated or run by the constituting organizations of ADHO in many parts of the world. I will only give one example here, that of a conference and seminar organized by the West Bengal University of Technology, Kolkata in 2007, where experts from ALLC were invited to participate. This conference dealt with the issue of digitization of a vast number of Indic languages, languages that either did not have at that time any encoding system or, on the contrary, had more than one but none of them appropriate for standard machine representation and analysis. The participation of delegates from ALLC was judged to be very useful in that, step by step, they were guided through actual and accomplished projects of digitization as possible examples of the use of standard methodologies. The list of local participants included a wide range of professions, from linguistics to IT to engineering and even nuclear physics, showing that these professionals deeply understood the needs of their country in the preservation of objects of their cultural heritage. Regardless of their academic orientation, they were ready to contribute to this magnificent goal by starting from the very basics and moving steadily towards accomplishment. ALLC was proud to be a contributing part of this—in a sense—historic moment.

(c) The essential strength of inter- and multidisciplinary approaches is clearly shown in joint projects requiring the contribution of DH (by itself multidisciplinary) to the accomplishment of tasks involving further disciplines beyond DH. Below, we will give an account of some leading ideas behind a fairly complex project involving traditional humanities, information science, and engineering, with computational linguistics playing a significant role.

The project HuComTech ("The Theoretical Foundations of Human–Computer Interactions": <http://hucomtech.unideb.hu/hucomtech>) at the University of Debrecen is based on the general observation that man–machine communication systems usually lack that "appeal" of naturalness which makes such an interaction easy and straightforward for the human participant. The reason is not just the fact that computer graphics are still in the phase of development (on the contrary, many games or even movies can now be made to appear realistic) or speech recognition systems are still restricted to a special or specialized vocabulary, but that we do not yet know enough about human–human communication in general. The underlying idea is that, if we know how to formally represent the structure of a given human–human interaction, we can build computer systems that will "behave" in a similar fashion. But the major problem is that, being dependent on many individual and in cases never repeated factors (profile, ontology, background knowledge on the one hand, and given psychological, cultural, moral, and so on, settings on the other), human–human interaction seems to be hard to represent in a regular form. The aim of the project, then, is to learn the regularities of human–human interactions based on type scenarios and respective ontologies, separate these regularities from their context-dependent individual characteristics, and finally build and interpret a corresponding structure for the given interaction. This task requires the collaboration of many people from various disciplines, and the project thus involves computer scientists, engineers, computational linguists, specialists in communication, as well as psychologists. The task is inspiring and at the same time challenging for all. The novelty of research is mainly represented by its special interdisciplinary nature and the way in which it contributes to the completion of the research program: it is its cross-disciplinary DH approach that unites the often seemingly incompatible counterparts. The major issue, as mentioned above, is that of the formal representation of human communication. Although several theories exist for communication, most of them miss the criteria of formal description necessary for implementation by the computer. Our task, then, is to search for and identify those building blocks of communication that, in an orderly fashion, contribute to what we can tell the computer as structure. It is the computational aspect of DH that leads us in the search for implementable structure and that does not let us go astray under the influence of certain functional features inherent in any communication, but that go beyond the scope of a technologically implementable human–computer interaction system.

Accordingly, the focus of the project is to propose a model inspired at the crossroads of the humanities, engineering, and information science, and to validate this model in a practical, working implementation. Supported by approaches aiming at unveiling the formal basic structure of communication and also at the model-based technological implementations of an arbitrary communicative event (cf. Polanyi, 1988, 2004; Jurafsky, 2004; Thione et al., 2004a, 2004b), but extending the scope to multimodality and bidirectionality, our model itself is generative (cf. Hunyadi ,2011): it inherits its approach from theoretical linguistics (the latter originally inspired by the needs of computational linguistics for language technology). The approach is modular, a significant property equally important and manageable for theoretical linguistics and technology. Namely, the complexity of the issue of understanding the basic underlying structure of communication and implementing it within technology can be reduced and, consequently, relatively conveniently handled by subdividing the flow of communication into a number of self-contained but structurally interrelated modules for the description and generation of appropriate and specific internal relations. In our model, these modules are assumed to be responsible for (a) the generation of the formal skeleton of all possible communication events, (b) the functional extension of the formal basis of a given event, and (c) the pragmatic extension of the functionally already extended, rich formal basis. This latter module contains the interface between the verbal (and, from a technological point of view, informal) description of an event and its formal technological implementation. All this is done in a unified manner: each module consists of a finite set of primitives only specific to the given module and a finite set of rules of derivation to derive the set of all possible structures within that given module. Modules are connected by applying the same unifying principles and rules to them within a structural hierarchy. The big challenge is how to map non-formal, practically verbal descriptions of events of communication onto formal, parametric data, the latter being the only possible input relevant to technology. This is where our approach is thought to offer a strong theoretical contribution to the problem. Applying to our model the theory of fuzzy systems to capture linguistic descriptions of certain cognitive concepts (cf. Zadeh, 1965; Bunt and Black, 2000), we map linguistic variables onto technological parameters in order to handle the two, conceptually apparently very distant, fields of human communication and technology in a single unified system.

In addition, a further benefit of applying a (humanities-based) generative model to the technology of human–machine interaction is that this model is then bidirectional: it equally models analysis and synthesis, two aspects of communication that virtually happen at the same time but that are usually implemented as two independent and (at least partly) incompatible models. Instead of building separate systems for analysis and synthesis using principally different models, our generative model allows for capturing the relevant aspects of human–human communication as they exist in unity in our own behavior. Even though the task is definitely highly complex, we believe that an attempt to technologically implement at least a restricted subset of communicative relations can serve as a means of validation for the model and its application.

The complexity of the issues described above suggests that this project can only be carried out in strong co-operation by a number of disciplines. There are many challenges: linguists, engineers, and IT people have radically different conceptual and working methodologies and cultures. We believe that DH that is inter- and multidisciplinary by itself can effectively contribute to the successful establishment of synergy between these groups that are professionally distant but closely related by the definition of the final goal.

Our virtual Center for Digital Humanities, which has already proved to be successful in making a proposal for the academic program MA in Digital Humanities and which has led further academic activities in virtual space, plays a leading role in this technological project, with the hope that the complex approach of DH will bring this project to successful completion.

Multidisciplinary Collaboration in a Virtual Lab

With significant advances in computing and the use of the internet, it has been made possible to share one and the same physical infrastructure among a number of researchers and research communities, both for individual projects that are connected by way of the use of the same infrastructure and for joint complex tasks. I will present here our current effort to build such a shared physical and virtual research infrastructure, where traditional disciplines of the humanities reach out to and become an integral part of engineering application development.

As a logical continuation of the HuComTech project mentioned in the previous section, we at the University of Debrecen are in the process of creating a cognitive robotic lab that is: (a) real (physical) in the sense that it is based on a real technological implementation of a primary lab, with all the necessary components like testing space, robots, external sensors, and a complex computing system; and (b) virtual in the sense that we can network into this system a number of "stripped down," secondary labs which lack the robots but which each has a testing space and is equipped with the necessary external sensors and the appropriate computing system. These two kinds of labs are integrated into a single research space using the VIRCA (Virtual Collaboration Arena; cf.) framework. There are at least two far-reaching benefits of this research setting: (a) each of the secondary, robotless labs can carry out experiments with the robot of the distant primary lab; (b) our labs (either the primary or the secondary) can also be integrated into a larger network of similar labs running the same protocol. As a consequence, it is not only the case that we can use the infrastructure of other distant labs, but we also have the opportunity to invite remote projects to join us and carry out joint research and experiments with and within our project.

What is the role and interest of humanities and digital humanities in building the above network of real and virtual labs, if the setting seems to be so technical and technology oriented? We learn something significant from engineering and the application of computing methodologies: it can be said that the humanities is strong in building theories such that their validation is usually done by testing their logical consistency. On the other hand, engineering and computing are also necessarily supported by theories, but the nature of their disciplines requires validation by testing them against their physical implementation. Second, whereas findings in, among others, physics or chemistry are verified in real-world tests and experiments, humanities will also have a significant contribution to engineering and especially robotics only if any appropriate theory aimed at engineering development is exposed to testing through and within technology. It is especially true of a theory of communication aimed at cognitive robotics, where any theory has to be tested against the "behavior" of the given robot. In this way a humanities theory can be verified, refined, or rejected as a result of exposure and testing against its technological, robotic implementation. The network of real and virtual cognitive robotic behavior with humans will be able to remotely manipulate the behavior of robots and observe their response, and, ultimately, test the validity of a given theory of human behavior.

We are aware that the use of a network of real and virtual labs as described above reaches beyond the scope of humanities and even digital humanities, but we also believe that the establishment of such a research environment is very much in line with the general purpose of DH: we need to include in humanities research the power and possibilities of computing in order: (a) to offer a more complete answer to some traditional issues in humanities; and (b) to reach out to multidisciplinary research where we believe our knowledge and methodologies can contribute to the understanding and implementation of more complex issues, that are traditionally non-specific to humanities. Time will show if this direction that we are taking now by building an infrastructure of real and virtual labs will indeed yield the results we are envisaging at present.

Summary

The purpose of this chapter has been to show through some concrete examples that humanities research has come a long way since the introduction of computational methodologies, to develop into a new discipline called digital humanities. The new technologies adopted from computing have made it possible to introduce novel scientific perspectives by facilitating the emergence of further forms of collaboration among scientists. Inter- and multidisciplinary research has become a "must" to solve certain emerging new issues, giving rise to virtual research collaboration as well. Research, academic education, and technological advances go hand in hand while transforming the whole long-established landscape of humanities, leading it into the digital era which promises so much. Pioneering institutions and organizations, as well as newly emerging ones, lead this march, with the indispensable participation and co-operation of a rapidly growing number of single individuals.

References

Bunt, Harry and William Black, 'The ABC of Computational Pragmatics', in Harry Bunt and William Black (eds), *Abduction, Belief and Context in Dialogue: Studies in Computational Pragmatics* (Amsterdam: John Benjamins, 2000): 1–46.

Hunyadi, László, 'Multimodal Human–Computer Interaction Technologies: Theoretical Modeling and Application in Speech Processing', *Argumentum* 20 (2011): 240–60.

Jurafsky, D., 'Pragmatics and Computational Linguistics', in Laurence R. Horn and Gregory Wards (eds), *Handbook of Pragmatics* (Oxford: Blackwell, 2004).

Krol, Ed, *The Whole Internet: User's Guide and Catalog* (Sebastopol, CA: O'Reilly & Associates, 1992).

Polanyi, L., 'A Formal Model of Discourse Structure', *Journal of Pragmatics* 12 (1988): 601–39.

Polanyi, L., 'A Rule-based Approach to Discourse Parsing', in *Proceedings of SIGDIAL '04* (2004), Boston, MA.

Thione, G.L., M. van den Berg, Ch. Culy and L. Polanyi, 'Hybrid Text Summarization: Combining External Relevance Measures with Structural Analysis', *Proceedings of the ACL Workshop Text Summarization Branches Out* (2004a), Barcelona.

Thione, G.L., M. van den Berg , Ch. Culy and L. Polanyi, 'LiveTree: An Integrated Workbench for Discourse Processing', *Proceedings of the 2004 ACL Workshop on Discourse Annotation*, 25–26 July 2004, Barcelona, Spain (2004b): 110–17.

Zadeh, I.A., 'Fuzzy Sets', in *Information and Control* 8.3 (June 1965): 338–53.

Chapter 7
Crowd Sourcing 'True Meaning': A Collaborative Markup Approach to Textual Interpretation

Jan-Christoph Meister

> Text markup is currently the best tool at our disposal for ensuring that the hermeneutic circle continues to turn, that our cultural tradition endures.
>
> Burnard (2001)

From Prejudice to True Prejudice

To state that something is a *text* implies, among other things, that it is not just a dispassionately perceived object, but one that has (or is supposed to have) a *function* for intelligent beings able to process it. In the following, the functional aspect of texts of major concern is that of their *meaning*, and the question motivating my deliberations is how digital humanities might facilitate a collaborative markup approach in textual interpretation.

But is markup in fact still relevant as an interpretive methodology in the first place? The exponential growth in digital source material has provided us with such substantial text corpora that data mining and information retrieval technology has shifted its focus from intelligent description, explication and categorization to semantically indifferent mathematical approaches, such as statistical analysis and stochastic calculus. Yet the new approach has of course its own inherent restrictions. For example, if the corpus is too small, too idiosyncratic or made up from elements whose functional logic keeps evolving and changing on every iteration in an unpredictable way, then human interpretation will always beat the algorithm. After all, the rules of language are defined by *us*, its users and inventors, more or less as we play and modify the language game. Long before behavioural patterns and regularities can be observed in how we construct and interpret texts, we will already have begun to develop non-explicit intuitions as to how the process works – intelligent speculation, after all, is the human forte.

When markup is intelligent, it is more apt to grasp and communicate our intuition concerning ongoing rule changes; it also acknowledges the functional spectrum of that which texts are made of, that is, language. This spectrum is multi-faceted and spans, in Roman Jakobson's view, at least six dimensions (sender, receiver, context, message, contact and code). The various disciplines that study texts and language each foreground the particular dimensions and aspects of textual and language functionality that are topical in relation to their own research interests. In the digital humanities, this practice is nowadays reflected not only in the design of different markup schemes and conventions, but also and on a more practical level by the fact that one particular textual object may be marked up in different ways and for entirely different purposes.

While the functional richness of texts may be an uncontroversial fact, the explication of their *meaning* is not, neither in terms of the explicated content, nor in terms of the methodology of explication. The progress from Plato's initial notion of *hermeneutic knowledge* as a type of belief-based intuition which, in contrast to *sophia*, is revealed or stated, but not proven by logical analysis, to Aristotle's fundamental philosophical reflections in his *De interpretatione*, and eventually our contemporary practice of analytical and critical *hermeneutics* as a proper scientific method of interpretation has been slow and painful, and even nowadays popular deconstructionism refutes the idea of a scientification of interpretation *per se* as an absurd and misguided project. But then that is a radical position of little practical relevance to the digital humanities whose methodology, by and large, is rooted in scientific rationalism.

Modern Western philologies only developed in the nineteenth century and were shaped by two major shifts in paradigm: one, a critical re-conceptualization of texts as historical artefacts that evolve in relation to man's own intellectual, social as well as psychological conditions and development; two, a methodological codification and theoretical reflection of the hitherto more or less intuitively practised *hermeneutike techne* from the perspective of the (Kant-inspired) German Idealism. The most advanced systematization of interpretive methodology prior to that had of course been developed in theological exegesis which in itself had witnessed an important methodological reorientation towards the original text some 200 years before when Luther postulated the principle of *sola scriptura*. This reorientation from dogma to text culminated in the 1838 posthumous publication of Schleiermacher's lectures on hermeneutics, under the programmatic title *Hermeneutik und Kritik*. Schleiermacher's 'idea of a critical turn in hermeneutics combined with the focus on the individuality of language-use' (Ramberg and Gjesdal, 2009) put an end to the quest for the identification of the absolute and eternally 'true' meaning of a text. While we must of course strive to identify the correct grammatical sense of an utterance and avoid a-grammatical reasoning about it, we must at the same time acknowledge the historical and psychological dimension of making an utterance, as well as of trying to understand it. As Schleiermacher (1977: 78–9) put it: 'Verstehen ist nur ein Ineinandersein dieser beiden Momente (des grammatischen und psychologischen)' – 'understanding is but the coexistence of these two moments (the grammatical and the psychological)' (my translation).

Since Schleiermacher, the psychological, cultural and historical contextualization of texts and their interpretations is generally seen as the fundamental methodological condition and insurmountable boundary of all hermeneutical activity. But it is not only a boundary, a limitation: it is also the source of the inexhaustible dynamics inherent to the twin pair of utterance and interpretation and their related methodologies, rhetoric and hermeneutics. If we wanted to describe the programme of any hermeneutics after Schleiermacher in computational parlance, it might be adequate to say that it no longer operates in the a-historical procedural paradigm of 'batch-mode interpretation', but in a context-sensitive dynamic paradigm of 'interactive interpretation': interpretation – that is, non-trivial, that is, non-deterministic interpretation – is not just an input–output or a database driven 'look-up' procedure, but a discursive process that produces results characterized by contingency. As a matter of principle, its outcome is non-predictable, though not irrational. On the contrary, the fact that it *has* been arrived at proves that it must have some rationality, idiosyncratic as this rationality might turn out to be. It is important here to point out the subtle difference between possibility and contingency, a differentiation which we owe to medieval authors such as John of Salisbury and Roger Bacon who, as Jozef Brams (2002: 22–3) has brought to our attention:

> ... make a distinction between the two expressions, *possibile* meaning that which is not but has the possibility to be, *contingens* meaning that which is, but has the possibility to not be. This is the modern conception of possibility and contingency, which we find elaborated in Leibnitz ... .[1]

A particular interpretation might not be realized and remain a mere possibility. An existing and non-trivial interpretation, however, is always worth considering, and particularly so if it has been arrived at in a methodologically controlled and transparent fashion that merits reasoning about it.

The scientific – that is, the methodologically transparent and falsifiable – interpretation of a text requires what all scientific activity and reasoning demand: systematic taxonomies and terminological concepts, defined and logically consistent analytic and synthetic procedures, a reflection of hidden assumptions as well as epistemic and theoretical limitations inherent to the chosen approach, and so on. Yet even a formalized and theoretically explicit hermeneutics that seems to emulate the dispassionate analytical approach of the natural sciences cannot factor out the subjective. The degree to which such a highly systematic decoding of textual meaning surpasses the mere 'finding' and extraction of pre-existent semantic atoms and becomes in itself constructive and creative was explored and demonstrated in a particularly fascinating way by Roland Barthes in his study of Balzac's *Sarrasine*. Barthes' exercise in structuralist close reading in his seminal book *S/Z* marks one of the first attempts to apply such a systematic approach to a literary text across five interpretive dimensions. It was undertaken in 1970 and thus long before PCs, the web and digital humanities came into existence – in other

---

1   Brams himself refers to Cfr. H. Schepers' important article 'Möglichkeit und Kontingenz. Zur Geschichte der philosophischen Terminologie vor Leibniz', *Filosofia* 14.iv, Supplement (1963): 901–14.

words, at a time when a distributed intelligence and human–machine interaction-based approach to textual interpretation was at best a utopian concept.

The idea of a computationally supported collaborative interpretation of complex texts may have seemed rather futuristic in those days; the idea of an automated interpretation of short utterances and in particular of machine translation (MT), however, was not. In fact, it had been around since the seventeenth century and Descartes' vision of a universal language. In the twentieth century, it was put into practice, for example, in the famous 'Georgetown Experiment' that involved the successful translation of some 60 Russian texts into English. Reading the original 1954 IBM press release, one wonders why we are still optimizing MT algorithms some 56 years later:

New York, January 7, 1954

Russian was translated into English by an electronic 'brain' today for the first time.

Brief statements about politics, law, mathematics, chemistry, metallurgy, communications and military affairs were submitted in Russian by linguists of the Georgetown University Institute of Languages and Linguistics to the famous 701 computer of the International Business Machines Corporation. And the giant computer, within a few seconds, turned the sentences into easily readable English. A girl who didn't understand a word of the language of the Soviets punched out the Russian messages on IBM cards. The 'brain' dashed off its English translations on an automatic printer at the breakneck speed of two and a half lines per second. 'Mi pyeryedayem mislyi posryedstvom ryechyi,' the girl punched. And the 701 responded: 'We transmit thoughts by means of speech.'

[...]

This amazing instrument [that is, the IBM 701; J-CM] was interrupted in its 16-hour-a-day schedule of solving problems in nuclear physics, rocket trajectories, weather forecasting and other mathematical wizardry. Its attention was turned at brief intervals from these lightning like numerical calculations to the altogether different consideration of logic in an entirely new and strange realm for giant electronic data processing machines: the study of human behavior – specifically, the human use of words. The result, as publicly proved today, was an unqualified success.

'The potential value of this experiment for the national interest in defense or in peace is readily seen,' Prof. Leon Dostert, Georgetown language scholar who originated the practical approach to the idea of electronic translation, declared to a group of scientists and United States government officials who witnessed the demonstration at IBM World Headquarters, 57th Street and Madison Avenue.

'Those in charge of this experiment now consider it to be definitely established that meaning conversion through electronic language translation is feasible.' Although he emphasized that it is not yet possible 'to insert a Russian book at one end and come out with an English book at the other,' Doctor Dostert predicted that 'five, perhaps three years hence, interlingual meaning conversion by electronic process in important functional areas of several languages may well be an accomplished fact.'

IBM Press Release, January 8, 1954[2]

It is trite to belittle such enthusiasm from today's perspective; we owe a lot to these pioneering efforts. For example, Dostert and his colleagues were clearly aware of the need to restrict their initial work to domain-specific texts, and also of some of the looming pitfalls like those presented by metaphor.[3] More importantly, they had come up with a particular idea as to how one could resolve the problem of language-specific grammatical rules and semantics. On this, we read in the 1954 press release:

What the electronic translators have actually done is to create an entirely new electronic language. They have taken normal words and attached to them tags or signs which give each word a precision it does not usually possess. These signs actually denote rules of grammar and meaning. Although only six rules were used in today's demonstration, the six were enough to cover all the words in all the sentences the 701 was asked to translate.

The IBM 'brain' could translate only because these rule-tags were hitched onto normal words. For the 'brain' cannot think independently. It can only perform tasks in obedience to detailed instructions prepared by human minds. And the minds of the Georgetown linguists (Dr. Dostert was assisted by Dr. Paul Garvin, a member of his Institute staff, just as the enormous detail work at IBM was done by Mathematician Peter Sheridan, under the supervision of Dr. Cuthbert Hurd, Director of IBM's Applied Science Division) could not give the 'brain' dependable instructions until they themselves had worked out foolproof means

---

2   <http://www-03.ibm.com/ibm/history/exhibits/701/701_translator.html> (accessed 6 October 2010).

3   'Doctor Dostert assumes that electronic translation will begin with separate dictionaries for each technical area, and that as experience with them grows, enough will be learned to permit accurate translation of our common everyday language, in which are such illogical and unpredictable words as "charleyhorse." "Charley" is a nickname for Charles. "Horse" is a type of quadruped. But "charleyhorse" does not mean a horse named Charley. It means a muscular contraction which may take place in the calf. And "calf" in this context does not mean the offspring of a cow.' <http://www-03.ibm.com/ibm/history/exhibits/701/701_translator.html> (accessed 6 October 2010).

of telling in advance how to translate a word which had more then [sic] one meaning.

The six rule-tags were the solution. Those particular six were chosen because they have a broader effect on language translation than any other rules studied by the Georgetown linguists. Doctor Dostert estimates that it may take as many as one hundred rule-tags to translate scientific and technical literature in general. But no matter how large the number becomes the six will remain basic.

The six rules govern transposition of words where that is required in order to make sense, choice of meanings where a word has more than one interpretation, omission of words that are not required for a correct translation, and insertion of words that are required to make sense.

The Georgetown Experiment's approach to resolving the problem of language-specific word order in fixed phrases and sentences was: add machine-readable markup. Glossary entries were augmented with a tag denoting, for example, a syntactic transformation rule that would then be interpreted by the machine during the actual translation; one of the first computational applications of natural language tagging.[4] Moreover, the crucial idea was to use the tags as triggers for the execution of generic syntactic rules, rather than as specific descriptors of the word or phrase to which they were attached. The markup thus operated on a higher level of grammatical abstraction than the object text, though it appears that Dostert and his colleagues made sure that the execution of the rules would always result in non-ambiguous, deterministic results. For the linguist, the approach's conceptual similarity to that of the Chomskyan generative grammar seems obvious; note though that Chomsky's earliest relevant publication only came out two years later (Chomsky, 1956: 113–24).[5] For the digital humanist, on the other hand, the Georgetown Experiment presents itself as the application of procedural markup, more than a decade before Tunnicliff's invention of 'generic coding' and almost two decades before Goldfarb's 1973 presentation of the IBM GML markup language.[6]

Today's computational simulations of our human natural language and text processing capabilities vary significantly in the degree to which they have mastered the hermeneutical challenge that the Georgetown Experiment had –

---

4   Renear's important article on 'Text Encoding' in the *Companion to Digital Humanities* (2004) gives a comprehensive overview of the early history and development of markup, yet it traces these back only to the early 1960s contributions in text processing systems and hypertext theory.

5   Chomsky's PhD dissertation on 'Transformational Analysis' was submitted in 1955.

6   On Tunnicliff's contribution, see Harvey Bingham and Charles Goldfarb's 1996 obituary notices posted under 'SGML: In Memory of William W. Tunnicliff', at <http://xml.coverpages.org/tunnicliffe.html> (accessed 7 October 2010).

wisely so – narrowed down to the problem of domain-specific machine translation of fully marked-up utterances. The modelling of a specific natural language grammar's rules for, say, the correct resolution of pronoun references via syntactic backtracking is a problem that can nowadays be considered resolved. By contrast, the computational identification of the correct interpretation of a metaphorical expression in a poem is certainly not so easy, although probabilistic algorithms and stochastic seem to have pushed back the boundary here as well. The availability of large digital corpora marks a significant breakthrough in this regard, and Google Books alone, with its currently approximately 12 million data sets, seems to provide us with a suitably large reference corpus. Shouldn't we feel encouraged to believe that the problem of text interpretation, too, can in principle and at some stage be handled automatically?

Satirical takes on this vision, as, for example, in Swift's *Gulliver's Travels* of 1726 which mocks the Leibnizian *ars combinatoria* (and the Academy of Leiden) in the chapter reporting on the protagonist's visit to the Academy of Lagado, are commonplace: to be able to produce all the books ever written in any of the world's languages by cranking some handles seems to be as absurd as the belief that some computational 'cranking of handles' might be able to do the job of textual interpretation for us. But wherein exactly lies the problem, apart from purely pragmatic considerations?

In a conceptual perspective, text interpretation poses at least two significant obstacles. The first is that of the complexity of statements; the second, and related, that of the underlying dynamics of text and language. Both problems were eliminated by design in the Georgetown Experiment which of course only operated on purpose-made example sentences: the 'girl who didn't understand a word of the language of the Soviets' did not type in just any sentence that came to her mind, but only those that had been fully pre-defined and pre-declared, character by character and word by word, by the human linguists. That this restriction has little to do with how the real-world phenomenon of text and language works is acknowledged in passing by Chomsky in his 1956 'Three Models for the Description of Language'. Couched in a mere footnote, we read: 'Note that a grammar must reflect and explain the ability of a speaker to produce and understand sentences which may be longer than any that he has previously heard.'[7] This caveat is certainly an understatement as the problem is not one of the mere length of sentences, but rather of the complexity of their grammatical structure: a grammar must enable me to formulate and understand sentences that take on a (grammatically correct) structure which I have not already encountered *in actu* in my language practice. So case-based reasoning will not suffice; the grammar must in itself be able to explore and verify as 'grammatical' new construction.

The second and even more fundamental problem is the one that Schleiermacher had already pointed out: language is more than just an execution of grammatical rules on the elements of a dictionary. Both its production and its interpretation are

---

7   Chomsky (1956): 124, n. 7.

embedded in a multi-dimensional and ever evolving context. Even if we were to discount any ongoing development in the rule sets of grammars *per se*, we do have to account for variance and fluidity in the *contexts* in which they are actualized. And even if, on top of that, we were able to define the historical and motivational context of the speaker or writer once and for all by way of historical-critical analysis, interpretation must, at the very least, still be able to take into consideration and reflect its *own* fleeting point of departure and the methodological implications which its particular and temporally bound perspective onto the textual object has (a postulate ignored in the adaptation of Schleiermacher by the Dilthey-inspired historicism).

Against this backdrop, the hermeneutic naïvety of some of the current methods employed in computational extraction of meaning is somewhat charming. Expert systems and concept ontologies in particular strike a humanist as encyclopaedic undertakings that clearly resemble the 'describe and define it all' positivism of the eighteenth century. On the other hand, one might equally well argue that in the reality of our pragmatic day-to-day use of language and texts, we *do* in fact operate on the legitimate assumption that grammar, lexicon and semantics are sufficiently regulated, stable and sort of finite, though this stability and reliability may of course only be enforced by conventions. In other words, a pragmatist might respond that the alleged hermeneutical problem of principle manifests itself only in rather specific contexts, such as the interpretation of historical or literary texts. Yet there is sufficient proof beyond the realm of literature for the ongoing complications encountered in our daily decoding of utterances and texts. The 'interpretation industry' is thriving and omnipresent – psychotherapy or law, to name but two examples, spend a good deal of effort on relating human actions to human utterances, and vice versa.

The problems posed by the interpretation of literary texts are thus not an exceptional, but rather an exemplary case. How, then, can a digital humanities approach help us to realize a hermeneutics that would live up to the postulate formulated in the seminal modern philosophical work on the methodology of interpretation, Hans-Georg Gadamer's *Truth and Method*:

> ... the discovery of the true meaning of a text or a work of art is never finished; it is in fact an infinite process. Not only are fresh sources of error constantly excluded, so that all kinds of things are filtered out that obscure the true meaning; but new sources of understanding are continually emerging that reveal unsuspected elements of meaning. The temporal distance that performs the filtering process is not fixed, but is itself undergoing constant movement and extension. And along with the negative side of the filtering process brought about by temporal distance there is also the positive side, namely the value it has for understanding. It not only lets local and limited prejudices die away, but allows those that bring about genuine understanding to emerge clearly as such. (1960: 298)

Is the discovery of a text's 'true meaning', after all, still and despite Schleiermacher's historical-critical intervention a realistic and worthwhile undertaking? The answer to this question depends on what we mean by 'true meaning'. As for Gadamer, he surely did not have in mind a positivist or historicist concept of interpretation. On the contrary, the crucial epistemological premise in his philosophy is that all understanding is – not in a normative, but in a logical sense – 'prejudice'-based, that is, based on prior judgements. The point is not to *avoid* prejudice; the point is to *make it transparent* to reasoning and thus to differentiate between productive and misleading prejudices:

> 'Often temporal distance can solve the question of critique in hermeneutics, namely how to distinguish the *true* prejudices, by which we understand, from the *false* ones, by which we misunderstand' (Gadamer, 2004: 298).

Productive prejudices are enablers for new ways of interpretation and understanding, whereas false prejudices are hermetic and terminate the process of exploration. For the digital humanist, the method of choice that leads to the fine-grained explication of such pre-interpretive 'prejudices', as well as of the declaration of the hermeneutic outcome of their application in processes of textual interpretation, is and remains: markup. This is the point which Lou Burnard rightly made in his article 'On the Hermeneutic Implications of Text Encoding', from which we took our motto (Burnard, 2001).

Conceptual Limitations and Implications of Markup

That a theory of text is by necessity inherent to any markup approach and practice is nowadays part of the digital humanities *communis opinio*.[8] But how did that critical awareness evolve?

In their 1987 article on 'Markup Systems and the Future of Scholarly Text Processing', Coombs, Renear and DeRose (1987: 933–47) presented a first in-depth methodological and philosophical reflection on markup that is still of relevance. The authors' point of departure was radical: 'there is no such thing as "no markup." All writing involves markup. "No markup" really consists of a combination of presentational and punctuational markup.' This premise not only motivated one of the first taxonomies of markup systems (which differentiated punctuational, presentational, procedural, descriptive, referential and meta-markup). More importantly, it also triggered some principal reflections concerning the cognitive relevance and conceptual consequences of an application of the various types of digital markup for scholars of texts.

---

8 See, among others, the TEI session on 'Markup as Theory of Text', at the TEI Members Meeting, 1–3 November 2007, University of Maryland, which presents important contributions by, among other, Sperberg-McQueen, Renear, Burnard, and so on.

Coombs et al. observed that the recent advent of PCs in the mid-1980s and the tendency to restrict their use to the emulation of traditional writing techniques and apply them mainly as 'electronic typewriters' had resulted in a counter-productive fixation on aspects of presentation. On the conceptual level, they warned, this would amount to the replacing of the 'model of scholar as researching and composing author' by that of the scholar as typist. In their view, the only type of mark-up that really served the intellectual purpose of academics had to be *descriptive* rather than *procedural*:

> Under the descriptive system of markup, authors identify the element types of text tokens ... the tag <lq> identifies the following text as a long quotation, and the tag </lq> identifies the end of the quotation. Authors who are accustomed to procedural markup often think of descriptive markup as if it were procedural and may even use tags procedurally. The primary difference is that procedural markup indicates what a particular text formatter should do; descriptive markup indicates what a text element is or, in different terms, declares that a portion of a text stream is a member of a particular class. (Coombs, Renear and DeRose, 1987)

This distinction between a type of markup that instructs a machine how to process a string of characters regardless of its intrinsic semiotic or rhetorical function, and another type of markup that informs a human reader about the correct categorization of that string in reference to some external system or purpose (a grammar, a lexicon, a pragmatic context, and so on) proved fundamental. The case in favour of descriptive markup made by Coombs et al. ('descriptive markup is not just the best approach ... it is the best imaginable approach') draws on two observations further elaborated upon in Renear (2004: 218–39). The first concerns the significant number of practical advantages which descriptive markup holds in terms of its flexibility and (re-)usability in a broad variety of contexts (authoring, composition, transcription, publishing, archiving, retrieval and analysis). The second and principal finding is that only descriptive markup implies an accurate model of what a text actually *is* from the point of view of the human reader: namely a means of communication. On this, Renear clarifies as follows:

> The objects indicated by descriptive markup have an intrinsic direct connection with the intellectual content of the text; they are the underlying 'logical' objects, components that get their identity directly from their role in carrying out and organizing communicative intention. (Renear, 2004)

However, if we disregard the fact of the different existential and cognitive status of the recipients of these two types of markup – simply put, procedural markup addresses the machine whereas descriptive markup addresses the human being – then this clear-cut distinction turns fuzzy. Telling a processing system what *to do* with an object always implies a prior conceptualization of what that object *is*; vice versa, declaring what the object *is* by necessity also implies formulating ideas and rules as to what could or should be *done* with it. Consider POS-tagging: a grammatical category such as NP (noun phrase) is by definition an explication of what, in a grammatical use of the particular language, may be done with the elements so defined. A similar argument concerning the question of the performative dimension led Renear to declare the procedural/descriptive distinction flawed already in 2000 and comment:

> It conflates questions of mood (indicative vs. imperative statements about a document) and domain (the kinds of objects named in those statements). It also fails to describe adequately the use of markup by authors rather than by later encoders. An adequate markup taxonomy must, among other things, incorporate distinctions such as those developed in contemporary 'speech-act theory'. (Renear, 2000: 411–20)

With a view to the question under discussion at current – that is, how digital humanities might facilitate a collaborative approach toward the exploration of textual meaning – it seems reasonable to take Renear's suggestion one step further than speech-act theory, and back to hermeneutics: in an extensively cross-connected and resource-rich, computationally highly performant digital environment in which humans and computers continuously interact and in which we can instantaneously switch back and forth from description to interpretation, the distinction of procedural versus descriptive markup should, I believe, be replaced by a scalar model that extends between the ideal-types of performative versus hermeneutic markup. The former type represents all markup practices intended to define the legitimate modes and procedures by which textual elements and textual objects on a whole may be *processed*; the latter stands for approaches to markup that are primarily motivated by the aim to define how these textual elements and objects ought to be *interpreted*.

But why must the 'performative versus hermeneutic' distinction be conceptualized as a continuum, not as a clear-cut opposition? Let us first consider the question whether an *exclusively performative*, that is, totally non-interpretive, markup is possible. Since not only machines, but also intelligent agents, are involved in creating or executing markup, this seems doubtful: most, if not all processing-oriented markup lays a foundation for interpretation (for example, structuring a text into chapters). Performative markup can be exclusively performative and nothing else under one condition only: it must not affect any intelligent processing agent, directly or indirectly. But then what would be the point of markup in the first place?

Approaching the question from the opposite angle, one must ask whether *exclusively interpretive* markup exists – but that seems even more impossible. No interpretation is *only* interpretation; in fact, highly interpretive markup in particular will imply, explicitly or not, declarations of what the object at hand is understood to be, consist of and relate to – that is, of *what one can do with it and how.* So beyond the ideal-type distinction, markup is always both performative and hermeneutic.[9] And all markup therefore constrains and delineates a text's pragmatic as well as interpretive potential, even where it is supposedly just an abstract categorization or a processing instruction issued to a non-intelligent agent – to quote Spinoza: *omnium determinatio est negatio.*

In this regard, the methodological issue of major concern to literary history and analysis is how to distinguish 'true' prejudices, that is, meaning-productive markup, from 'false' markup prejudices that will prematurely terminate our interpretive process. Of course, it would be naïve to ignore the fact that in most day-to-day contexts it is exactly the fiction of such hermeneutically 'false' and finite 'markup' (taken in the metaphorical, not in the technical, sense) that we rely upon. We act and interact as if it were possible to define in an absolute manner what things are and what may be done with them, and what they are not and what is not permissible to do. Moreover, we try to rule out conflicting definitions and interpretations through institutions and by way of sanctions. Yet it turns out that court cases, criminal laws, national constitutions, contracts – let alone personal symbolic communications such as declarations of love or hate – are regularly subjected to revision and reinterpretation. In reality, our everyday 'markup' and interpretation of empirical as well as symbolic phenomena always seems to come with a hidden time-stamp, an expiry date and an agenda attached to it.

State-of-the-art digital humanities markup – now again understood in the proper technical sense – makes such conditions explicit by way of a declaration of the relevant markup scheme and conventions, the definition of document types, the embedding of process-related context information in XML-headers, and so on. However, despite the important self-reflective and critical dimension which meta-markup represents, it is questionable whether the conceptual paradigm in which we currently operate when applying or analysing, say, TEI markup has really changed that fundamentally. In reality, meta-markup is considered in the main as a pragmatic necessity to ensure portability and reusability, rather than as a truly hermeneutic *sine qua non.*

Arguably, the most fundamental philosophical critique of the restrictions inherent to contemporary approaches to markup was formulated by Dino Buzzetti (2002: 61–88) in his reflections on 'Digital Representation and the Text Model'.[10] In Buzzetti's view, strongly embedded markup implies a data model that can only capture the expression plane of literary texts, but is inherently inadequate to model the content plane. While the symbolic material that represents the expression is organized in a linear, sequential fashion clearly emulated by embedded markup,

---

9   Burnard (2001, 1998) gives an excellent demonstration of this and illustrates how a single markup spans the three functional domains of compositional features, contextual features and interpretive features.

10   The question has also been raised with a particular view to the adequacy of the SGML sequential data model. On this, see Renear et al. (2002).

the semantic content is organized as a non-sequential and multidimensional continuum that takes on the form of a matrix. Buzzetti concludes that:

> ... a suitable digital representation of the text seems to require a weakly embedded markup system and a non-linear data model. The markup system must be capable of projecting the non-linear structure of the model upon the linear expression of the text, and the model must be able to represent the non-linear structure of its content. ... The data model upon which the digital representation of the text is founded must be capable of transposing, by way of algorithms, the procedures for textual criticism and interpretative textual analysis. The model must be able to satisfy the needs of the philologist and the editor, as well as those of the historian and the literary critic. (Buzzetti, 2002: 76–7)

Buzzetti further points out that markup tags can equally well be considered as elements of a descriptive meta-language explicating certain features in an object text, and interpreted as expressions belonging to a second-order object language that represents an interpretation of the first-order object text – a point which we have just made ourselves. But the conclusion which Buzzetti draws from this goes beyond the acknowledgement of the dialectic of performative/hermeneutic: in conceptual terms, the key criterion for an adequate markup of literary texts is, in his view, the ability to model and define not only the sequential representational material from which texts are made, but more importantly, the *one-to-many relationships* that are characteristic of texts both in terms of textual pragmatics (construction, distribution, editing, critique, interpretation, and so on) and textual semiotics:

> Just as the relation one-to-many between the expression's identity and the content's variation can be turned into the relation one-to-many between the expression's variation and the content's identity, in the same way the markup can be considered a varying expression of a content which is always identical to itself, or a manifestation of the content's variation of a single and always identical expression of the text. In this way, markup becomes an instrument for use in transforming the implicit variation of the interpretation of an identical expression into the explicit fluidity of the expression of an identical content. Variously encoded textual portions, generated by different interpretations of one single expression, may be considered synonymous expressions of one single content. (Buzzetti, 2002: 83)

One-to-many: A Vision of Collaborative Markup

This is where the vision of collaborative markup comes into play – a vision already sketched out by Christian Wittern in a *Humanist* posting more than a decade ago:

> With the application of markup, we have become used to ask a processing software to generate multiple, entirely different views of a text, depending on

what we want to do with the text. I think, we have to carry this notion one step further, to extend the creation of views to the markup itself: Of course, I could in theory have one densely marked up text with linguistic markup, markup for the needs of historians and yet another type for literary studies. Instead of loading all this into one file, I suggest we think of different layers of markup, from which one instance is generated depending on the needs we have at a certain moment.

Although the source sharing is important and needed, this should not be the only perspective of collaboration: What we need to develop is also some protocol through which distributed layered portions of markup, which might be located on entirely different physical locations, can be used to generate a view of a text. We might also want to think of 'open workgroups', where markup can be added remotely to texts located somewhere in cyberspace.[11]

Most of what Wittern suggested sounds very do-able today in practical as well as in technical terms, and so one should expect collaborative markup to have become a reality hence. Let us consult the modern day oracle then.

Unfortunately, the number 1 hit which a Google search for the keyword *collaborative markup* produces at this point in time (October 2010) has absolutely nothing to do with what we have in mind: CAML (Collaborative Application Markup Language), we learn, 'is an XML based markup language used with the family of Microsoft SharePoint technologies'.[12] So CAML is not about collaborative markup, it is about marking up collaborative applications. The number 2 ranking entry points to an XML editor software named 'Topologi Collaborative Markup Editor'[13] – from our perspective another misnomer, as in this case 'collaboration' boils down to enabling computer lab users to exchange messages and screenshots while they perform tagging duties. Apparently the purpose of facilitating such exchange is to arrive at an agreement as to how a specific passage in a document ought to be tagged correctly. In other words, collaboration is aimed to guarantee (albeit by way of discourse) that everybody not only adheres to the same norms and conventions, but also produces results that can be reliably reproduced by any other member of the team. Here collaboration equates to normative validation.

The current number 3 listing is closer to the target, albeit only conceptually. It advertises a software for web-based collaborative reviewing of 'shop drawings, product data and RFI sketches' by way of adding annotations, sketches, arrows, and so on to a single pdf document. The developers explain their goal as follows:

---

11   <http://www.digitalhumanities.org/humanist/Archives/Virginia/v13/0289.html> (accessed 10 October 2010).

12   <http://en.wikipedia.org/wiki/Collaborative_Application_Markup_Language> (accessed 8 October 2010).

13   <http://www.topologi.com/resources/pdfs/Training.pdf> (accessed 8 October 2010).

The question we always get is 'can multiple people review simultaneously?' and the answer is 'yes.' AEC-Sync allows for concurrent markup and the software automatically notifies you when other users have added comments, so you never worry about overlapping your stamps and markups.

The markups are completely secure so there is no need to be concerned that other users could edit or delete your markups. Each markup is tagged to a user and is time-stamped down to the minute for accurate history tracking.[14]

Of course, this type of freestyle annotation has little in common with fully declared approaches to text markup such as TEI-XML. But if we ignore the fact of a missing syntax and rule set for the moment, the approach (at least in theory) amounts to a somewhat different conceptualization of markup in two important aspects. One, the ideal of an authoritative and 'correct' markup seems no longer to be in force; the paradigm is indeed one of (again, theoretically) open-ended and unrestricted collaboration by means of discursive annotation. Two, by overlaying all individual markup instances and mapping them onto one single source document, and at the same time tagging them with a user-specific session ID, the system allows for iterative procedures and conflicting markup layers that can be stacked and configured in many different ways. Contradiction across layers at least does not necessarily amount to a system anomaly or a syntax error.

Neither of these characteristics constitutes a new idea or phenomenon, for this is exactly the *modus operandi* not just of Wikis, but in fact of all critical post-enlightenment discourse. Indeed, in a philosophical and methodological perspective, the normative approach inherent to conventional text markup, if we allowed its practice to become an entity unto itself and de-contextualized its results into a-historical categorizations of texts and their constitutive elements, is conceptually quite simply at odds with critical rationality. On the other hand, the idea of a completely intuitive and idiosyncratic approach to markup is not an option either if we want to exploit the possibilities of information retrieval, computational analysis and computational modelling. We do want a defined syntax and procedural rules.

What, then, would the ideal scenario for a hermeneutically productive collaborative approach to text markup look like? Here are some key requirements:[15]

1. Collaborative markup must adhere to best practice in terms of meta-declaration of objects and procedures (DTDs, XML header declarations, workflow models, and so on).
2. Collaborative markup must use a standardized, but infinitely extendable, markup syntax (which TEI already provides in the form of feature structure tags).

---

14 <http://www.attolist.com/online-markups> (accessed 8 October 2010).
15 Requirements 1 to 5 have been met in part or full in the development of CATMA (Computer Assisted Textual Analysis and MARKUP); see <http://www.catma.de>.

3. Collaborative markup must be based on a one-to-many relationship model in which one object text is related to *n* associated markup instances. For practical reasons, this makes stand-off markup a more feasible choice than inline markup.
4. Every markup instance generated in the course of collaborative markup practices must be preserved as a unique data set; it must also point to a unique and persistent object text as its original source document.
5. Collaborative markup software must allow for iteration, duplication, review, contradiction and ambiguity *within and across* markup instances. While the form of the markup has to adhere to an agreed syntax, the assessment of the validity of its individual statements in terms of their content constitutes a hermeneutic operation that falls outside the scope of the process of collaborative markup itself.
6. All original source documents and all the markup instances related to these must be handled by an integrated document management system in order to make it possible to:

    • map a particular markup onto other variants of the original document;
    • analyse the full set or subsets of the markup for patterns, trends, variations, and so on;
    • exploit the data, in a meta-analysis, for machine learning purposes, so that over time certain parts of hitherto manually effected markup can be handed over to automated procedures. This frees human hermeneutic resources that can thus be deployed to identify and markup other features in the textual objects.

In technical terms, all of this is well within reach, and some current developments in linguistic markup – such as XCONCUR – are potentially moving in this direction.[16] Yet it must be stressed that the collaborative search for 'true meaning' requires more than approaches and tools that can handle concurrent and layered markup: what is required now amounts to conceptualizing and enabling *conflicting* markup.

While big numbers and excessive data storage requirements no longer awe digital humanists, ambiguity somehow still seems to. In this regard, we are perhaps still under the influence of an engineering paradigm that is foreign to the humanities, a paradigm in which 1 cannot at the same time be 0. Yet 'true meaning', in Gadamer's perspective, is indeed a moving target that defies this binary logic and whose continuous repositioning is effected by those who consciously pursue

---

16   See Schonefeld (2007). While XCONCUR is designed to handle layered markup, the emphasis of this article lies on constraint-based validation of layer-specific markup which the developers consider to be a key requirement. In other words, a markup layer is not supposed to be capable of handling mutually excluding tags for one and the same character string.

it. I am not advocating deconstructionism here; rather, the point I am trying to make is that our traditional markup methodologies cannot suffice to generate and exploit opposing 'true prejudices' in a methodologically controlled fashion. Of course, we do already allow for overlap, for different markup schemes and layers, and we do collaborate – but in the conceptualization and implementation of markup, we have not yet fully acknowledged the importance of dissent and the richness of the one-to-many paradigm that refutes disambiguation.

Markup has to learn how to generate and render as hermeneutically productive ambiguity and contradiction, from its conceptual model right to the level of its computational application. For the digital humanist, this will open up a new perspective on how we might use computation to elevate our hermeneutic undertaking to a new and more complex level – and thus to 'crowd source' true, that is, critically reflected, meaning in a joint venture that involves us all and takes every contribution seriously.

References

Note: In all instances where a freely available electronic version is indicated by an URL, any verbatim quotes from the respective text have been taken from this electronic version (therefore lacking page numbers).

Barthes, Roland, *S/Z* [1970], trans. Richard Miller (New York: Hill and Wang, 1974).

Brams, Jozef, 'Between Translation and Interpretation: The Concept of Contingency in the Aristotelian Tradition', *Medioevo: rivista di storia della filosofia medieval* 27 (2002): 22f.

Burnard, Lou, 'On the Hermeneutic Implications of Text Encoding', in D. Fiormonte and J.Usher (eds), *New Media and the Humanities: Research and Applications* (Oxford: Humanities Computing Unit, 2001): 31–8, available in the 1998 version at <http://users.ox.ac.uk/~lou/wip/herman.htm> (accessed 12 October 2010).

Buzzetti, Dino, 'Digital Representation and the Text Model', *New Literary History* 33 (2002): 61–88.

Chomsky, Noam, 'Three Models for the Description of Language', *IRE Transactions on Information Theory* 2 (1956): 113–24, available at: <http://www.chomsky.info/articles/195609--.pdf> (accessed 7 October 2010).

Coombs, James H., Allen H. Renear and Steven J. DeRose, 'Markup Systems and the Future of Scholarly Text Processing', *Communications of the ACM* (ACM) 30.11 (1987): 933–47, available at <http://xml.coverpages.org/coombs.html> (accessed 7 October 2010).

Gadamer, Hans-Georg, *Wahrheit und Methode. Grundzüge einer philosophischen Hermeneutik* (Tübingen: Mohr Verlag, 1960).

Gadamer, Hans-Georg, *Truth and Method*, 2nd rev. edn (London and New York: Continuum Publishing, 2004).

Ramberg, Bjørn and Kristin Gjesdal, 'Hermeneutics', in Edward N. Zalta (ed.), *The Stanford Encyclopedia of Philosophy* (2009), available at <http://plato. stanford.edu/archives/sum2009/entries/hermeneutics/> (accessed 12 October 2010).

Renear, Allen H., 'The Descriptive/Procedural Distinction is Flawed', *Markup Languages: Theory and Practice* 2 (2000): 411–20.

Renear, Allen H., 'Text Encoding', in Susan Schreibman, Ray Siemens and John Unsworth (eds), *A Companion to Digital Humanities* (Oxford: Blackwell, 2004): 218–39, available at: <http://www.digitalhumanities.org/companion/vi ew?docId=blackwell/9781405103213/9781405103213.xml&chunk.id=ss1-3-5&toc.depth=1&toc.id=ss1-3-5&brand=default> (accessed 10 October 2010).

Renear, A.H., D. Dubin, C.M. Sperberg-McQueen and C. Huitfeldt, 'Towards a Semantics for XML Markup', in R. Furuta, J.I. Maletic and E. Munson (eds), *Proceedings of the 2002 ACM Symposium on Document Engineering*, McLean, VA, November 2002 (New York: Association for Computing Machinery, 2002): 119–26.

Schleiermacher, Friedrich Daniel Ernst, *Hermeneutik und Kritik*, Mit einem Anhang sprachphilosophischer Texte Schleiermachers, ed. Manfred Frank (Frankfurt am Main: Suhrkamp, 1977): 78f.

Oliver Schonefeld, 'XCONCUR and XCONCUR-CL: A Constraint-Based Approach for the Validation of Concurrent Markup', in Georg Rehm, Andreas Witt and Lothar Lemnitzer (eds), *Data Structures for Linguistic Resources and Applications – Proceedings of the Biennial GLDV Conference 2007* (Tübingen: Gunter Narr Verlag, 2007).

Swift, Jonathan, *Gulliver's Travels Into Several Remote Regions of the World* (London: Jones & Company, 1826).

Chapter 8

From Building Site to Building: The *Prosopography of Anglo-Saxon England* (*PASE*) Project[1]

Janet L. Nelson

At a symposium on prosopography sponsored by the British Academy in London in 2000, one historian remarked that a prosopographical project 'allows, in principle, a universal record'. Another historian issued a timely reminder that a database was 'only as comprehensive as the available data themselves'. Ten years on, the aspirant to universality, who happens to be the present writer, has learned to be more realistic – Anglo-Saxon historical records have proved curiously resistant to inquiries for information about women – and learned, too, new ways of thinking about data and database.[2] Among my many teachers, two must be named here. One, whose teaching was delivered despite his having died before I was born, is Walter Benjamin (1892–1940). His *Arcades Project*'s relevance to my belated re-tooling lies less in its foreshadowing of digital technology (interesting though that is) than in its suggesting of new ways of doing history. Benjamin began with deconstruction: began from fragments, as if it were bits on a building site. Evoking the steel supports of a bridge, he proposed a new 'building': 'the historian today has only to erect a slender but sturdy scaffolding – a philosophic structure – in order to draw the most vital aspects of the past into his net.'[3] The second name is that of Harold Short, whose intent in humanities computing generally has been to create 'new dynamics of collaboration', and, in more than a decade's work on *The Prosopography of Anglo-Saxon England* (*PASE*) in particular, 'to push the historians to reassess their data, their methods,

---

1 I would like to thank the following colleagues, present and past, for comradeship over many years, and for help in preparing this chapter: Stephen Baxter, John Bradley, Simon Keynes and Susan Kruse; and Marilyn Deegan for decades-long friendship and, more recently, editorial patience.

2 Cameron (2003). The first quotation is from Nelson (2003): 158; the second is from A. Cameron, in the same volume's Preface, at xvii. For the record: out of 31,565 named persons in the *Prosopography of Anglo-Saxon England* database, there are only 1,736 women. The new project mentioned below will identify women in Domesday.

3 Benjamin (1999): 459, convolute N1a, 1. I am very grateful to Stuart Airlie for introducing me to Benjamin's work.

their purposes'.[4] This offering to Harold's *Festschrift* acknowledges no mere nudge, nor just 'invigorating tension', but an experience of impulsion which in the short term was hard and unsettling, but whose longer-term effects have provided me and many others with a wholly beneficial form of further education.

A happy conjuncture at King's College London from the late 1980s changed the landscape on the Strand and produced the idea from which *PASE* grew. The Centre for Computing in the Humanities (CCH) was created and Harold Short arrived in 1988. Collaboration soon followed: colleagues, including Susan Kruse in CCH and me in the Department of History, co-taught an optional introductory computing course to History undergraduates. The area in which Susan's and my interests overlapped (she, a Viking-Age archaeologist, I a mainly Carolingian historian) was Anglo-Saxon England. The *Prosopography of the Byzantine Empire* (*PBE*), funded by the British Academy, had begun at King's in 1987 thanks to the leadership of Averil Cameron, successively Professor of Ancient History (1978–89) and Late Antique and Byzantine Studies (1989–94), and the expertise of John Martindale, whose work on the *Prosopography of the Later Roman Empire* predated the application of digital technology, but whose later career, on *PBE*, embraced it.[5] *PBE* inspired the turn of Susan's and my lunchtime conversations to a possible Anglo-Saxon equivalent. But it took Harold to turn a wild wish into a hard-edged plan. By 1998, the Arts and Humanities Research Board (AHRB) had emerged as the major national funder, and Harold was involved in planning another big prosopographical database project, *The Clergy of the Church of England*, jointly nurtured by another King's historian, Arthur Burns, with colleagues at Kent and Reading. *PASE* was an idea whose time had come. For unmatched Anglo-Saxon historical expertise and a confident way with computing, a collaborator outside King's was needed: Simon Keynes combined the requisite qualities with unquenchable enthusiasm, generosity of spirit and mind, and a base at Trinity College Cambridge where 50 per cent of our project meetings were scheduled to happen, and where the lunchtime hospitality was legendary, inspiring concerted thinking and plenty of cheer without need for alcohol. His willingness to take on the co-directorship of *PASE* was key to the success of an application for AHRB funding put together by Simon, Harold, as prospective technical director, and me, as co-director and lead applicant. The project was designed, we said, as: 'a relational database aiming to provide structured information relating to all the recorded inhabitants of England between 597 and 1042, based on a systematic examination of the available written sources for the period, and intended to serve

---

4   Short (2003): 163.

5   See the other contributions to Cameron (2003), especially Magdalino, at 44–7, with the encouragingly prescient comments: 'The time has come for prosopography to move up front, so as to make it impossible for any student in the twenty-first century to graduate with a history degree without knowing what prosopography is'; and 'Thanks to the electronic revolution ... the *PBE* is going to be the ultimate reference work for the history of Byzantium ...'

as a research tool suitable for a wide range of users with interests in the Anglo-Saxon period.' In 1999 *PASE* was awarded £517,839 by the AHRB, to run for five years, from 1 January 2000 to 31 December 2004. *PASE* went online in May 2005.

PASE's successor project (originally entitled *PASE II*, or *PASE2*) was submitted to the AHRB under its resource enhancement scheme in 2004, and was designed to follow seamlessly on from *PASE* itself, by: (i) continuing the chronological coverage of all recorded inhabitants of England beyond 1042 to 1066, and adding coverage of all English persons down to c. 1100;[6] (ii) adding information derived from available written sources for the period between 1042 and 1066, as well as information derived from major sources written after 1066 (especially in the early twelfth century); (iii) incorporating various improvements to *PASE*, including a new, more user-friendly web interface and more powerful search functions; and (iv) adding information on landholders recorded in Domesday Book for 1066 (*TRE, Tempore Regis Edwardi*) and 1086 (*TRW, Tempore Regis Wilhelmi*). Because of the importance of the Domesday material, Stephen Baxter, a King's historian with special expertise in Domesday studies, joined the three co-directors of the original *PASE*. In 2005, the AHRB (which shortly thereafter became the AHRC) awarded *PASE II* £317,246, to run for three years from 1 October 2005 to 30 September 2008. For reasons to be examined below, but especially the decision to create a separate *PASE Domesday* area of the *PASE* site, the completion of *PASE II* was subject to delays, and successive no-cost extensions were secured from the AHRC to cover these. The new data entered for *PASE II* was published on the existing web platform in December 2009, *PASE Domesday* was published online in July 2010 and formally launched on 9 August 2010, and *PASE II* and *PASE Domesday* were finally officially launched together on 26 October 2010 (in a pleasing coincidence with the 1,111th anniversary of the death of King Alfred of Wessex).

These projects, now collectively known simply as *PASE*, have been hailed as major achievements in humanities computing and Anglo-Saxon studies. Called by assessors 'a model project', the original *PASE* was approved at every annual reporting stage; and *PASE II* won similar approval. There is good evidence (mainly in the form of references in learned works) that the original *PASE* has been widely appreciated by the international scholarly community, and rather shakier evidence (numbers of website hits, and anecdotal information of use by schoolteachers and sixth-formers) of wider impact. It is too soon to measure *PASE II*'s impact; but *PASE Domesday* has already received very wide publicity thanks to Stephen Baxter's BBC2 TV appearance on 10 August 2010 in an hour-long programme, 'Domesday', which among other things featured the project, and which was

6   In proposing Englishness as an identity pre- and post-1066, we followed: Campbell (1986); Williams (1995); van Houts (1996); Wormald (1999); Gillingham (2000); and Thomas (2003). It is good to be able to say that all the above scholars, and also, pre-eminently, Nicholas Brooks, have given active support to *PASE* in one capacity or another. I am in no position to say whether the dedication of databases is customary in digital humanities, but *PASE Domesday* has been dedicated to Nicholas Brooks and Ann Williams.

associated with other media attention. Further, Stephen has gained Leverhulme Trust funding (from 2010) for a two-year research project, 'Profile of a Doomed Elite', that stands on the shoulders of *PASE II*. In sum, *PASE* can be considered a resounding success for all involved, including, signally, CCH and Harold Short, *PASE*'s technical director throughout. This makes *PASE*, I hope, a suitable subject for this contribution to Harold's *Festschrift*.

It is first worth briefly considering, since Harold has helped steer so many large projects into port, what was and is distinctive about the *PASE* enterprise. Though large, it could be represented at the outset as clearly delimited by the long-established parameters of the Anglo-Saxon period, as recorded in written sources. This would be no voyage of discovery, but rather of more thorough trafficking over and trawling of well-charted waters. Modern academic Anglo-Saxon studies, as developed by (largely) anglophone scholarship since the nineteenth century and embodied in the late twentieth by the International Society of Anglo-Saxonists (ISAS), rested firmly on a corpus of texts mostly in Latin, but including some important items (notably the *Anglo-Saxon Chronicle*) in Old English.[7] The chronological start-point was an iconic given for *PASE* as for Bede: the arrival in Kent in 597 of the mission of Augustine sent by Pope Gregory to the English.[8] True, in 1999 there was some fuzziness about the final destination: 'it is not intended at this stage to cover the material in Domesday Book', wrote the applicants. But though a realistic estimate of the time required for data entry at that point prescribed an end-date of 1042 (hence excluding the reign of Edward the Confessor), the even more iconic date of 1066, the Norman Conquest, was already envisaged for 'a later stage', and, as noted, was to be grappled with and incorporated *con brio*.

The strong disciplinary prevailing wind behind the craft and its scholarly direction explains why the identification of the items to be included in *PASE*'s source-base was relatively readily accomplished. The technical team were much impressed by the palpable sense of Anglo-Saxonist identity that permeated existing editorial and cataloguing work.[9] *PASE*'s initial source-inventory, which grew to just over 2,000 items, was the sturdy work of the two researchers on

---

7   For the history of Anglo-Saxon scholarship and its institutionalised embodiments, see Frantzen (1990); and for ISAS (founded in 1983), see its admirably well-maintained website. Both the book and the site well represent the place of history in that scholarly tradition, while fairly reflecting its literary, linguistic and philological elements – as does its flagship in the UK, the Department of Anglo-Saxon, Norse and Celtic, based in the Faculty of English at the University of Cambridge.

8   The importance of information given by Bede in his *Ecclesiastical History* is evident in *PASE*, thanks to the scrupulously thorough researching of Francesca Tinti, while David Pelteret extracted some less obviously available prosopographical material from Bede's exegetical works, as well as from Alcuin's letters and Ælfric's sermons: see Pelteret (2003): 160.

9   See, for instance, Biggs, Hill and Szarmach (1990); and Szarmach and Rosenthal (1997).

board when *PASE* weighed anchor, David Pelteret and Francesca Tinti. Especially notable on the initial five-year phase, but extending through into the second, was the remarkable stability of the research complement, and the consistency of the support given throughout by the International Advisory Committee and the wider Anglo-Saxon studies subject community. This continuity was fundamentally important to the outcome of a voyage on what was to prove an exceptionally long haul: a full two years beyond the eight as planned and hence as funded.

The two senior researchers developed significant sub-areas of their own: David on the *Anglo-Saxon Chronicle* (the differing versions of which posed data-entry problems), and Asser's *Life of Alfred*; Francesca on saints' *Lives*, from Cuthbert's interestingly different two, and those of Anglo-Saxons on the Continent, in the eighth century, through to those of the tenth-century reformers, and on correspondence between the papacy and English churchmen and kings. Two younger scholars, Alex Burghart as postgraduate researcher, then postdoctoral researcher, on *PASE* from 2001 to 2009, and Arianna Ciula, as a research associate at CCH working on *PASE* between 2005 and 2009, both contributed in formative ways not only to *PASE* itself but to creating an 'Anglo-Saxon Cluster' linking *PASE* with projects applying digital technology to Anglo-Saxon charters, specifically through text-encoding. Alex entered most of *PASE*'s rich data from charters, and then worked on the pilot project *ASChart* ('Anglo-Saxon Charters'), funded by a British Academy small research grant in 2005. Arianna made invaluable technical contributions on *LangScape* ('The Language of Landscape: Reading the Anglo-Saxon Countryside'), a database of land boundaries (most of them in Old English) detailed in Anglo-Saxon charters, funded by the AHRC and created at King's by Joy Jenkyns and Peter Stokes, with CCH collaboration.[10] The benefits of such a cluster in terms of integration and interoperability are already becoming very clear – at the same time demonstrating the vision of the projects' technical director and prime link-maker, Harold.

PASE's innovations are not just exemplary intended products of collaboration in the digital humanities. In several respects, they are responses to challenges generated within the process of *PASE*'s making. What has come to be known as the factoid approach to prosopography (that is, the identifying of discrete items of information in the sources of the period as assertions about individuals and groups, and the structuring of these items in a relational database), pioneered in *PBE*, was substantially developed in *PASE* (it is currently being deployed in four other projects involving CCH), and extended in *PASE II*. The 'Event' category, devised for the original *PASE* and restructured in the later stages of *PASE II*, groups

---

10   The cluster brings together *PASE*, *ASChart* and *LangScape* with the *Electronic Sawyer*, in a one-year project funded by the Joint Information Services Committee (JISC), in 2008–09, and now receiving ongoing support from CCH. The relevant websites are at: <www.pase.ac.uk>; <www.aschart.kcl.ac.uk>; <www.langscape.org.uk>; and <www.trin. cam.ac.u/kemble/index.php?menuitem=2&opagename=02>. See Ciula and Spence (2009), and Spence, Bradley and Vetch (2006).

factoids and hence facilitates searches. In very recent years, the development of faceted browsing, which, as John Bradley has put it, 'usefully blurs the distinction between browsing and searching', has been enabling users to combine different facets, that is to say, selection criteria, and hence, again, to select and relate highly structured data more efficiently. A faceted browser has been an uncovenanted blessing bestowed by CCH on *PASE* as a whole.

Changes of a substantial kind, however, have been not just desirable but necessary for the part of *PASE II* that is *PASE Domesday*. For it became evident during the early months of *PASE II* that the unique characteristics of Domesday Book data could only be catered for by substantial technical innovations. These were: a custom-built exceptionally large spreadsheet form of data capture; a consequent need to restructure the collection spreadsheets and reload them into a new relational structure in *PASE Domesday*; a way of incorporating *PASE Domesday* data into the main *PASE* database as well (so that, for instance, identifications of individuals could be made across the entire database); the provision of a specialised Domesday browser; and a suite of solutions to the problems involved in mapping Domesday land-holdings and land-holders. All the above entailed building the relevant software, and in the case of Domesday mapping, supporting the application of GIS software to the data. The volume added of *PASE II* and *PASE Domesday* data relative to *PASE* data can be expressed statistically: a 38 per cent increase in the number of sources used, a 243 per cent increase in the number of recorded names, a 186 per cent increase in named locations, and a 233 per cent increase in the number of factoids.[11]

Read my list! The uniquely detailed nature and the sheer scale of the Domesday data, combined with the complexities of representing it in interactive tables and maps, freely available online, had defeated previous researchers (and there have been a fair few). The amount of innovation necessary had been unforeseen and unapplied for by the co-directors; and the uncovenanted benefits were therefore also unfunded by the AHRC. Risk assessment had not yet been demanded from applicants to humanities funding bodies in 2005, let alone 1999. Yet despite the risks, and despite the huge technical difficulties and hugely time-consuming quests for solutions, the work has been done and the project completed – as I said earlier, after extra time, and thanks to no-cost extensions. It hardly needs to be spelled out that this outcome could not have been achieved had not all the researchers and technical team members involved in *PASE Domesday* gone many extra miles and foregone (we hope only temporarily) easier lives. It hardly needs to be added that Stephen Baxter, as the effective lead director, had to draw on leadership qualities and inner resources that, fortunately for us all, proved equal to what sometimes seemed an impossible task, nor that the technical director needed to find ever cleverer and more elastic ways to make CCH resources go further. It remains to summarise and emphasise the significance of all this. The whole culture of the project was defined by Harold's gift for collegiality, his almost unfailingly cheerful demeanour and his

11   See the Database Statistics link at the PASE website.

ever-constructive response to difficulties. He had, and diffused, the vision of *PASE Domesday* in particular as a strategic investment for CCH, for King's and for the wider world of humanities computing. For the ability to visualise complex data-sets *simultaneously* as interactive tables *and* as maps has the power to transform the way history is done. So far, the lead in this field had been taken by big corporations with powerful but very expensive software: to deliver something comparable online and gratis is a major breakthrough, wholly in line with the hope we nourished in 2000 of 'transforming what might otherwise have been for specialists only, and thought interesting only to them, into something fundamentally democratic and empowering'.[12] CCH and King's are now in a position to capitalise on a well-placed investment through the new 'Profile of a Doomed Elite' project: thanks to Harold's judgement, and the sparkling synergy he summoned forth from Stephen Baxter and John Bradley, a classic problem – the impact on England of the Norman Conquest – can be approached efficiently at last.

I have set out as clearly as I can (given limited space) the story of the making of *PASE* and *PASE II*, and the nature of the achievement which those projects represent. I want to use the rest of this chapter to reflect no less frankly, with whatever objectivity someone closely involved can muster, on some of the difficulties encountered (to use a pleasantly evocative Haroldian phrase) *along the way*. I will deal with these difficulties under three headings, all arising from the way we were determined to operate, and inherent in the cause under whose flag we flew: that of collaboration. To assert this is to say that strains and tensions were unavoidable, but that they were coped with, eventually and after a fashion. My hope is that an attempt to record our experience may help colleagues in other large digital humanities projects to take effective action (which could sometimes be preventive action) sooner than we did, and hence to reduce the symptoms and side effects.

Intradisciplinary Collaboration

In this area were to be found the most predictable and most easily resolved of tensions. I have already referred to multidisciplinary characteristics of Anglo-Saxonism (and I could have added archaeology, epigraphy and numismatics). Different strands can cause differing priorities to pull against each other. The annual meetings of *PASE*'s International Advisory Committee and our annual Colloquia of Anglo-Saxonists, both meeting at King's, showed up intradisciplinary divides, and differential levels of computing expertise (where generational difference too is often conspicuous), between researchers with different intellectual formations. The more or less philologically and more or less historically inclined, for instance, are not always natural or very thoroughgoing collaborators: they bring distinct types of expertise, and expectations, to the table when distinctions between rank,

---

12 Nelson (2003): 158.

office, occupation and status are in question.[13] Formational difference can be inflected by national difference too, very much more for good than ill when held up for inspection; and national in this context can refer to the subject of study rather than the student's place of origin. With relatively amateurish and partial interests in Anglo-Saxon history, and never a paid-up member of ISAS, I brought a comparativist's approach to *PASE*. All told, however, this kind of collaboration was genuinely close and very seldom other than constructive; and in the constellation that is *PASE* (as Marc Bloch said of the social science constellation), the 'queen and mistress is history'.

Interdisciplinary Collaboration

More familiar to digital humanists than the particular intradisciplinarity of Anglo-Saxonists is working collaboration on any given project between themselves, as members of a 'technical team', and subject-specific researchers in, say, music, or classics, or English literature, or – in *PASE*'s case – history. Our technical colleagues were alert listeners, thoughtful responders and adept negotiators. If the historians had a fault, it was to assume that the arcana of their Anglo-Saxonist trade were known, or easily explicable, to the technical team. A tremendous amount of communication went on, in both directions, as each group first learned to talk the talk, and ultimately to walk the walk, of the other. By project's-end, Bede and Wulfstan, *TRE* and *TRW*, were coming as trippingly off the tongues of CCH men and women as Æ's were rife in their print-outs, and the researchers for their parts had become equally fluent in attribute tables, projection and the language of GIS. Appropriately, it was on *PASE Domesday* that such intellectual collaboration went deepest, and the shared commitment and mutual respect of Stephen Baxter and John Bradley were most crucial. Inevitably, it was here that the tensions between the historical researchers' ambitions and the technical team's funded time became most painfully exposed. Here, too, sometimes a half-incredulous indignation became explicit: the value-added amount of technical work over and above what had been estimated, as calculated by John, was 'more than 1.5 person-years'. And what had not been estimated had not been funded. *PASE*'s gain was, transparently, at the expense of other CCH commitments. Amidst much nail-biting and some gnashing of teeth, the irresistible energy and drive of Stephen and John's steady grip and genial responsiveness drove this through. Though this was King's, whose foundation was achieved by victory in a duel, *PASE*'s fate never hung on pistols at dawn. In the end, I believe all who worked on *PASE* were convinced that the unique quality of the Domesday data, and the unique importance of the historical findings drawn from that data thanks to *PASE*, more than justified the price paid, short-term, by other projects and other less dramatic, but basic, CCH work.

---

13   Pelteret (2003): 161.

Administrative Collaboration

This bit of the story is not so happy. It is becoming increasingly common for large research projects to involve participants from different universities. The *PASE* experience was that the administrators in the two institutions – at School or College level in King's case, at Faculty level in Cambridge's – operated with different costing and accounting systems and procedures, and different pay-scales, for what appeared to be corresponding grades. The resultant problems had not been foreseen, and often proved tricky and very time-consuming to reconcile, despite the best efforts of the staff concerned. On *PASE II* especially, the relatively rapid turnover of research staff, which is a characteristic feature of large research projects in the humanities, as distinct from the sciences, exacerbated what were already complicated mismatches of information.

Difficulties also arose within King's, between School- or College-level administrators and their counterparts at departmental (CCH or History) level. Problems were especially severe when quite distinct conceptions of financial management seemed to be harboured by College finance officers and CCH managers. A kind of cognitive dissonance between professional cultures seemed, in my view, to inhibit understanding at College/School level of the imperatives under which CCH operated: that is to say, CCH's dependence on a large variety of different funding streams for projects, each of which had timings of demand for CCH support which were hard, even impossible, to predict. Digital humanities is quite exceptional in the rate and scale of technological changes that have opened up in recent years: developments which drive increased needs for CCH support as well as CCH's increased capacity not only to respond but to generate very large sums of additional funding for cutting-edge projects. *PASE Domesday* is a particularly good instance of this new virtuous circle. Standard financial/accounting procedures are, compared with the light cruiser that is CCH, like proverbial tankers: simply unable to adapt quickly enough to these changes. The dissonance diagnosed above has caused a failure to acknowledge appropriately creative and adaptive alternatives which, though necessarily unconventional, are not less rigorous and are certainly the more effective for being at once slender and sturdy. A paradoxical consequence has sometimes seemed to make the best of times the worst of times for the world-class digital humanist. It cannot be said that these *décalages* have yet been fully addressed, let alone resolved, by all at the most senior management level of the Higher Education Institution.

What this all adds up to is very much more than an everyday story in the lives of academic folk. It is an exceptional story of collective effort, to which scores of people contributed; of challenge and response; of collective achievement. It is a story set in a time of very rapid technological change, which seems on course to continue ever faster – a time, too, of generous state funding, the like of which, by contrast, will probably not recur soon, if ever. Harold Short is at the very heart of this story. He was responsible for the ultimate success – both because of his technological mastery and leadership, and because he picked the men and women who came up with and implemented solutions to the problems. He was not responsible for the risk underestimate. As lead applicant, I must shoulder blame for that (and please note that I use the word 'blame' in no other context). But if risk was discovered belatedly, we also came to learn a lot about trust: most crucially of all, about trust, on the funder's part, in CCH and so, in Harold. Without the AHRC's no fewer than three extensions, the Domesday site would have remained a building site, and a history in fragments. Those extensions were, you will recall, of the no-cost variety. So who paid the salaries of the CCH staff? The answer, built into the two-pronged funding structure of humanities research in the UK, was the Higher Education Institution – King's. The College too had trust – in its outstandingly resourceful employees and their director. When push came to shove, it was willing to allow some leeway, to cut some slack. Perhaps not willingly enough, though. This is not the place for more crystal-ball gazing. But it is absolutely the place for plain speaking. Harold Short has been liberated by retirement to work on; but whatever the merits of his successor, and they are great, Harold's leaving is ill-timed, and a loss to the College, nevertheless. It is a premature dropping of the pilot. A university that does not encourage its world-class research towards blue-skies thinking and risk taking, that is not prepared to use some perfectly legal and rigorous, but flexible and nifty, accounting procedures, that will not acknowledge the unknowns, that ignores the inbuilt frictions and tensions and juggling with timing and funding that inevitably arise in big projects, could be accused of the same short-sightedness that in 1890 caused young Kaiser Wilhelm II to drop wise old Pilot Bismarck, or – to come closer to the world of academe – that in 1925 led the Goethe University at Frankfurt-am-Main to reject *Ursprung des deutschen Trauerspiel* (*The Origin of German Tragic Drama*) as Walter Benjamin's *Habilitationsschrift*, his university teaching credential, thus, as it turned out, denying him forever the chance of an academic post. Walter Benjamin's chronic problems with timing (unkept) and funding (lack of) were the direct and finally tragic consequences.

I will end with some reflections, inescapably wry, on similarity and difference: Walter Benjamin's chronic problems with timing and funding, which were truly not of his own making, were quite different from those that have confronted Harold and over which he has triumphed. In other respects, though, there is some similarity. Harold is, as Walter was, ahead of his time. Harold is, as Walter was, an original, with charisma, and creative flair that, in its own sphere of operations, can strike you as genius. Harold can, and Walter could, imagine a methodological revolution which was also an intellectual one. But there, again, similarity ends – for Walter, unlike Harold, lacked the cool-headed judgement and practical skills to help, fundamentally, in bringing his revolution about and seeing it through in the long haul. Enough of comparisons which are bound to be unfair. Our times may feel and be threatening to values that we scholars believe in, but they are not catastrophic, as Walter's were for so many intellectuals and free spirits. Walter Benjamin could not choose. The inscription on his tombstone – he killed himself at 48, in flight from the Nazi terror – is chilling and dark: 'There is never a document of culture which isn't at the same time one of barbarism.' Harold's happier destiny is to have been liberated by retirement, not only to work but to choose where and on what to work. He will, we cannot doubt, continue working for and enjoying the humanistic culture to which he has devoted both his career and his personal life so far: a culture as free as he can make it of contemporary forms of barbarism.

References

Benjamin, Walter, *The Arcades Project*, ed. R. Tiedemann, trans. H. Eiland and K. McLaughlin (Cambridge, MA: Harvard University Press, 1999).

Biggs, F.M., T.D. Hill and P.E. Szarmach (eds), *Sources of Anglo-Saxon Literary Culture: A Trial Version* (Binghamton NY: MRTS, 1990).

Cameron, Averil (ed.), *Fifty Years of Prosopography: The Later Roman Empire, Byzantium and Beyond*, Proceedings of the British Academy 118 (Oxford: Oxford University Press, 2003).

Campbell, J., *Essays in Anglo-Saxon History* (London: Hambledon Press, 1986).

Ciula, A. and P. Spence, 'Threads of Integration: The Anglo-Saxon Charters Pilot Project at the Centre for Computing in the Humanities', in G. Vogeler (ed.), *Digitale Diplomatik. Neue Technologien in der historischen Arbeit mit Urkunden* (Cologne, Weimar and Vienna: Böhlau, 2009): 40–55.

Frantzen, A.J., *Desire for Origins: New Language, Old English, and Teaching the Tradition* (New Brunswick, NJ: Rutgers University Press, 1990).

Gillingham, J., *The English in the Twelfth Century* (Woodbridge: Boydell & Brewer, 2000).

Magdalino, P., 'Prosopography and Byzantine Identity', in Averil Cameron (ed.), *Fifty Years of Prosopography: The Later Roman Empire, Byzantium and Beyond*, Proceedings of the British Academy 118 (Oxford: Oxford University Press, 2003): 41–58.

Nelson, Janet L., 'Medieval Prosopographies and the Prosopography of Anglo-Saxon England', in Averil Cameron (ed.), *Fifty Years of Prosopography: The Later Roman Empire, Byzantium and Beyond*, Proceedings of the British Academy 118 (Oxford: Oxford University Press, 2003): 155–9.

Pelteret, David, 'Medieval Prosopographies and the Prosopography of Anglo-Saxon England, II: Forming the Factoid: The Historian Conceptualizes Database Entities', in Averil Cameron (ed.), *Fifty Years of Prosopography: The Later Roman Empire, Byzantium and Beyond*, Proceedings of the British Academy 118 (Oxford: Oxford University Press, 2003): 159–62.

Short, Harold, 'Medieval Prosopographies and the Prosopography of Anglo-Saxon England, III: "Humanities Computing" and New Dynamics of Collaboration', in Averil Cameron (ed.), *Fifty Years of Prosopography: The Later Roman Empire, Byzantium and Beyond*, Proceedings of the British Academy 118 (Oxford: Oxford University Press, 2003): 163–7.

Spence, P., J. Bradley and P. Vetch, 'Joining Up the Dots: Issues in Interconnecting Independent Digital Scholarly Projects', session presented to Digital Humanities 2006, Université Paris-Sorbonne, 5–9 July 2006, accessible at: <http://www.allc-ach2006.colloques.paris-sorbonne.fr/DHs.pdf>.

Szarmach, P. and J.T. Rosenthal, *The Preservation and Transmission of Anglo-Saxon Culture: Selected Papers from the 1991 Meeting of the International Society of Anglo-Saxonists* (Kalamazoo, MI: Medieval Institute Publications, Western Michigan University, 1997).

Thomas, H.M., *The English and the Normans: Ethnic Hostility, Assimilation and Identity 1066–c. 1200* (Oxford: Oxford University Press, 2003).

Van Houts, E.M.C., 'The Memory of 1066 in Written and Oral Traditions', *Anglo-Norman Studies* 19 (1996): 167–79.

Williams, A., *The English and the Norman Conquest* (Woodbridge: Boydell & Brewer, 1995).

Wormald, P., *The Making of English Law: King Alfred to the Twelfth Century* (Oxford: Blackwell, 1999).

Chapter 9

Crowdsourcing the Humanities: Social Research and Collaboration

Geoffrey Rockwell

Introduction

The phrase "Web 2.0" is supposed to have been coined at a conference brainstorming session about the new types of websites emerging after the dot.com collapse.[1] Web 2.0 sites, like the Wikipedia and Flickr, are often characterized by broad participation in content creation. They leverage the web to enable content to be created, not by those who manage sites, but by a community of participants. Web 2.0 participatory technologies are now being used by humanists to structure collaborations for research. This chapter will look at the opportunities for collaborative research in the humanities through two humanities computing projects that enabled collaboration through crowdsourcing. This will be framed by a discussion of collaboration in the humanities.

Humanists, in comparison to the sciences, are reputed to not collaborate on research. The image of the humanist as a "lone ranger" can be traced through images like Rembrant's "The Philosopher in Meditation"[2] or stories like Descartes' *Discourse on Method*, where he tells his story of original research when he "spent the entire day closed up alone in a room heated by a stove, where I had all the leisure to talk to myself about my thoughts."[3] By contrast, the digital humanities are supposed to be characterized by collaboration, partly because of the need for different skills to complete digital projects and because we have technologies that facilitate collaboration.[4] As Lynne Siemens summarized it:

---

1   O'Reilly (n.d.)
2   Rembrandt van Rijn, 1632, Musée du Louvre.
3   Descartes (2006), Part 2: 12.
4   See, for example, the HASTAC "About HASTAC" page where they define the network thus:
HASTAC ("haystack") is a network of individuals and institutions inspired by the possibilities that new technologies offer us for shaping how we learn, teach, communicate, create, and organize our local and global communities. We are motivated by the conviction that the digital era provides rich opportunities for informal and formal learning and for collaborative, networked research that extends across traditional disciplines, across the boundaries of academe and community, across the "two cultures" of humanism and technology, across the divide of thinking versus making, and across social strata and

Traditionally, research contributions in the humanities field have been felt to be, and documented to be, predominantly solo efforts by academics involving little direct collaboration with others ... However, Humanities Computing/Digital Humanities is an exception to this. Given that the nature of research work involves computers and a variety of skills and expertise, Digital Humanities researchers are working collaboratively within their institutions and with others nationally and internationally to undertake this research.[5]

In this chapter I will start by clearing the ground for crowdsourcing by discussing the limitations and promises for collaboration in the humanities. The point is not to praise collaboration, but to ask how it can be structured through social media for research. I will then discuss two social media projects I was involved in which used information technology differently to structure participatory or social research, and the lessons learned in these projects about collaboration. Both of these projects represent different ways of collaborating while thinking through technology. This will lead to general reflections on crowdsourcing in the humanities. The chapter will conclude by arguing that we need to rethink our models for how knowing is done in the humanities to account for the distributed knowing illustrated by social research projects.

Weed Control

In a section of the introduction to *Humanities Computing* called "Weed Control," Willard McCarty takes exception to the way in which collaboration has been taken as a "transcendental virtue, to be applied regardless of context" (2005: 9). He agrees that even so-called solitary scholars are indebted to the work of others, but that that indebtedness does not mean that collaboration should become an end in itself, something it seems to have become. One could add that we already collaborate in all sorts of ways: in departments to deliver the curriculum, in program committees when we organize conferences, when we correspond, when we edit journals, and when we review the work of others. These collaborations seem so obviously part of our academic life that we have ceased to notice them, calling instead for the new types of collaboration mediated by technology.

McCarty goes on, however, to make a stronger point about collaboration, that "[i]n the humanities, scholars have tended to be physically alone when at work because their primary epistemic activity *is* the writing, which by nature tends to be solitary activity."[6] McCarty seems content to leave the epistemological issue there, without questioning the primacy of writing in the generation of

national borders. ("About HASTAC" <http://www.hastac.org/about-hastac>). You can also see the importance of collaboration in Svensson (2010).

5   Siemens (2009): 225.
6   McCarty (2005): 12; emphasis in the original.

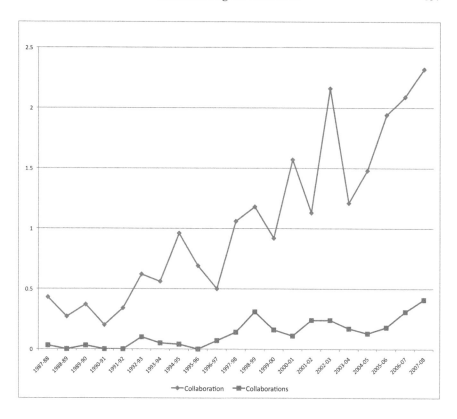

Figure 9.1   Growth of "collaboration" and "collaborations" across the
***Humanist* corpus**

Note: This graph was generated by Voyant Tools, S. Sinclair and G. Rockwell (2009)
<http://voyant-tools.org>. The corpus was created using the text files from the *Humanist*
discussion group archive at <http://www.digitalhumanities.org/humanist/>.

knowledge as he questions the perceived primacy of collaboration. I will return
to the epistemological issue at the end of this chapter, but for the moment I note
that McCarty concludes the control of the weed of collaboration with Ursula
Franklin's distinction between "holistic" and "prescriptive" technologies.[7]
McCarty, like Franklin, favors the holistic craft approach to technology where
the (solitary) individual controls the process (and technologies) over the threat
of prescriptive and industrial approaches where the individual is managed by
technology. McCarty wants to defend solitary epistemic writing as research
against enforced and managerial collaboration, and is right to do so. In this
context, one can see why his model for humanities computing is that of a

---

7   McCarty (2005). The distinction he draws on from Ursula Franklin is from *The Real
World of Technology*.

methodological commons where research methods are adapted for application to the problems of the traditional humanities without challenging the disciplines or their research practices.[8]

By contrast, digital humanists like Patrik Svensson, building on Cathy Davidson, believe the traditional ways of doing computing in the humanities for which McCarty is an advocate have been supplemented by a new wave of doing digital humanities or "Humanities 2.0," where technology is used to undermine practices and epistemic assumptions.[9] The very shift in names from "humanities computing" to "digital humanities" is indicative of the change from a model of applying computing in the humanities to a model where the digital is the catalyst triggering changes in the disciplinarity of the humanities. The new digital humanities for Davidson, like the Web 2.0 phenomenon, is characterized by the collaborative weeds of interactivity and participation.[10] The digital decenters authority, challenging peer review, solitary writing and authority, and broadcast ways of teaching. One man's weed is another woman's spice. She is aware of some of the perils of social media like Facebook, but in the end she favors experimenting with forms of participation that the network enables as a way of renewing the humanities.

Crowdsourcing the Humanities

I tend to agree with both sides and believe that they can be reconciled. Collaboration is not a transcendent value, as McCarty points out, but it can, if properly structured, advance research and achieve valuable research ends—ends which the solitary scholar might not achieve writing alone. Both the 1.0 and 2.0 type projects are valuable—one builds on the other. Talk about collaboration should not squeeze out the traditional curiosity-driven practices, despite what funding agencies may want. The interesting question is how to structure collaboration properly so that it contributes to, rather than hinders, research. This is a variant on Steve Fuller's fundamental problem of social epistemology:

> How should the pursuit of knowledge be organized, given that under normal circumstances knowledge is pursued by many human beings, each working on a more or less well defined body of knowledge and each equipped with roughly the same imperfect cognitive capacities, albeit with varying degrees of access to one another's activities?[11]

---

8   See McCarty (2005): 119, figure 3.1: "An intellectual and disciplinary map of humanities computing.".
9   Svensson (2010), paragraph 15.
10   Davidson (2008).
11   Fuller (1987): 145.

One particularly promising way of organizing the pursuit of knowledge through technologically mediated Web 2.0 collaboration is what Jeff Howe calls "crowdsourcing."[12] Crowdsourcing uses social media tools like wikis to enable a "crowd" or group of people to create something of value. The crowd of volunteers enabled becomes the human resource whose small contributions, if properly co-ordinated, can make a real difference. Perhaps the best-known crowdsourcing project is the Wikipedia, where volunteers have authored, edited and argued millions of encyclopedia articles in less than ten years without being paid to author and without editorial supervision.[13] Before the Wikipedia, few people believed that any resource as important as an encyclopedia could be created through unsupervised volunteer work. As Shirky puts it: "Skepticism about Wikpedia's basic viability made sense back in 2001; there was no way to predict, even with the first rush of articles, that the rate of creation and the average quality would both remain high ..."[14] But the Wikipedia proved the skeptics wrong; now everyone is trying to figure out how to leverage crowdsourcing for commercial advantage, as it has been noticed that some of the most valuable internet assets are built on content that is not paid for, but voluntarily contributed. YouTube, Facebook, Flickr and other Web 2.0 phenomena are all built on our content. They provide us with a structured site to place content and connect it with others, but these companies also mine our data and return it to us with embedded ads.

It should be noted, however, that crowdsourcing projects are not free. While the labour of many generously contributes to them, they still need support for the center that designs the application, maintains the software and runs the servers. Even the Wikipedia has to raise funds like a public broadcaster. Even further, the design of a crowdsourcing application significantly constrains the contributions of the crowd. There is a way in which crowdsourcing applications combine the vision of a solo researcher or small team with the broad contributions of the many in a distribution of work that has a "long tail." Crowdsourcing is not the opposite of solo work; it is an extension, where some have more influence than others.

Not all social media projects are commercial, nor are they all structured like the Wikipedia. A number of digital humanities projects have adapted crowdsourcing to research tasks in the humanities. One of the first was the *Suda On Line* (SOL) project that Anne Mahoney discusses in "Tachypaedia Byzantina: The Suda On Line as Collaborative Encyclopedia."[15] This project organized professional and amateur classicists to help translate passages from the Suda, a Byzantine Greek historical encyclopedia. This project was not, like the Wikipedia, completely open. Instead it had a workflow where translations were checked. Other projects include the *Transcribe Bentham* project that is engaging the public in the transcription

12   Howe (2009).
13   See the Wikpedia at <http://www.wikipedia.org/>.
14   Shirky (2008): 117.
15   The website for the crowdsourcing project is <http://www.stoa.org/sol/>. To learn more about the project, see Mahoney (2009).

of the 60,000 papers by Bentham in the library of University College London,[16] and the *Australian Historic Newspapers* project run by the National Library of Australia, that encourages the public to correct OCRed text of old newspapers.[17] Crowdsourcing, despite the skeptics, clearly works even in the small scale for serious research projects. What, then, can we learn from existing research projects?

Dictionary of Words in the Wild

At this point I will turn to two projects that I have worked on. They are by no means the only experiments in crowdsourcing in the humanities as noted above, but they both illustrate a way in which crowdsourcing can be used in research.

The first project I will outline is a social research site, the *Dictionary of Words in the Wild*[18] where users can get accounts and upload pictures of public textuality which they tag according to the words that appear. This site resembles social photo sites like Flickr, but it has a research purpose which is to document the forms of text that appear outside of print, on signs, as graffiti, tattoos, and so on. The project does not start with a hypothesis of what public textuality (in the wild) is—it allows contributors to define it through participation.

Figure 9.2   Home page of the *Dictionary of Words in the Wild*

The *Dictionary* was developed with support from the TAPoR (Text Analysis Portal for Research) project at McMaster University. The first version was programmed by Andrew MacDonald in Ruby on Rails in 2006. Since then Lian Yan and Kamal Ranaweera have added to the code for the project and it has been transferred to the University of Alberta with the new domain name of <lexigraphi.ca>. The *Dictionary*

---

16   For more, see <http://www.ucl.ac.uk/transcribe-bentham/>.

17   See Trove, <http://trove.nla.gov.au/>, or read Holley (2009).

18   Dictionary of Words in the Wild, <http://lexigraphi.ca>.

has been reported on at *Digital Humanities 2008* at the University of Oulu and elsewhere.[19]

Figure 9.3 **"Add word" screen where you tag the image with the appearing words**

Users who sign up for a free account can upload as many pictures as they want, though we downsize very large images for the sake of storage. Users tag the images with the words that appear and can add a description to the image.

The tagging allows us to offer a dictionary interface to the images of words. You can select a letter as you would in a dictionary (the image below shows "words beginning with E"); you can search for a word; or you can "Create a Phrase" out of words.

Figure 9.4 **First screen of "Words beginning with E"**

Some of the features we have added over time include:

- A commenting feature so that users could comment on each other's images, similar to what Flickr offers. This has not been used much.

---

19   Willard McCarty presented a paper which we co-authored, "A Carnival of Words: The Dictionary of Words in the Wild and Public Textuality" (McCarty et al., 2008).

- In order to accommodate people who were uploading longer passages of public text, we added a feature called "Phrases in the Fields." When a user tags an image, they have the choice of tagging it with a list of words or with a phrase.
- As we were getting a number of spam accounts created by bots, we had to add a simple Captcha-like feature to the screen where potential users sign up for new accounts. To sign up, you need to type in letters seen on an image like this: JABjJV. Alas, automated spam vandalism is a problem with crowdsourcing projects.

The *Dictionary*, as of October 2010, has over 6,000 images uploaded by 59 participants with over 7,000 unique words tagged. Like other crowdsourcing projects, there is a "long tail" effect where a small number of the users have uploaded most of the images, while most users have only uploaded one or two. According to the literature, this is common and in fact is one of the features of successful crowdsourcing projects—they harness not only the committed contributor but the long tail of less committed contributors.[20]

How is the *Dictionary* a social research project? The project was started as an alternative way of asking about the text outside of print—the text in the wild. Compared to the river of research about published textuality, there is little written about the noisy textuality that surrounds us in our everyday contexts.[21] Considering how much of it we read everyday, it is surprising that literary theory has not considered as discourse the text on T-shirts, signs, posters and painted on our walls. The *Dictionary* is a first step that tries to document textuality in the wild so that we can theorize it. Rather than simply post my photographs of what I considered public textuality, by creating a crowdsourcing project, the *Dictionary* invites others to contribute to the documentation without unduly constraining their imagination about what constitutes public textuality. The *Dictionary*, by enabling participation, has therefore gathered far more images of public textuality, but has a much greater diversity of images than if it had been a research project conducted by one person or a small team.

An important aspect of the project is that it is exploratory in the sense that it does not start from an assumption or theory. Instead, the project makes a simple point about the rich variety of textuality outside of the traditional covers within which we usually look. The sheer exuberance of the uploaded makes a visual argument about the importance of words in the wild that no narrative could. The project invites the reader to explore the variety of images or participate by adding new images, if you think we have missed forms of public textuality. As participants have noted, if you then start carrying your digital camera and looking for interesting examples of digital textuality, it changes your perception of the

---

20   See the section in Shirky (2008): 122–30, titled "A Predictable Imbalance."
21   An interesting exception is Scollon and Scollon (2003).

urban landscape.[22] In short, the *Dictionary* can work as a different type of rhetoric that changes your perception through participation.

Day in the Life of the Digital Humanities

The second project I will discuss is the *Day in the Life of Digital Humanities* (*Day of DH*) project which brought together digital humanists around the world to blog one day of their work as a way of answering the question "Just what do computing humanists really do?" This project has been run twice, first in 2009, when we had 84 participants, and again in 2010, when we had just over 150. The project was organized by a team that included me, Stan Ruecker, Peter Organisciak, Megan Meredith-Lobay, Julianne Nyhan, and Kamal Ranaweera.

List of Day of DH 2009 Participants

Below, in alphabetical order by surname, is a list of colleagues who are expected to participate in A Day in the Life of Digital Humanities on 18 March 2009.

- William Allen ⟨ℰ⟩ - Arkansas State University
- Rafael Alvarado ⟨ℰ⟩ - Dickinson College

- Jon Bath ⟨ℰ⟩ - University of Saskatoon
- Craig Bellamy ⟨ℰ⟩ - King's College London
- Brett Bobley ⟨ℰ⟩ - National Endowment for the Humanities
- Matthew Bouchard ⟨ℰ⟩ - University of Alberta
- John Bradley ⟨ℰ⟩ - King's College London
- Susan Brown ⟨ℰ⟩ - University of Guelph
- Kai-Christian Bruhn ⟨ℰ⟩ (link to user page) - University of Applied Sciences Mainz
- Lou Burnard ⟨ℰ⟩ - Oxford University Computing Services

Figure 9.5   Alphabetical list of participants in the 2009 *Day of DH* project, with map

Participants who signed up agreed to blog their digital humanities work on the same day, March 18, with text and images. Before the day, we used an email list to prepare participants and to discuss issues like securing permissions from people appearing in photographs. We used a wiki page as an anchor site for the project, with explanations and links to documentation. Here is the main page for the project in 2009.

Before the day itself, we created a blog for each participant. They were encouraged to enter an About entry before March 18 to introduce themselves and to test the system. This also gave participants a way to talk about projects that might not be dealt with on the particular day when we were all going to blog. The blog, of course, was primarily for participants to enter reflections as the day in question progressed. Many participants, including myself, ended up having to

---

22   See Peter Organisciak's blog post of April 20, 2009, "Words in the Wild" at <http://www.porganized.com/blog/words-in-the-wild>.

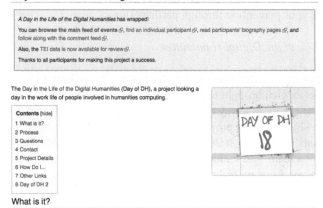

Figure 9.6   Home wiki page for the 2009 *Day of DH* project

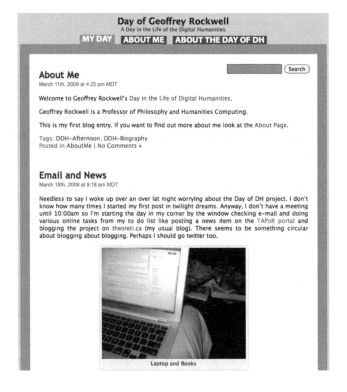

Figure 9.7   Day of Geoffrey Rockwell

continue editing their entries and uploading photographs after March 18, but the idea was still to use the day as an organizing principle. Here is the start of my *Day of DH* in 2009 (see Figure 9.7).

On the day itself in 2009, we were surprised to find that the project got attention as it was happening, primarily through Twitter. A number of people hearing about it asked to join on the day of the project. In the second iteration, we tried to take advantage of this by suggesting a Twitter Hashtag.

Once the After the Day in question was over, the organizing team slowly exported all the blog entries, proofed them, and tagged them, creating a dataset or collaborative publication available for others to read or analyze.[23] The hope is that we can sustain the project, repeating it each year with the help of others. This would add a diachronic dimension to the project, where people could compare reflections on the digital humanities over time.

The *Day of DH* project, unlike the *Dictionary*, was developed using off-the-shelf tools. The website that documents the project is a wiki created with MediaWiki. The individual blogs that participants used to document their day were set up using WordPress MU, which allowed us to rapidly create all the needed blogs. The only tools that we had to write ourselves were the scripts for processing the output from all the WordPress blogs.

The idea of the project was to document what we do in the digital humanities through a participatory project. The project can be seen as a form of autoethnography, where a community writes its own ethnographic narrative, or it can be seen as a type of one-day conference, since what effectively happened in both iterations is that the participants blogged about the digital humanities while reading each other's blogs.

This project, like the *Dictionary*, is also exploratory in the sense that it does not start with a hypothesis or theory about the digital humanities, but uses crowdsourcing to provide a communal answer. The *Day of DH* is, in effect, a different kind of answer to the question of what do digital humanists do, a collective answer rather than a reflective one. The project could have been conceived of as a survey, where people would be polled as to what they do and the answers summarized and reflected on, but that would not have had the same impact, and I doubt that we would have had as many volunteers if we had asked people to fill out a survey. Instead, through crowdsourcing, participants could negotiate the answer with each other and they could be assured that their voice would not be drowned in the summarization. For that matter, the full dataset of blog entries is available for analysis and summarization by everyone. We even provided a live RSS feed of the entries for those who wanted to run real-time analytical tools, as some like Stéfan Sinclair did. The *Dictionary* makes possible summative or reflective answers, but in and of itself it is a different type of answer, one that is communal and dialogical.

We chose the name *Day in the Life of the Digital Humanities* for the project, not only because it would indicate the expected commitment of participants, but

---

23   The 2009 dataset, as we call the complete collection of blog entries, is available at <http://dl.dropbox.com/u/128635/Day%20of%20DH/DayOfDHwithoutImages.zip>.

because it might resonate with readers. The title, for example, was partly influenced by a lecture that a prominent digital humanist, Ed Ayers, gave on "What Does a Professor Do All Day, Anyway?"[24] It should also remind readers of Solzhenitsyn's *One Day in the Life of Ivan Denisovich,* Joyce's *Ulysses,* and Woolf's *Mrs. Dalloway,* all of which are structured around one day. Finally, it might remind people of *The Day in the Life of ...* series of photography books, which bring together images of a country by many photographers, all taken on the same day. In the *Day of DH,* we also encouraged participants to upload pictures, though we had to worry about ethics requirements. The hope was that participants and readers would see the *Day of DH* as being in a tradition of organizing understanding around a day.

This project raises questions about authorship and academic recognition. We have submitted a paper about the project, "A Day in the Life of the Digital Humanities 2009," to a peer-reviewed online journal in the field. This, of course, raised questions as to the authorship of the project. While this is still being negotiated, the solution that we hit upon was to have the organizing team as the co-authors of the paper that describes the project, and to also submit the dataset, along with a short "About the Dataset" document, as co-authored by all the participants and organizers. It was important as we were setting up the project that all participants felt that this was a collaborative online publication where all were co-authors. It is doubtful that any of us will get significant academic recognition for this project itself (as opposed to any papers in journals about the project). This, alas, is one of the many challenges that we face when collaborating in a humanities academic culture that still considers sole-authored written works as normative.[25] It is not, however, a problem particular to crowdsourcing projects—any co-authored project or digital project suffers the same problems when evaluated.

Making Crowdsourcing Work

Crowdsourcing projects, as attractive as they may be, run the risk of falling flat if no one volunteers to participate. The big question behind the design of social media projects is motivation—what motivates participation and how to design for motivation.[26] From my experience and from the literature, here are some general guidelines for developing crowdsourcing projects for humanities research.

---

24   Ayers (1993).

25   Another collaborative project that I was involved in was the development of a wiki on "The Evaluation of Digital Work" for the Modern Languages Association, to deal with issues around evaluation and recognition of digital work. I started this on my personal wiki at: <http://www.philosophi.ca/pmwiki.php/Main/MLADigitalWork> when I was on the MLA Committee on Information Technology. The MLA then took it over and runs it now at: <http://wiki.mla.org/index.php/Evaluation_Wiki>, so that others can maintain it.

26   See Organisciak (2010) for an extended discussion of motivation.

Ask for Help. No one will help you in a research project unless you ask. Social research projects depend on volunteers to achieve research ends. To get volunteers, whether for a computer-supported project or not, you need to ask for help, and when asking, you have to be able to quickly explain what help is needed. Don't be afraid to promote your project and outright ask for help.

High Concept, Good Title. For volunteers to decide to participate in a crowdsourcing project, they need to understand what they are committing to. It is important, therefore, to communicate efficiently the idea of the project. A title for a project like "Wikipedia" goes a long way towards describing the project—that is, it is an encyclo-pedia created with a wiki. I chose the name *Day in the Life of the Digital Humanities* for a similar reason; it would communicate the commitment asked for (a day) and remind people of the "Day in the Life of ..." photography series, to give them a sense of what could be achieved.

Small Autonomous Tasks. Crowdsourcing is suited to tasks that can be broken into smaller, relatively autonomous tasks. Jeff Howe's sixth rule is "Keep It Simple and Break It Down."[27] Malcolm Gladwell, in a welcome critique of the revolutionary claims made for social media like Twitter, points out that social media are not suited for sustained and complex tasks, especially ones that carry significant risk (like real revolutions).[28] Instead, they are suited for lots of little tasks that carry little risk, are relatively quick and easy to complete, and do not call for lots of collaboration between participants. That is not to say that crowdsourcing cannot achieve complex things, but it often does so through leveraging many doing small tasks.

Support Imbalance. An imbalance between contributors is normal, so you should plan for it. A small number of participants will contribute a lot each, while a large number will contribute a little. Crowdsourcing projects should not neglect the long tail of participants who just want to give a little time. They are your word-of-mouth advertising and their contributions add up, so support them as well as the power contributors.

---

27 Howe (2009): 285.

28 Gladwell (2010). Gladwell's essay is an antidote to the generally enthusiastic press that social media have received. In particular, it deals with revolutionary claims made for social media. Gladwell does not think that social media is very effective at serious change:

It [social media] makes it easier for activists to express themselves, and harder for that expression to have any impact. The instruments of social media are well suited to making the existing social order more efficient. They are not a natural enemy of the status quo. If you are of the opinion that all the world needs is a little buffing around the edges, this should not trouble you. But if you think that there are still lunch counters out there that need integrating it ought to give you pause.

Interpretative and Creative. Crowdsourcing in the humanities does not have to be used only for interpretative tasks like correction, transcription, and translation. It is tempting to want to manage the chaos of a social project so that the crowd can only contribute safe tasks that can be moderated. But why not imagine projects that encourage original contributions. Crowdsourcing can also be used for creative tasks where users contribute new material to an open-ended project, like the *Dictionary of Words in the Wild*. The trick is to make small original contributions possible.

Support Diversity. Crowdsourcing should be structured to maximize diversity, not to flatten it. Collaboration isn't necessarily a good thing if it leads to erasing difference. Eliot Smith (2007) discusses how groups can perform worse than individuals or fall prey to biases similar to those of individuals. For example, too much communication can lead to a convergence of opinion in a group, rather than maintaining healthy diversity.[29] Communication should be managed to avoid "bandwagon" convergence.

Vandalism. Vandalism of different sorts can be a real problem for crowdsourcing, especially automated or spam vandalism. For this reason, it is useful to anticipate and prepare for misuses of your site in ways that do not undermine the participatory character of the project. Holley (2009) gives an example of a thorough risk analysis.

Use Custom and Open Tools. You don't have to create custom software for your crowdsourcing project. You can creatively use existing tools or customize tools. For the *Day in the Life of the Digital Humanities* project, we used off-the-shelf tools from a wiki to WordPress Mu. The *Transcribe Bentham* project has adapted MediaWiki rather than build a custom system. I expect that there will soon be good open-source crowdsourcing tools available that can be adapted easily to humanities projects.

Recognize Community. Crowdsourcing creates a community, even if the project is intended to be utilitarian. You need to support that community, without harassing it, through appropriate communication vehicles. How you do that will vary, depending on the project, but the sense of community is one of the motivations for volunteers to participate.

Organizational Team. You need a team to set up and run a crowdsourcing project—don't try to do it alone. Some members of the team might emerge from

---

29   Smith (2007): 28. Smith is not writing about crowdsourcing projects, but about group work in general. He writes: "group members tend to have their opinions drawn in toward that average. Ultimately this process can lead all group members to converge, creating a destructive uniformity of opinions within the group, leading to the disregard of relevant evidence, and possibly even to what has been termed 'groupthink' ..." (2007: 28).

the crowd of participants. Find ways to recognize the organizing team, whether they contributed programming, wrote documentation, helped others, or cheered you on.

Small Crowds Work Too. The success of a crowdsourcing project need not depend on large numbers of contributors. The numbers of collaborators in the projects discussed above are small, especially when compared to large-scale projects like the Wikipedia, but the numbers were sufficient to achieve progress on the research task.

Knowledge in Process. Like many digital projects, crowdsourcing projects should be thought of as processes not products. Articles in the Wikipedia are continually being edited—often, but not always, for the better. If you see an error, fix it. Crowdsourced knowledge is therefore more of a relationship than a finished object. It starts out tentative and then slowly gets refined. The history of that process is often available, which adds an open dimension to the knowledge in process. With Wikipedia articles, you can see their editing history and unwind it.

Distributed Knowing

The real limitation to the adoption of crowdsourcing is our imagination about what research is in the humanities. This brings us back to the question of epistemic activity raised by McCarty when he writes that, for the humanist, the "primary epistemic activity *is* the writing, which by nature tends to be solitary activity."[30] While this may be true now, it has not always been that way and it need not continue to be this way. One could argue that dialogue was the primary epistemic activity from the Platonic Academy up until the emergence of the research university and its emphasis on publication. Or one could argue that the primary activity of the humanist is reading not writing, at least in terms of time spent by most people, and that writing is a specialization by professional humanists. Or one could argue that teaching is the primary epistemic activity by which ideas are transmitted. My point is that the usual move to argue for the primacy of writing is historically contingent and possibly not even true today, depending on what metric you use to establish primacy.

Nor is the primacy of writing a normative truth in the sense that writing should be our primary activity. Just as McCarty calls us to guard against treating collaboration as a transcendental value for the humanities, so we should also guard against writing becoming the fetish of a humanities driven by single-authored publication. A philosopher like Heidegger would call us to thinking as the primary activity. Heidegger and Wittgenstein would warn us against writing as a way of grasping the truth. For both there are dangers to writing, especially about truths

---

30   McCarty (2005): 12.

that may be ineffable. Ironically, we know this through their writings, but that shows how important writing has been for the transmission and preservation of knowledge over time.

More recently, there has been a convergence of fields around the idea that thinking can be distributed, and much has been published on this.[31] Fields like social epistemology and the sociology of knowledge look at how knowledge is formed by groups. Traditional epistemology is concerned with how individuals can know and specifically how they can be certain of the truth of their beliefs. This view has been challenged on two fronts: social epistemologists have argued that there is also knowledge in groups independent of the individual knowing, and some cognitive scientists have argued that distributed cognition is possible, where the act of thinking is distributed across different individuals, be they ants collaborating, nodes in a neural net, or people in some structured context like a law court. As Fuller argues, in the face of the common view of the primacy of solitary thinking:

> I reject the Cartesian gesture of withdrawing from all social intercourse as a means of getting into the right frame of mind for posing foundational questions about the nature of knowledge. For even though the social world may appear to be a confusing place from which to deliver epistemic judgments—certainly more confusing than the privacy of one's own study—it is nevertheless the *normal* (and really the *only*) place in which such judgments are delivered.[32]

Psychologists and cognitive science researchers are also considering distributed cognition through technology, or how technologies can extend the cognition of individuals and co-ordinate the cognition of groups.[33] This convergence should interest digital humanists since it brings society, culture, technology, and history back to cognition. It turns out that one cannot understand cognition by studying the brain alone and that one needs to understand how thinking is social, contextual, and technologically extended. It may not even be the case that writing is best described as a solitary Cartesian activity. It could be that the real activities of knowledge are best understood as distributed, in which case the question is again, how to best organize distributed cognition?

This brings us back to the problem of the imagination of knowing. To understand crowdsourcing in the humanities, we need to provide alternatives to the primacy of the solitary writer as the image of how knowledge is organized. One alternative image would be a trial in a law court. A trial is a classic example of the social generation of knowledge where a group of people with different roles negotiates

---

31   One place to start is Hutchins (1995a), or for more, his book *Cognition in the Wild* (1995b).

32   Fuller (1987): 146.

33   For an introduction to distributed cognition, see Gureckis and Goldstone (2006). For distributed cognition and computing, see Hollan, Hutchins and Kirsh (2000).

actionable knowledge about a defendant. The judge manages the process, lawyers present arguments for and against the defense, and a jury deliberates. The end result is a verdict that goes on record as the best available knowledge judgment about the situation that can be acted upon. A trial is a way of organizing distributed cognition that has a long history. It is an alternative paradigm for understanding human knowledge that illustrates the importance of the organization of the group.

Now what we need are convincing paradigms of what crowdsourced research might look like that do not just treat it as a way of distributing labor in order to get traditional results. While we might use crowdsourcing this way, achieving traditional Humanities 1.0 aims, the promise of Humanities 2.0 is that it will offer new aims, new types of knowledge, and new outcomes. Not all these novelties will stand the test of time, but the possibilities are worth the exploration so that we can learn about research practices. The two projects described above were both imagined to be such exploratory projects. They were designed not to deliver traditional writings, but to develop collaborative knowings that work rhetorically as responses in the dialogue of the humanities. In trying to understand how they are a different type of research, we might better understand the epistemic activity of writing with which they are contrasted.

Conclusion

To conclude, the challenge of collaboration is not, I believe, to traditional individual research, but to the organization of professional scholarship in general. Clay Shirky (2008) describes how social media like blogs and Twitter call into question the social bargain around journalism as the fourth estate. Journalists were accorded special privileges, like the protection of sources, because we valued their investigations. Now that anyone with a blog is some sort of journalist and social media seem to be undermining the newspaper business, it is unclear that there is support for the social bargain that protected journalists. We do not know what will replace the newspaper, but the line between a professional journalist and an amateur is vanishing.

Likewise, I believe that the distinction between the professoriate and amateur researchers will also blur as more and more research is shared through social media.[34] While we never believed that the professoriate should have special legal privileges, we have acted as if we were a special caste of intellectual worker who should be supported by society and protected with administrative mechanisms like tenure. Unfortunately we live at a time when our social contract with society is being challenged and the humanities have not found a satisfactory way to answer utilitarian questions from the larger community.

The good news is that social research models offer one way to show relevance through involving a larger community. Crowdsourcing projects

---

34 See the chapter in Howe (2009) on "The Rise of the Amateur."

provide structured ways to involve the growing numbers of well-educated amateurs with time on their hands, so that they can contribute and be recognized for their contributions. As Howe points out: "An exponential rise in education has coincided with the emergence of the greatest mechanism for distributing knowledge the world has ever seen: the Internet."[35]

Such projects do not just provide educated amateurs with a meaningful way to use their leisure time, but they can create small communities of inquiry interested in advancing knowledge about a phenomenon—and that is what should matter. Such projects can create the network of friends that understand the value of the humanities because they are part of the community of inquiry. Such participation, where people understand the value of humanities inquiry, is a far better response to our critics than any "gotcha" argument is likely to be. These amateurs vote with their feet, creating knowledge with us that is then available back to the larger community.

Further, crowdsourcing projects, especially in times of diminished funding, provide ways of doing "big humanities" without needing big grants as most digital humanities projects do. As Stanley Katz writes: "Let's not whine about the humanities. Let's watch, think and act."[36] One way of acting when there is little funding is to imagine and develop projects that are inclusive and participatory. Both of the projects described above were not grant-funded. They were developed with the resources at hand.[37]

Above all, crowdsourcing erases differences between professional scholars with degrees and those who are self-taught amateurs without formal training. This is the decentering of authority that Davidson writes about. That does not mean that the professoriate is likely to become irrelevant; after all, we are given time to do research and we have significant resources to help organize research projects, including the resources needed to set up crowdsourcing projects. What it means is that a different relationship between the professoriate and amateur researchers is emerging. The digital humanities is one of the sites where a collaborative relationship is being prototyped using networking. We have the skills to imagine different configurations that bring together professionals and amateurs in new forms of knowing together. Along with the opportunities, there is the danger that if the academy does not meaningfully reach out to amateur researchers, starting with our students, amateurs will organize social research sites on their own or crowd to commercially developed services. In either case, the academy could find itself left behind like print encyclopedias in the era of the Wikipedia. We could find ourselves irrelevant to and, what is worse, bypassed by the public that

---

35   Howe (2009): 29.

36   Katz (2009).

37   I have posted an online essay, "Computing with the Infrastructure at Hand," (Rockwell, n.d.) that goes into more detail about how we should consider what we have at hand. To be fair, both of these projects benefit from resources secured by other grants, especially infrastructure grants like those that funded TAPoR.

public universities depend on for support, when we could have evolved research gatherings that bridge the imbalances and support diversity of commitment. In short, I believe the best scholarship is done when professionals and amateurs are provided with mechanisms to collaborate for the advancement of knowledge. That is the real promise of collaboration, that it cross-sectors, and the digital humanities are in a unique position to help construct the needed bridging mechanisms.

> Great ages of science are great ages of the humanities because an age isn't a historical period but a construct, and constructs are the work of humanists.[38]

References

Ayers, E.J., 'What Does a Professor Do All Day, Anyway?' [Lecture] University of Virginia (1993), <http://www.virginia.edu/insideuva/textonlyarchive/93-12-10/7.txt>.

Davidson, Cathy N., 'Humanities 2.0: Promise, Perils, Predictions', *Publications of the Modern Language Association of America* 123:3 (2008): 707–17.

Descartes, René, *A Discourse on the Method of Correctly Conducting One's Reason and Seeking Truth in the Sciences*, trans. Ian Maclean (Oxford: Oxford University Press, 2006).

Franklin, Ursula, *The Real World of Technology*. CBC Massey lectures series. (Concord, ON: House of Anansi Press Ltd, 1992).

Fuller, Steve, 'On Regulating What Is Known: A Way to Social Epistemology', *Synthese* 73 (1987): 145–83.

Gladwell, Malcolm, 'Small Change: Why the Revolution Will Not Be Tweeted', *New Yorker*, October 11, 2010, <http://www.newyorker.com/reporting/2010/10/04/101004fa_fact_gladwell?currentPage=1>.

Gureckis, Todd M. and Robert L. Goldstone, 'Thinking in groups', *Pragmatics & Cognition* 14:2 (2006): 293–311.

Hollan, James, Edwin Hutchins and David Kirsh, 'Distributed Cognition: Toward a New Foundation for Human–Computer Interaction Research', *ACM Transactions on Computer–Human Interaction* 7:2 (2000): 174–96.

Holley, Rose, *Many Hands Make Light Work: Public Collaborative OCR Text Correction in Australian Historic Newspapers*, National Library of Australia, 2009, <http://trove.nla.gov.au/work/22531631>.

Howe, Jeff, *Crowdsourcing: Why the Power of the Crowd Is Driving the Future of Business* (New York: Three Rivers Press, 2009).

Hutchins, Edwin, 'How a Cockpit Remembers its Speed', *Cognitive Science* 19 (1995a): 265–88.

Hutchins, Edwin, *Cognition in the Wild* (Cambridge, MA: MIT Press, 1995b).

---

38 Davidson (2008): 707.

Katz, Stanley, 'Let's Not Cry for the Humanities—Yet', *The Chronicle Review's* blog Brainstorm, February 25, 2009, <http://chronicle.com/blogPost/lets-not-cry-for-the-humanities-yet/6687>.

Mahoney, Anne, 'Tachypaedia Byzantina: The Suda On Line as Collaborative Encyclopedia', *Digital Humanities Quarterly* 3:1 (2009).

McCarty, Willard, *Humanities Computing* (New York: Palgrave Macmillan, 2005).

McCarty, Willard, Geoffrey Rockwell, Andrew MacDonald and Eleni Pantou-Kikkou, 'A Carnival of Words: The Dictionary of Words in the Wild and Public Textuality', conference paper at *Digital Humanities 2008*, University of Oulu, Finland, 2008.

O'Reilly, Tim, 'What is Web 2.0: Design Patterns and Business Models for the Next Generation of Software', <http://www.oreillynet.com/pub/a/oreilly/tim/news/2005/09/30/what-is-web-20.html>.

Organisciak, Peter, 'Why Bother? Examining the Motivations of Users in Large-scale Crowd-powered Online Initiatives', MA thesis in Humanities Computing at the University of Alberta, defended August, 2010, <http://crowdstorming.wordpress.com/2010/08/17/on-the-motivations-of-crowds/>.

Rockwell, Geoffrey, 'Computing with the Infrastructure at Hand: Collaborative Research for the Arts and Humanities in Times of Scarcity', online at *Philosophi.ca*, <http://philosophi.ca>.

Scollon, R. and S. Scollon, *Discourses in Places: Language in the Material World* (London: Routledge, 2003).

Shirky, Clay, *Here Comes Everyone: The Power of Organizing with Organizations* (with an updated epilogue) (London: Penguin, 2008).

Siemens, Lynne, '"It's a Team If You Use 'Reply All'": An Exploration of Research Teams in Digital Humanities Environments', *Literary and Linguistic Computing* 24:2 (2009): 225–33.

Smith, Eliot R., 'Social Relationships and Groups: New Insights on Embodied and Distributed Cognition', *Cognitive Systems Research* 9 (2007): 24–32.

Svensson, Patrik, 'The Landscape of Digital Humanities', *Digital Humanities Quarterly* 4:1 (2010).

Chapter 10
Why Do We Mark Up Texts?

Charlotte Roueché

One of the challenges in introducing computing to practitioners in the humanities is to explain how digital scholarship relates to the traditions of scholarly work to which they are accustomed. Those of us who have worked at King's have been hugely fortunate in having colleagues at the Centre for Computing in the Humanities (CCH) who understand humanities scholarship as well as computing: and this offers me a welcome opportunity to express my gratitude to Harold Short, who has transformed understanding for so many of us.

Even so, there are barriers to be overcome. The very terminology is problematical. Humanities scholars do not very often compute; but many of them do categorise and analyse, and those are aspects that they can appreciate. More profoundly, perhaps, they do all communicate. Marking up a text involves both analysing it and communicating that analysis.

If I read alone, a bookmark is all I need: I want to know my own location in a text – perhaps even marking several places. The need for markup begins when I need to refer to something: either for myself, because I want to move between multiple locations, or, more often, when I want to talk to someone else. In a book, we use page numbers for this purpose, and they have the advantage of being supported by the physical reality, as long as we all use the same edition. It is in working with texts produced in more than one format, or with documents which are each unique, that it becomes valuable to have materials marked up on consistent principles.

Such markup is not essential, as is clear from some of the oldest documents we have. Greek inscriptions were commonly presented all in capitals, with no breaks between words. In the early stages of inscribing texts, the masons experimented with a variety of layouts, including lines which went as an ox ploughs – *boustrophedon* – you read along the line until you get to the end, and then return back along the next line in the other direction. That approach assumes that the determinant is the eye of the reader. Another early style, *stoichedon*, makes no concessions at all to the reader, but focuses on appearance: each letter is placed precisely below the letter above it. The effect is elegant, but it is very demanding to read. The presentation of inscribed texts in Greek gradually became more nuanced. Words continue to be presented in capitals, with no word-breaks. But, at least by the Hellenistic period, there is some grouping: masons worked to ensure that the break at the end of a line made syllabic sense.[1] The same principle extended to manuscripts. One of

---

1   Robert ([1961] 1989): 93.

our earliest surviving manuscripts is Codex Sinaiticus, a Bible manuscript of the fourth century CE. The wonderful images on the British Library website show a lavishly prepared and presented text, in an unbroken flow of capital letters;[2] only the different books of the Bible are distinguished. The apparent uniformity is readable to a trained eye, but recognition of words or syntax does not seem to be a prime consideration.

Interestingly, Latin texts were originally more user friendly. Although very few early Latin texts survive in manuscript or papyrus, the few datable between the late first century BCE and the first century CE show punctuation – interpuncts separating words, marks to show the limits of sentences, and even marks within sentences.[3] Seneca mentions the practice: *nos etiam cum scribimus, interpungere adsuevimus*: we too, when we write, normally punctuate (*Ep.Mor.* 4.11.11). In inscribed documents, paragraphs were demarcated, often by a larger initial letter, outset;[4] and there was also punctuation. In the great memorial inscription of Augustus (emperor 27 BCE–14 CE), the *Res Gestae*, there is extensive punctuation: of 57 sentences whose end survives, 44 are punctuated. But these signs were not standardised. Altogether, there are 21 different marks used in the inscribed text of the *Res Gestae*.[5]

What is really remarkable is that Latin abandoned these marks in the early imperial period. During the first to second centuries CE, Latin documents and inscriptions came to adopt the unbroken style, *scriptio continua*. As one scholar notes: 'For this amazing and deplorable regression one can conjecture no reason other than an inept desire to imitate even the worst characteristics of Greek books.'[6] It may also have been easier to abandon such marks precisely because there was no agreed standard. But it is important to bear in mind how easy it is for such regression to take place, influenced by appearances more than by practicality. There is a kind of academic snobbery detectable here – Greek being seen as culturally superior to Latin – which we can recognise in our own day. Those of us who aim to publish in electronic form know well that this is not seen as having the prestige of book publication. Parkes, in his history of punctuation, also observed that the copying of texts was an activity for inferior classes of people, who should not be encouraged to add to the text the level of interpretation that punctuation brings;[7] this raises interesting and familiar questions, for us, as to who should be entrusted with the marking up of a text.

But a continuing requirement for punctuation was to help in reading aloud. Reading aloud was, of course, not just for public reading of a text: most people in antiquity read aloud even in solitary reading. So such punctuation could be useful

---

2   <http://www.codexsinaiticus.org>.
3   Oliver (1951): 241; Wingo (1972): 132–3.
4   Parkes (1992): 10.
5   For a detailed analysis, see Wingo (1972): 29–49.
6   Oliver (1951): 242.
7   Parkes (1992): 11.

simply to an individual: examples survive of texts marked up for a particular reader. Parkes suggests that late antique scholars started to add punctuation marks to important classical texts in response to a perceived diminution in learning – these understandings needed to be preserved.[8] But for texts which were to be read to others, standard marks could ensure a consistent sense; they were particularly important for copies of sacred texts which were to be read aloud, and required to be read correctly. In the late fourth century, Jerome, the great scholar who translated the Bible, claimed to be setting out his texts in 'a new kind of writing': *novo scribendi genere distinximus.*[9] A text written with punctuation – *per cola scriptus et commata* – offers a 'clearer sense to those reading';[10] a comma represented a pause, a colon a stop. Both marks contribute to the understanding of a passage, and mark places where the reader can draw breath.

These observations were remembered and had a profound influence. In the mid sixth century, Cassiodorus was developing a major monastic library in Italy; he required his scribes to record – or, when necessary, add – such marks, referring to Jerome:

> We believe this also ought to be noted: St. Jerome, led by consideration for the simple brothers, said, in the preface to the Prophets, that he had arranged his translation as it is now read today by *cola* and *commata* for the sake of those who had not learned punctuation from teachers of secular learning. Guided by the authority of this great man, we have judged that his procedure ought to be followed and that the other books be supplied with these divisions. St. Jerome's divisions by *cola* and *commata* in place of punctuation provide sufficient guidance for easy reading. We do not, therefore, presume to surpass the judgment of such a great man. I have left the rest of the books which were not arranged in such system of punctuation to be examined and corrected by the scribes who are responsible for this exacting task. (*Institutes* I.9)

So punctuation had some recognised value, and the authority of Jerome meant that it became increasingly standard as part of the transcription of texts, particularly the Bible.[11] While it had a function of making private reading easier, an important motive was the need to communicate, in reading aloud. Sharing is made easier by agreed standards.

One reason to share texts beyond the individual is, of course, in teaching: and the larger the group, the greater the problems. A first revolution came with the development and increase of academic study. In medieval Paris, students started to gather together for the study of texts; they often arrived from different regions, and brought differing versions of the Latin translation of the Bible, the Vulgate.

---

8   Parkes (1992): 12–13.
9   Jerome, Prolegomena to Isaiah (PL 28.771), cited by Parkes (1992): 13.
10   Jerome, Prolegomena to Ezekiel (PL 28.938–9), cited by Parkes (1992): 13.
11   See Parkes (1992): 16ff; Vezin (1987). For liturgical MSS, see Gilles (1987).

This led to the development of the Paris text of the Vulgate, which standardised the order of the canon.[12] There were copyists who specialised in producing quick cheap copies: but joint study of multiple copies makes it necessary to know where you are. It was almost certainly Stephen Langton – later to be famous as the driving force behind Magna Carta, but who was teaching in Paris until 1206 – who introduced numbered chapter divisions to the Latin Bible: Ranulf Higden († 1364) wrote in his Polychronicon, a history of the world, which was printed in English in 1495: 'Stephen the archebysshop ... quoted the Byble at Parys. and marked the chapters.'[13] The earliest dated version of such a text is 1231.[14]

Fixed numbers make possible systems of analysis, lexica or concordances. The Hebrew Bible had for centuries been presented in verses, which were demarcated by the system of accentuation.[15] This is, however, punctuation as reading aid, as in the library of Cassiodorus: it does not provide for references. In about 1440, Rabbi Isaac Nathan produced a concordance of the Hebrew Bible, using the chapter numbers established by Langton, and indicating verses, which could be calculated by counting down within the chapter.[16] The chapter divisions were also adopted in the Hebrew Bible printed by Bomberg in 1517–18.[17] In 1528, Santes Pagninus, an Italian scholar, produced a new Latin translation of the Old and New Testaments, from Hebrew and Greek, in which he gave numbers to the verses already found in the Hebrew text;[18] and in the following year he produced a Thesaurus of the Hebrew Bible. In the edition of the Hebrew Bible which Bomberg produced in 1547–48, he printed the numbers of every fifth verse.[19] It is interesting to consider that some of the first Greek and Latin text collections to be put into electronic form were digitised primarily in order to be analysed, rather than to be read – so the Thesaurus Linguae Graecae was devised, in 1972, as a body of searchable texts,[20] as were the various collections of Latin epigraphic texts now forming part of the EAGLE Electronic Archive of Greek and Latin Epigraphy,[21] or of Greek epigraphic texts created by the Packard Humanities Institute.[22] At present, only the last of these invaluable collections has now made provision for users to cite and link to particular texts, and places in those texts, since they were conceived as tools for analysis, not as corpora for reading and referring to.

---

12   Loewe (1969): 145–8.
13   Polychronicon Ranulphi Higden [1865–86]: 302v.
14   Loewe (1969): 147.
15   Penkower (2000).
16   Meir Nativ (1437–45; printed Venice, 1523).
17   Moore (1893).
18   Rosenthal (1954): 90–91.
19   Moore (1893): 76.
20   <http://tlg.uci.edu/about>.
21   <http://www.eagle-eagle.it>.
22   <http://epigraphy.packhum.org/inscriptions>.

The increasing multiplication of texts created by printing came to drive an increased need for markup;[23] this came from the need not only to refer analytically, as in a concordance, but also to refer between versions of texts. This of course implies the acceptance that a text can exist in versions, with variants; there is a concept of comparison here which may be profoundly subversive. The next step was taken by Robert Estienne, a printer and publisher.[24] He edited and produced several Bible texts, the first in 1532. In 1539, he was appointed Printer/ Publisher to the King of France for Latin and Hebrew: 'Imprimeur et libraire ès letters Hebraiques et Latines'.[25] By 1544 he was 'typographus regius' in Greek.[26] He became increasingly concerned to present textual variation, and in 1545 he published an edition of the Latin Vulgate, with a facing modern Latin translation from the Hebrew. This was already a complicated process, and his work was starting to draw unfavourable attention from the church authorities. In March 1547 his patron, François I, died, and in October of that year the Faculty of Theology in Paris condemned all Estienne's Latin Bible editions.[27] In 1548 the ban was renewed, and Estienne started planning to move; in November 1550 he obtained permission to reside in Geneva, where such investigations were not just allowed, but encouraged.

In 1551, presumably in Geneva (although this is not indicated), Estienne printed a Greek New Testament, with both the Vulgate text, and the Latin translation of Erasmus, all presented on the same page. In this edition, for the first time, the verses are numbered, to help the reader identify the corresponding passages. He followed this, in 1552, with French and Latin versions of New Testament Psalms and Proverbes, 'Tant en Latin qu'en François; les deux translations traduictes du Grec' *or* 'de l'Hebrieu respondantes l'une à l'autre, verset à verset, notez par nombres', so illustrating the usefulness of the verse-numbering system.[28] In 1557 he published a Latin Bible with complete concordances.[29] The system rapidly became widespread: it is found in the English translation of 1560.

Robert's son, Henri, took over the printing business. In 1578 he published an edition of the works of Plato. Since then, the text of Plato has always been numbered with reference to his page numbers and section letters. Similarly, the works of Plutarch are numbered by reference to the pages of the Stephanus edition of 1572, as reprinted in 1624. This became a standard procedure as the publication of Greek and Latin texts multiplied: the works of Aristotle are numbered in a similar way, following the page numbers and columns in Augustus Bekker's Berlin edition of 1831. That process represents how multiplication of copies requires

---

23 Saeger (1999).
24 See the full study by Elizabeth Armstrong (1955/1986).
25 24 June 1539; see Armstrong (1955/1986): 117–23.
26 Armstrong (1955/1986): 124–30.
27 Armstrong (1955/1986): 184.
28 Armstrong (1955/1986): 228.
29 Armstrong (1955/1986): 232.

more identifying markup, and how an entirely random structure can be perfectly sensible. The resilience of this system is a wonderful proof of the value of arbitrary but consistent and agreed systems.

When we now mark up texts in consistent XML, we are therefore acting within a long tradition of scholarship; we are responding to the acceleration of systems of exchange and systems of analysis created by digital resources. To exploit these possibilities, it is essential to have agreed identifiers, however arbitrary. Just like spies decoding a secret message, we would need the text of Bekker to *explain* the numbers in the text of Aristotle: but once we know how they work, we do not need to know why they do.

This set of standards worked very well for re-editions of texts, and it evolved at a time when a hunger for knowledge was driving frequent publication and republication of texts. It has been noticeable that such conventions are slower to develop when texts are not republished with great frequency. Some Byzantine Greek texts, for example – republished perhaps three times in two centuries – have not adopted any convention, so that you can find a reference which has to be presented in three forms to reflect three different editions.

A further development, during the nineteenth century, was an increase in the publication of documentary texts, existing in only one exemplum, where editors felt the need to use extended systems of markup to convey information about the state of the text: so using, for example, square brackets for supplied material, or underdots for doubtfully read letters. This began with the regular publication of Greek and Latin inscriptions; it was accelerated by the discovery of the papyri, from the late nineteenth century, which further encouraged the use of markup to represent characteristics which could only otherwise be expressed by drawings or – in due course – photographs.

The papyrologists first started producing agreed conventions at the 18th International Congress of Orientalists, meeting at Leiden in 1931.[30] Inscriptions on stone had been recorded over a longer period, so that there were pre-existing conventions to deal with; gradually the epigraphers came to agree to use the 'Leiden' conventions. But there are still differences in practice between scholars from different countries, or working on different periods.[31] It is sobering to see how hard it is to reject an 'imperialist' approach to the adoption of norms of this kind.

The digital publication of inscriptions and papyri is now gathering pace, using TEI-compliant XML to represent the many nuances that papyrologists and epigraphers wish to express. But there is no doubt that the kind of presentation on which documentary scholars have traditionally insisted, and which are therefore being carefully replicated, is one of the things which makes 'normal' scholars quite uncomfortable with these texts. They are overloaded with information, rather like

---

30   Van Groningen (1932).

31   Cf, for example, Dow (1969); Krummrey and Panciera (1980); Robert and Robert (1983): 9–11, on 'Signes critiques du corpus et édition'.

Estienne's third Bible. A consequence of this is that they have been kept carefully separate from 'real' literature – that which has come down to us by the manuscript tradition, and is normally encountered in a fluent presentation, with annotations subordinated.

In the city of Aphrodisias, in the late fifth century CE, a local citizen was honoured with two epigrams, inscribed on stone.[32] Of these two epigrams, one was also recorded in the literary tradition and entered the collection known as the Anthologia Palatina (*AP* 9.704): this work is normally shelved in the literature section of the library. The inscribed texts, however, are only ever shelved under inscriptions. It is to be hoped that a markup system which actually subordinates markup – which does not have to be displayed unless it is wanted – can help to break down this arbitrary barrier, and other barriers which scholars have so carefully erected.

That should become easier as more and more material goes online, in trustworthy editions. Scholars will increasingly expect to be able to search across a body of materials from the literary and documentary traditions. The exciting thing is the chance to make rich support materials available to the reader, without imposing them: readers can exercise choice, in a way which is subversive of many established norms – just as subversive as the sixteenth-century Bible editions and translations.

Markup, as long as it is consistent, develops through the demands of people to communicate with one another, to discuss and understand texts. The determining essential is consistency – across kinds of material, across languages and historical periods. That simple discipline is enabling us to communicate what we know and care about to new and unimagined audiences – just as the texts which survive on parchment or on stone are being read by generations of whom their authors never dreamt. Humanities need this new accessibility, if we are to justify and preserve the scholarship that we value: digital humanities are essential to our survival.

References

Armstrong, E., *Robert Estienne, Royal Printer* (Cambridge: Cambridge University Press, 1955; revised edition, with the same pagination, Abingdon: Sutton Courtenay Press, 1986).

Dow, S., *Conventions in Editing: A Suggested Reformulation of the Leiden System* (Durham: Duke University Press, 1969).

Gilles, A-V., 'La ponctuation dans les manuscrits liturgiques au moyen âge', in A. Maieru (ed.), *Grafia e interpunzione del latino nel medioevo* (Rome: Edizioni dellíAteneo, 1987): 113–34.

Krummrey, H. and S. Panciera, 'Criteri di edizione e segni diacritici', *Tituli* 2 (1980): 205–15.

---

32 Roueché, ala2004, no. 53.

Loewe, R., 'The Medieval History of the Latin Vulgate', in G. Lampe (ed.), *The Cambridge History of the Bible* II (Cambridge: Cambridge University Press, 1969): 102–54.

Meir Nativ (1437–45; printed Venice, 1523).

Moore, G.F., 'The Vulgate Chapters and Numbered Verses in the Hebrew Bible', *Journal of Biblical Literature* 12 (1893): 73–8.

Oliver, R.P., 'The First Medicean MS of Tacitus and the Titulature of Ancient Books', *Transactions and Proceedings of the American Philological Association* 82 (1951): 232–61.

Parkes, M.B., *Pause and Effect: An Introduction to the History of Punctuation in the West* (Aldershot: Scolar Press, 1992).

Penkower, J.S., 'Verse Divisions in the Hebrew Bible', *Vetus Testamentum* 50 (2000): 379–93.

Polychronicon Ranulphi Higden monachi Cestrensis, ed. J.R. Lumby (London 1865–86).

Robert, L., 'L'épigraphie', in Charles Samaran (ed.), *L'histoire et ses Méthodes, Encyclopédie de la Pléiade* (Paris: Gallimard, 1961): 543–97; also in L. Robert, *Opera Minora Selecta* V (1989): 65–110.

Robert, L. and J. Robert, *Fouilles d'Amyzon en Carie* (Paris: De Boccard, 1983).

Rosenthal, F., 'The Study of the Hebrew Bible in Sixteenth-Century Italy', *Studies in the Renaissance* 1 (1954): 81–91.

Roueché, C., *Aphrodisias in Late Antiquity: The Late Roman and Byzantine Inscriptions*, revised second edition, 2004, available at <http://insaph.kcl. ac.uk/ala2004>.

Saeger, P., 'The Impact of the Early Printed Page on the Reading of the Bible', in P. Saeger and K. van Kampen (eds), *The Bible as Book: The First Printed Edition* (London: British Library, 1999): 31–52.

Van Groningen, B.A., 'Projet d'unification des systèmes de signes critiques', *Chronique d'Égypte* 7 (1932): 262–9.

Vezin, J., 'Les divisions du texte dans les Évangiles jusqu'à l'apparition de l'imprimerie', in A. Maieru (ed.), *Grafia e interpunzione del latino nel medioevo* (Rome: Edizioni dellíAteneo, 1987): 53–68.

Wingo, E.O., *Latin Punctuation in the Classical Age* (The Hague: Mouton, 1972).

Chapter 11

Human–Computer Interface/Interaction and the Book: A Consultation-derived Perspective on Foundational E-Book Research[1]

Ray Siemens, Teresa Dobson, Stan Ruecker, Richard Cunningham, Alan Galey, Claire Warwick and Lynne Siemens, with Michael Best, Melanie Chernyk, Wendy Duff, Julia Flanders, David Gants, Bertrand Gervais, Karon MacLean, Steve Ramsay, Geoffrey Rockwell, Susan Schreibman, Colin Swindells, Christian Vandendorpe, Lynn Copeland, John Willinsky, Vika Zafrin, the HCI-Book Consultative Group and the INKE Research Team

This piece is a team-written effort, involving – singly and in group – the efforts of a considerable number of people comprising the HCI-Book Consultative Group (2004–2008) and the subsequently-formed INKE Research Team (2009–).

Contexts for Electronic Book Research

More than half of all people living in developed countries make use of computers and the internet to read newspaper, magazine, and journal articles, electronic books, and similar materials. The next generation of adults already recognizes the electronic medium as its chief source of textual information. Our knowledge repositories increasingly favor digital products over the print resources that have been their mainstay for centuries. Moreover, a chief priority of those professionals who produce and convey textual information is to make such information available electronically in ways that meet the standards of quality, content, and functionality that have evolved over half a millennium of print publication. The movement toward the use of the digital medium is an inevitable one, with clear benefits associated with the production, dissemination, and reception of the record of human experience,

---

1 Reporting on a major collaborative project's extended stage of inception, this chapter does so as an implicit homage to Harold Short's exceptional academic community-building insights and abilities, and itself reflects very early conversations with him that led to the more formal deliberations that founded the research team.

as well as the ultimate impact of these processes on our knowledge-based society. However, for all the good we perceive, we also realize that there is much still to know about this new media form. We must gain this knowledge in order to make the best use of what the digital has to offer us. What do we really know about the ways in which we interact with these new texts that replace the print artifact, re-present to us the knowledge and experience of the past, and deliver the direct-to-digital record of the present? Do we understand the ways in which we interact with these knowledge objects, and the information that they contain—and do we understand the impact that the confluence of media formats in these digital objects has on our use of them, such that we may best facilitate interaction with the new digital artifact?

In short, there is much that we still need to learn about the "new knowledge machine," as some term it, presented to us by the computer. More specifically, at the moment there is a real need to understand the principles involved in dealing with digital artifacts, so that we may interact in an effective way with the digital representations of the objects of human experience. This chapter reports on the efforts of a working group to identify issues central to the digitization of the human record and to act on that identification, with the aim of:

- understanding and describing the basic principles of humanistic interaction with knowledge objects (digital and analog alike);
- articulating core strategies for the design of humanistic knowledge objects, especially electronic books, based on this understanding;
- suggesting basic principles for evaluating and implementing current technologies, and exploring future ones.

Possibilities for human–computer interaction and the electronic book may be examined from a range of interrelated perspectives, which are approached in several essential ways:

- via a process that seeks to identify, quantify, and evaluate print and electronic books in terms of their features and uses;
- via a process that explores the material, symbolic, and formal aspects of the book, toward the end of computational modeling;
- via a process of prototyping computational models and simulations of the book, both literal models and metaphoric.

The authors of this chapter aim to make observations and to raise questions about these issues, as the first step toward determining the best ways in which to structure the basis of our seven-year research project which endeavors to understand these issues more fully, theoretically, and, more pragmatically, via functional prototypes and illustrative models.

Audience

Perspectives on the relationship of audience to the electronic book come from a number of disciplines, and debates about reading in hypermedia environments often become mired in philosophical disagreements among these disciplines regarding what constitutes a satisfactory reading experience—or, put another way, what constitutes a usable text. For instance, early research on reading hypertext, conducted by researchers concerned with interface design and software engineering, tended to focus on articulating best practices to prevent reader disorientation and cognitive overload in complex, highly networked multimedia environments. Navigational supports such as site overviews and hierarchical structures were promoted as a means by which to improve usability.[2]

A sustained conversation between the fields of scholarly editing and empirical reader studies is long overdue, especially since scholarly editing inevitably involves a process of informed speculation about who will read an edition (and for what purpose), and about the reader's use of paratextual elements such as cross-references, foot- or endnotes, and so on. The reader studies component of our project is in part concerned with how scholars come to trust or distrust digital resources—a question of major and perhaps unexpected importance to digital scholarly editors (Best, 2004), just as the socially constructed trustworthiness of print has been an important research question for scholars in book history (Johns, 1998). Nevertheless, the figure of the reader in much editorial theory often remains abstract and even mystified, even though readers' habits are often invoked to justify certain ways of presenting the text. Decisions such as modernizing spelling versus retaining the original orthography, conflating texts into a single ideal form versus presenting multiple versions, providing one kind of annotation but not another, and silently emending an apparent error versus leaving the text unchanged, all serve to configure the relationship between reader, editor, and text.[3] Reader studies provides a formal vocabulary to describe these relationships, an important task for textual scholars given the capability of digital editions to reach new audiences, as well as the need for digital scholarly editors to engage with interface design and usability.

Interface and Design

The design of computer interfaces for researchers working with electronic texts requires a combination of specialist areas of inquiry, including the ethnographic study of information-seeking behaviors, diagnostic performance evaluation of existing interfaces, and iterative design and usability study of new design

---

2   Foss (1989); Leventhal et al. (1993); Astleitner and Leutner (1995); Kim and Hirtle (1995); Rouet and Levonen (1996).

3   See the articles in Best (1998), especially those by Werstine, Anne Lancashire, Ian Lancashire, and Siemens.

prototypes (Ruecker, 2003). Some interfaces are intended to provide researchers with access to collections of materials. Others aim to facilitate research tasks once an appropriate subset of materials has been selected by the user. One of our goals is to bring together expertise in the areas listed above in order to inform the design of new "affordances" (Gibson, 1979) for people working with digital texts.

Following Gibson's definition, an affordance is an opportunity for action, and the design of a new digital affordance provides people with a tool that was not previously available. An example of a widely successful digital affordance is the cut-and-paste function, which had not been available to writers using typewriters, but was adopted wholesale by those using word processors. As soon as the technology was able to support it, people learned that it was available, and a function that had been reserved for the editorial process became indispensable as part of the writing process. On the other hand, a digital affordance that is not yet widely available is the dynamic table of contents (Ruecker, 2005), which would allow the reader to perform a variety of research tasks by interactively adding or subtracting content.

Form and Content

A key question for those interested in the representation and re-presentation of texts in any form has been whether content exists abstractly, independent of its representation by an interface, or whether it exists only concretely, as the sum of its instantiations. One of the problems currently evident in the field is the document-mindedness of ideas inherited from (mostly literary) hypertext theorists, who tend to speak of content in abstract terms, as links and lexias, but almost never as material objects, identifiable classes, and specific instances. On the other hand, the field also contains many examples of idealistic approaches to content such as can be seen in the guidelines of the Text Encoding Initiative (TEI). The TEI is an international project developing guidelines for encoding machine-readable electronic texts, with the aim of facilitating activities such as text analysis and sophisticated searching, and ensuring long-term accessibility. While the TEI is well suited to encoding print objects (for example, a novel), it is less useful when dealing with ontologically complex texts such as plays, which are both documents and events. As F.W. Bateson famously phrased the problem, "if the Mona Lisa is in the Louvre, where [is] Hamlet?" (quoted in Greetham, 1994: 342). And if an edition of *Hamlet* is an interface between the readership and the content, where then does the content begin?

Readers and Users

To begin, we think it is important to consider that "user-centered" approaches to information systems need to be "user-in-context" approaches. That is, we must take into account variations in use and interaction patterns that depend upon specific scenarios, tasks, roles, subject domains, and socio-cultural frames. To cite Andrew Dillon: "it makes no sense to describe a tool or technology as usable or unusable in itself. Any tool is made for use by certain users, performing particular tasks in specific environments. Its usability can only be meaningfully evaluated in relation to such contextual variables" (2004: 17). Examples of this approach to system design are contextual design and cognitive work analysis, but the approach itself has also become a focus of research, as evidenced by the recent *Information Seeking in Context* and *Information Interaction in Context* conferences (Ingwersen and Jarvelin, 2005).

In this light, one of the goals of our investigation should be to identify and test the impact of contextual variables of interaction with electronic texts. This would include conducting task analyses and developing taxonomies of interaction types, use scenarios, and user roles. The starting point for this can be the two scenarios (comprehension and engagement) and the two user groups (scholars and readers), but we aim to develop a more robust model of user testing that is specifically relevant to the e-book. The development of these taxonomies would provide a framework for an ongoing discussion of how "use" and "interaction" can be interpreted with respect to the e-book.

User Studies and Usability Assessment

The wide adoption of "use" as a descriptor for engagement with hypermedia reflects the challenges inherent in understanding and facilitating interaction with complex multimedia artifacts. It also points to a potential problem with research in this area: when we attempt to accommodate the digital artifact's complexity by devising terms like "use," which synthesize the range of processes involved in human–computer interaction, does that deter us from realizing the distinctiveness of those processes?

One component of our research will entail close examination of how literary structures and reading processes are extended and modified in digital environments. As many theorists have observed, a close look at modern print and electronic texts reveals a shift away from conventional narrative logic, and toward indeterminacy, fragmentation, and open-endedness.[4] At the same time, current theories concerning how readers engage with texts tend to be derived from studies of readers working with "normal" prose or other conventional narratives.[5] To develop appropriate models of reading complex print or digital narratives, we must examine how people engage these texts, and revise our perspectives of narrative structure and literary reading processes.

In discussing empirical research related to how people engage books and e-books, then, we envisage two main types of reading: 1) the type in which the

---

4   For example, Landow (1997); Bolter (2001); Van Peer and Chatman (2001).

5   For example, Chatman (1978); Rabinowitz (1987); Kintsch (1988); Zwaan, Magliano and Graesser (1995).

economization of comprehension is the aim; and 2) the type in which engagement with an aesthetic artifact is the aim. With respect to the first, information-seeking in the humanities is a well-researched area (for example, Dalton and Charnigo, 2004). Nevertheless, our understanding of how humanities scholars engage computer-based information resources is in continual need of refinement as new research resources are developed. An overview of research in this area is provided below. With respect to the second scenario mentioned above, models of reading based on observing readers of complex print narratives, or emerging hypermedia genres, do not yet exist.[6]

The Importance of User Studies in the Humanities

The technical world has been slow to realize that users matter, not just in the field of digital humanities, but in broader areas of system design. As long ago as 1971, Hansen called for software engineers to know their users (Hansen, 1971), and for the last 30 years the advantages of software projects whose systems are designed with an eye to the user have been well documented (Shneiderman and Plaisant, 2005). Yet some are still inclined to assume that users might not know what they want, and thus it is better not to ask them, in case they answer the wrong question.

If users are integrated into system design at all, it happens late in the process. Typically the user is presented with a late-stage prototype that the designers hope she will like. This can be of limited use, since at this point system designers may be unwilling to make significant alterations. Thus, late-stage user input can only have a relatively minor impact, since the radical redesign of a system costs time, money, and enthusiasm, all of which are often in short supply. It is much easier to make minor adjustments and get the system into production. In scenarios of this sort, if users lose their enthusiasm for the product, it is they and not the designers who tend to be blamed. As a result, the failure rate of software in the commercial world is still staggeringly high (Dalcher and Genus, 2003; Flowers, 1996).

In the humanities, as Warwick notes (2004), scholars have too often been branded as digitally unskilled or even backward looking, because they have been slower to adopt digital tools than scientists. This is a fundamentally flawed assessment of the situation: when technologies fit well with what scholars do, they will use those technologies (Bates, 2002).[7] At present, general information

---

6   Further, Douglas has questioned whether there are even a dozen "studies or considerations of how hypertext may transform the way we read or write texts, and, indeed, our whole conception of a satisfactory reading experience" (2000: 73). See also Dobson and Miall (1998); Miall and Dobson (2001); Dobson and Luce-Kapler (2005); Luce-Kapler and Dobson (2005); Dobson (2006).

7   Several recent studies of humanities users and digital resources in the UK have found many humanities scholars reporting that they are enthusiastic users of digital resources. However, what they define as digital resources tend overwhelmingly to be generic informational resources, such as library and archive websites, or large online

resources are better suited to humanities researchers' needs. If we would like those researchers to use future electronic books, they must be equally fit for the purpose. To produce such a resource, we must understand what users in the humanities do, what they like, and what they might like in future.

Previous Studies of Humanities Users

The study of digital resource usage in the humanities is well-researched. As Dalton and Charnigo (2004) show, in recent years there has been a flood of literature about scholars' information needs and seeking behaviors. Although useful recent work on humanities scholars has been done,[8] much of the literature tends to conflate information seeking and information needs in relation to humanities scholars.

The earliest work on humanities users was on their information needs and patterns of use, and it is only very recently that research has been conducted on their actual behavior in digital environments. Seminal work done by Stone (1982) and later by Watson-Boone (1994) showed that humanities users need a wide range of resources of different ages and types.[9] Humanities scholars also rely on face-to-face information gathering, from colleagues and at conferences. They may also use personal collections of knowledge built up over years of study.[10]

If we are to design an e-book that humanities scholars may regard as fit for their research purposes, then it follows that we must understand what they do in digital environments, what kind of resources they need, and perhaps most importantly, what makes them decline to use resources. These questions are not well understood, and very few people have studied what humanities scholars do when they carry out research in an online environment.[11] There is even less concern with what they do offline and how connections may be made between the two fields of activity. Some of these questions are being addressed by researchers involved in the HCI-Book project. However, a great deal more research remains to

---

reference collections such as the O-DNB or Literature Online, rather than the kind of digital object that might be compared to a scholarly book (Warwick et al., 2007).

8   Green (2000); Talja and Maula (2003); and Ellis and Oldman (2005).

9   This is still true in a digital environment, where humanities users continue to need printed materials and manuscripts, the latter implying older materials than those generally used by scientists (British Academy, 2005).

10   They do not necessarily expect to create new data or discover new facts, but reinterpret and re-express ideas, where the expression itself is as important as the discovery (Barrett, 2005). A major theme of the literature about humanities users is that they are not like those in the sciences or social sciences, although many systems designers of electronic resources have assumed that they are (Bates, 2002). Humanities scholars are much more likely to use what Ellis has called "chaining;" that is, they proceed by following references that they have found in other literature (Ellis and Oldman, 2005; Green, 2000). See also Chu (1999); Wiberley (1983 and 1988); Dalton and Charnigo (2004); Whitmire (2002); Lehmann and Renfro (1991); Wiberley (2000).

11   Bates et al. on the Getty project (Siegfried et al., 1993) is a notable exception.

be done on such areas before we may be confident of designing digital resources that will be of genuine utility to the humanities researcher.[12]

In addition to the above-mentioned projects, two major Canadian undertakings have influenced our thinking. Both TAPoR (Text Analysis Portal for Research) and ECO (Early Canadiana Online/Notre Memoire En Ligne) have investigated how humanities researchers use online tools, whether text-specific or not. Two major findings emerged. First, scholars are most concerned with accomplishing their tasks; the interface must present things in the context of tasks that they might wish to accomplish, rather than of the tools that might do the job, or the technical details of the text that they might be using. Secondly, graduate students behave differently and have different needs from more senior scholars. These findings highlight the need for the HCI-Book project to identify different categories of users in order to meet their needs; these categories may be more fine-grained than we expect.

Features of Books and E-Books

The task of enumerating generalized features of the electronic book becomes very difficult when we take into account the two distinct concepts embodied by the word "book." On one hand, a book is an empirically measurable type of physical object; on the other, it is a powerful and comprehensive metaphor. The book, as the phrase appears in terms like "history of the book" or "culture of the book," inevitably simplifies a range of textual materials. Meanwhile the value of these materials (scrolls, manuscript and print codices, newspapers, magazines, fascicles, broadsides, bound quires of manuscript poems, and unpublished archival materials) lies for many scholars in their diversity. Members of our research group study all these materials and more, and yet humanities scholarship still assigns the co-ordinating metaphor of the book to a number of heterogeneous texts. As a result, in many areas of the humanities the book has of necessity tended to remain an abstract idea that emphasizes common features over historical particularities. Broad histories of writing tend to group texts into major categories based on what are perceived as primary technologies. Typically these categories are manuscript (including the shift from papyrus to parchment, and from scroll to codex), print (including the shift from hand-press to machine-press printing), and, more recently, digital writing.

The book remains a metaphor with potency even in a digital culture. We continue to make cultural investments in structures of information that offer, as features, closure and containment matched with navigability and connectivity. A book has physical boundaries—its covers set its contents off from other books—

---

12   In thinking about how best to conduct a study of humanities users, we have benefited from the experience of two previous UK-based projects: UCIS and LAIRAH. See Warwick et al. (2005); Makri et al. (2007); Warwick et al. (2006); Blandford et al. (2006).

and yet its text invariably refers beyond those boundaries, such that the book becomes a metaphorical stand-in for the entire bookshelf, library, or archive. Institutional models such as libraries and publishing houses likewise depend upon books as discrete units of manageable content. As bibliographers such as D.F. McKenzie have argued in recent years, the cultural perception of the book as a discrete unit of production is thus at odds with the heterogeneity implied by a term such as "textuality;" yet "textuality" carries none of the symbolic force of the book (McKenzie, 1999).

Our use of the term "book" throughout our discussions comes with an appreciation of the term's ambivalence and hidden complexity. The same terminological challenges arise with the term "e-book," which for our purposes means not only the book-like electronic simulations of past decades, but also electronic texts generally, from transcriptions in electronic archives to born-digital electronic texts. With this sense of complexity in mind, we propose to study the features of books and e-books, not by assigning features exclusively to print or to digital textuality, but by identifying the features most at stake in the textual economy that print books and e-books now form together. The most salient of these features include:

1. **Tangibility**, or the capacity of a book to convey information about itself through physical indicators such as size and format. E-texts are often regarded as intangible, or tangible in different ways, but still possess a physicality that should be considered in their analysis (see Kirschenbaum, 2004a).
2. **Browsability**, or the book's ability to provide random access through tactile means such as flipping pages to move within the text—a feature amplified in digital text by speed, scale, and browsing tools such as rich-prospect browsing interfaces (Ruecker, 2003).
3. **Searchability**, a feature available in all texts through optical scanning, which is dramatically enhanced in machine-readable digital text by tools for algorithmic analysis and retrieval.
4. **Referenceability**, a text's propensity for intertextual linking (explicit or implicit), as well as the degree to which parts of a text may be referenced by other texts; in print, the addition of chapter and verse numbers to the Bible made it referenceable, while on the web, the use of encoded tags allows linking to other web pages.
5. **Hybridity**, or the composite nature of books as being composed of various discourses, genres, sources, and textual formations; literary miscellanies and anthologies, for example, might include poetry, prose, and drama by various authors; electronic forms, which are less fixed and definite, allow for a potential increase in hybridity.

In drawing an analogy between printed books and e-books as artifacts, we might also consider how developments in technology enable and sometimes direct changes in the features and characteristics of the book. For example, the advent of columns and printable margins on the printing press enabled marginalia, leading to notes, which eventually became footnotes, and then (as tastes changed) endnotes. In other words, the relationship and means of connection among text, context, paratext (such as an accompanying preface or glossary), and intertext (such as a text with close thematic or allusive links to another)—verbal and non-verbal elements—has changed over time (Greetham, 1997; Maclean, 1991). Similarly, in the short history of e-books, technological developments have enabled new ways of relating and linking texts. The result is a series of changes in the format and features of texts, and in how they are presented to the user. Theoretically, just as changes in marginalia changed reading practices in the early history of printing, so too have changes in e-book technology affected reading practices (Slights, 2001).

The Uses of Books

The history of the book is the history of how people have shaped the intellectual tool of writing in order to make it more efficient, more versatile, and easier to use. In Greece, before 600 BC, there was no clear decision regarding whether writing should go from left to right or from right to left (or even boustrophedon, where the direction of writing followed the path of the plough in a field and lines had to be read in alternating directions).[13]

Gradually, the text departed from the linearity of the spoken word and became organized in a visual way, giving more control to the reader. The codex, invented in the first century AD, took four centuries to completely replace the less efficient scroll format and to evolve from an essentially linear format to a tabular one. This evolution gradually gave the reader more control over the pace and form of reading.

The changing practice of reading, from *ruminatio* (pondering at length) in the medieval age to "extensive reading" with the advent of newspapers and magazines, helped to shape the book as it is today. Each medium in the evolutionary chain puts varying emphasis on the visibility of the text and on the reader's interactions with that text, making different operations easier for the reader to perform. In this regard, text is the nexus of a fundamental tension between the limitations of language and the freedom provided by its visual elements.

The Uses of E-Books

Among the features pertaining to books and e-books, tangibility is strongly associated with the book as a physical artifact, while hybridity is strongly associated with digital texts. Browsability, searchability, and referenceablility are dramatically enhanced in digital media. Perhaps because e-books are particularly well suited to the needs of researchers, efforts in the digital humanities have

---

13   Romans read aloud, or were read aloud to by slaves.

focused on developing searchable digital archives and databases, establishing a consistent method of encoding digital texts, and establishing a new knowledge economy related to electronic scholarly publication.

Other research areas concern the affordances of digital media for collaborative knowledge production and for the literary arts. The first of these, collaborative knowledge production, is increasingly facilitated by various emerging forms of social software, such as wikis and weblogs. The most obvious example is Wikipedia, a popular web-based free-content encyclopedia that maintains a relatively open policy regarding contributions. Wikipedia's model for contribution clearly interrogates notions of authorship and intellectual property rooted in print culture.[14]

Meanwhile, electronic literature refers to "works with important literary aspects that take advantage of the capabilities and contexts provided by the stand-alone or networked computer" (ELO, 2006: para. 2). Electronic literature includes genres such as hypertext fiction, reactive poetry, and blog novels.[15] Emerging genres such as reactive poetry, on the other hand, intermingle literary arts and multimedia design. Often presented as Flash files, works in this latter class employ animated images and text accompanied by sound, in an effort to produce visually dynamic pieces. We will study further the nature of these emerging genres and how readers interact with them.

Aspects of the Book

Material Aspects

Understanding the material aspects of the book is a crucial pre-condition to developing e-books. The very name "e-book" alerts us to this fact. When the movable-type press created the opportunity for mass-producing texts, its operators aimed to make books look like manuscripts. It took decades for books to become something other than mechanically produced manuscripts. During these early years of e-books, it is crucial that we attend closely to the processes and products that have, over the 500 years of print culture, established the printed book as a standard physical medium.[16] Readers will be best served if we imagine radical departure from the printed volume. To help ourselves make this paradigm shift, we

---

14   This is not a new model: it is one that was displaced by the formalized diffusion of academic writing, which saw its genesis in seventeenth-century Europe (see Siemens et al., 2002).

15   Older forms, such as hypertext fiction, have their roots in text adventure games (such as Will Crowther's 1975 Adventure and Infocom's Zork) and Bantam's Choose Your Own Adventure series of children's books.

16   Revising the printed book into electronic format while keeping to the conventions of print is not the best use of resources.

might juxtapose the set of practices carried out in producing printed texts and the set of practices necessary for the production of electronic texts.[17]

Changing means of production fundamentally alter cultural notions of authorship, readership, and literary form. For example, the substantial cost of the materials required to produce the early printed book necessitated selective publication according to any number of criteria (content quality, author's status, marketability, and so on). The cost of the end product also determined the readership of printed materials: as technological developments reduced production costs, readership expanded and changed, as did the types of books that were produced.[18] Conversely, electronic publishing began with a cost advantage over print production. The cheaper electronic publishing process does not require a large infrastructure of dedicated printers, editors, and publishers. Consequently, the practice of "self-publishing" that was once regarded with a certain amount of stigma is now increasingly legitimized. Selective publication is no longer necessitated by technology or economics. This new means of production forces a reassessment of cultural assumptions about authorship, readership, genre, accessibility, and usability (including quality control and censorship).

Symbolic Aspects

The concepts of e-book and electronic text can be defined in many ways. Most traditional definitions are based on the functional and material characteristics of e-book technology. From this perspective, e-books are defined by the following characteristics: they are electronically searchable, they are dynamic in terms of content updateability, they are adaptable in terms of cross-platform portability, they are physically portable, they are user-interactive, and they are non-sequential— provided they use hypertext technology.

E-books are currently available in a variety of formats; most e-book formats allow for multilinear navigation. So, hypertextuality seems to be a characteristic feature of e-book technologies. However, most of the work on hypertext has considered it from a technological perspective; very few research initiatives have tried to formalize the substantial impact of hypertextuality on the symbolic aspects

---

17   To discuss the material aspects of the book, then, is to discuss not only paper, ink, formatting, binding, and content, but also the processes that are required to produce a book.

18   With the advent of machine-made paper, for example, periodical and newspaper publication proliferated in the nineteenth century (Rose, 1995). Another consequence of reduced printing costs was the emergence of the so-called popular press. In the late sixteenth and early seventeenth centuries, small and cheap books, chapbooks, pamphlets, and broadsheets brought a new demographic to the book market. This in turn enabled new means of influence upon the reading public in sociopolitical matters such as religion, and new forms of writing to meet the interests of an increasingly diverse reading public (Chartier, 1994; Spufford, 1982; Watt, 1991).

of the way we read texts, especially from a semantic point of view.[19] Hypertextuality may be an important feature of e-book technologies, but hypertexts themselves are heterogeneous, and can be defined from many perspectives.[20]

Formal models of hypertext can offer tools for an understanding of its main characteristics, but they can also neglect the importance of the user (the reader in the context of e-book technology), particularly when the objective is to understand and model the meaning of hypertext. The challenge is to model or formalize both e-books and hypertextuality, as the latter is one of the former's main characteristics, at the same time taking the reader into consideration as an interpretative agent.

Formal Aspects

Possibly the most immediate way in which a reader interacts with a book is through its material aspects. Readers tend to enjoy the feel of the pages, the cover, and the design of the book. The physical aspects of the book are important to consider when imagining how to transfer the reading experience to a digital environment.

In addition to length, there are other material properties typically associated with books. There is, for instance, the cover—the upper and lower boards, and the spine—which plays a role in communicating the contents of the book. We say that a book cannot be judged by its cover precisely because the natural human response to covers is to use them to judge books. Designers use this tendency to communicate various kinds of information, such as genre, author and title, publisher, and often something about the narrative content. Immediately beneath the cover are the pages that constitute the front matter. These reiterate in more standardized formats some of the suggestions made by the cover, and provide additional information such as the metadata required for cataloguing, as well as an outline of the contents.

The body of the text contains significant layers of design, such as white space and page numbers, that exist in addition to the text itself, but make the act of reading more efficient. White space in the margins, for instance, allows the book to be held without obscuring any text, and provides room for binding. Sequential page numbers allow the pages to be accessed non-sequentially with the aid of a table of contents or an index. Page numbers also serve to allow the reader to track progress through the book.

Experimentally developed over centuries, these conventions are now subject to remediation in the digital environment. We have an opportunity to reconsider

---

19   Most of the time, hypertext is explained in terms of nodes, links, markup language, and so on.

20   For instance, the concept of hypertext can be defined as a hardware- or software-based computer technology, or as an abstract textual structure. In the lexical database Wordnet, for example, hypertext is defined as machine-readable text that is not sequential but is organized so that related items of information are connected. Although incomplete, this definition is a very good example of hypertext as an abstract textual structure.

them, and to decide which are important enough to keep and which have become irrelevant. We also have the chance to extend and elaborate on the features that are most valuable, reconceiving them in ways impossible in print. Electronic searching is one such enhancement; hyperlinking is another.

Prototyping

Interface

It is in some ways unusual to discuss the book as though it were an interface, but the term begins to seem more appropriate when we shift our focus into the discussion of the e-book. An interface is the intermediary technology between a set of services or functions on one side, and a person on the other. For the conventional book, the service consists of the text and its apparatus, and the interface consists of paper, ink, binding, typography, and so on. The set of services provided by the e-book has the potential to expand in a wide range of directions, from the inclusion of more sophisticated hyperlinks, to audio and video clips, to metadata of various kinds, to data mining processes and their results, to visualizations of information. Ruecker (2005) points out, for instance, that the e-book's table of contents has the potential to develop into a sophisticated research tool, where the reader can add or subtract elements of interest in order to obtain a dynamic overview of the contents.

Our research into e-book interfaces will include developing prototypes in several directions, from content visualizations, to overview displays coupled with tools for manipulating the displays, to experimental browsers that allow exploration of both collections and content. Our research questions primarily involve remediation and new affordances. That is, what elements of print books are valuable or even indispensable in the new digital context, and what new functions are significant enough to readers and researchers that they should be developed? Furthermore, how should the conventions of reading and scholarship influence the design of the e-book form and function?

We have already been making progress in a number of these areas, with projects for dynamic text playback, for nuanced browsing of collections and files encoded in XML (eXtensible Markup Language)—the Mandala browser (Cheypesh et al., 2006)—and for making data mining tools accessible to humanities scholars (Ruecker et al., 2006). In addition, members of our team have been working on online tools to support editors and readers of scholarly editions (for example, Best, Galey, Werstine), and we are working with a wide range of researchers who are actively editing such editions (for example, Flanders, Schreibman, R. Siemens).

Interface work often involves technical software and hardware development that are not research contributions, but that are needed to answer new research questions. Our methods will help us to obtain a useful academic result without engaging in extensive development activities. We recognize that the research life cycle moves from theory and sketches to interactive prototypes to development projects. By coupling the design research strategy of iterative constructive diagnostic research (Sless and Wiseman, 1997) with approaches based on the affordance strength vector model (Ruecker, 2006), we hope to maximize exploration of novel research questions at the early stages of the life cycle, while avoiding getting drawn into expensive, time-consuming development tasks.

Reading Culture

Early discussions of new media from the perspective of literary theory devote much time to a consideration of how reader and writer roles are modified in the fragmentary, multilinear writing spaces of the digital medium. Such discussions frequently propose that engaging with networked texts requires more active participation by the reader. Some of these same discussions conclude that technology is destined to improve the experience of literary reading.[21]

Readers have always been actively involved in reconstructing texts within their own worldviews, and hypermedia clearly extends such processes in important ways.[22] In spite of calls for more careful attendance to the nature of reading–writing relations, the subject has been largely overlooked by hypermedia theorists, who often promote metaphors suggesting the conflation of the two processes, but who fail to examine whether or how those metaphors play out in practice. Questions regarding the interdependencies of reading and writing, what sort of cognitive processes each demands, and how the two might effectively be combined to promote learning, have long been a subject of study among literacy researchers.[23] What is clear is that reading and writing, while related, are cognitively and experientially separate. Metaphors conflating the two fail to consider the complexities of both processes, the phenomenological and cognitive differences between the two, whether one or the other process might be better for facilitating acquisition of particular forms of knowledge, how the two may support each other in knowledge acquisition, and so on. Computer-based environments for reading and writing offer an interesting venue in which to consider anew the question of reading–writing relations. Tasks related to manipulation (the material dimension of reading), comprehension, and interpretation lie at the forefront of this discussion, as well as the active, physical processes that underlie these tasks.[24] At the moment,

---

21   See, for example, the roots of electronic literature in computerized text adventure games (Bolter, 2001: 126 ff; Douglas, 2000: 23).

22   Rosenblatt (1938/1968); Iser (1978). Landow's "active, even intrusive reader" is a key point in this consideration (1997: 90). See also Landow (1994: 14) and Rosenberg (1994), relating to the coinage of the term "wreading," which has roots in Barthes (1974), Derrida (1976) (as in, for example, "Plato's Pharmacy") and Derrida (1981).

23   See Fitzgerald and Shanahan (2000), who provide a useful overview of such research, as well as Stotsky (1983), and, related, Ganong (2003).

24   Thérien (1985) lists three tasks and five distinct processes that are active every time we read a text. Tasks include: (1) manipulation (the material dimension of the

what is at stake with e-books is the mastery of basic forms of manipulation. We still do not know how to read, manipulate, and work with e-books. To establish a reading culture of e-books, we must find ways to help establish robust forms of manipulation, which is the first step in facilitating strategies of comprehension and enabling interpretations to be put in motion; comprehension- and interpretation-based issues flow from this understanding and the modeling that reflects it.

Afterword: Consultation, Consensus, and the Needs of Interdisciplinary Research

Interdisciplinary and multidisciplinary approaches are key to this research, because of the complex and sophisticated nature of the questions being asked—which are beyond the capability of any one individual or even one discipline to answer. This interdisciplinarity stands in contrast to traditional research contributions within scholarly fields, where academics tend to make solo efforts with little direct collaboration with others—a model often reinforced through the conventional structure of doctoral studies and of hiring and promotion decisions (Hara et al., 2003; Newell and Swan, 2000). At the same time, however, funding agencies are providing incentive for collaboration between researchers in universities and other research institutions, as well as members of the community, through their funding programs (SSHRC, 2004; Newell and Swan, 2000). As a discipline, digital humanists are capitalizing on these trends, undertaking collaborative research projects that require a variety of skills, both technical in nature and content/discipline-specific. These collaborations draw upon individuals who are based at single institutions, as well as with others who are located at institutions across the country and internationally. Interdisciplinary collaborative research projects of this kind offer clear benefits; however, the very nature of collaboration presents challenges which must be managed carefully if the success of such a project is to be ensured. A successful research team must develop mechanisms to maximize those factors that contribute to success while minimizing the potentially negative impact of the associated challenges (Amabile et al., 2001; Cuneo, 2003). Examination of the experience of the HCI-Book team—now, at the time of writing, the INKE team—provides insight into the nature of interdisciplinary research and suggests potential "best practices" for other teams to consider.

---

reading process); (2) comprehension; and (3) interpretation. Processes include: (1) neuro-physiological (eye movements, the brain's functions, and so on); (2) cognitive (the basic cognitive functions as studied by cognitive science); (3) argumentative/narrative (the act of following a complex sign such as a discourse, a narrative, and so on); (4) affective (emotional response); and (5) symbolic (interpretation of the text within the context of our own body of knowledge and establishment of relations between the text being read and other texts). On interpretation, see the symbolic dimension of the reading process: Kim and Hirtle (1995); Foss (1989); Rouet and Levonen (1996); and Eco (1992).

Consultation Process

This particular research team has been in development for approximately six years. The first meeting brought together several individuals who had previously worked together and had similar research interests, though from a variety of academic disciplines, to explore potential areas of collaboration. From this initial discussion, others with similar research interests were drawn in. In the second year, we met again to discuss potential research questions and potential team members. Over the next year, we continued online discussions and met for another weekend to further the conversation of proposed research directions. These efforts were supported by a week-long symposium held the following summer, which resulted in a more refined research question and set of methodologies, and more fixed team membership. Later that fall, the research question, methodologies, and team membership were finalized, along with rules for interaction and collaboration, which were articulated in an application for the first stage of the granting program. In the fourth year of the collaboration, we were then invited to write a complete grant application. We were ultimately successful on our second attempt to the granting program, nearly six years after the first conversations had occurred. The final research team has 35 active researchers across four countries, several universities and institutions, and almost 90 academic disciplines and sub-disciplines, with a budget of approximately C\$13 million in monetary and in-kind contributions. The represented fields range from philosophy and cultural studies to visual communication design and robotics.

Challenges

As we developed our collaboration, we had to negotiate several key challenges stemming from the disciplinary differences within the team. Disciplines play a very important organizing role within the academy. First, disciplines provide guidance to scholars within a particular field on the nature of appropriate research questions, methodologies, research output, quality standards, funding levels, and career progression. These factors tend to be unique to each discipline (Bruhn, 2000; Cech and Rubin, 2004; Russell, 1985).[25] As the number of disciplines within a research project increases, the greater the potential for conflict becomes. Key issues that create conflict include, but are not limited to, the definition of research problems, the level of interdependence among team members, the determination of appropriate methodologies, the authorship attribution, the selection of appropriate publication and dissemination venues, and the development of effective work and communication patterns among the collaborators.

---

25   In many respects, this disciplinary insularity creates a common understanding of the "world" which allows members within the discipline to communicate easily and quickly in short-hand. However, as discussed above, some research questions require collaboration among a variety of disciplines, and this creates a potential for conflict and miscommunication.

Ultimately, to collaborate effectively, researchers from different disciplines must find common ground in areas of theory, language, value system, methodology, and research style.[26] In some cases, the research team may even need to develop a new working vocabulary specific to the interdisciplinary/multidisciplinary project.[27] Even a common term such as "model" may be understood very differently in different disciplines (Derry, DuRussel and O'Donnell, 1998). As a result, team members must exhibit flexibility, an eagerness to communicate, and a preparation for compromise (Bracken and Oughton, 2006; Bruhn, 1995). In early papers on their collaboration, Liu and Smith (2007) suggest that the analogy of ambassador may be appropriate in this context. An effective ambassador must be willing to bridge cultures and understand differences, while finding the similarities upon which relationships can be built.[28]

Our research team dealt with the challenges associated with disciplinary differences in the following ways, before they became potentially damaging conflicts.[29] First, through the almost six years of discussion that took place before our successful grant application, we met face-to-face and through online mechanisms such as e-mail, project planning spaces, and Skype. Through these conversations, we found that while team members used the same words, they often defined the terminology in very different ways. The terms "book," "text," "reading," "authority," and "prototype" presented particular difficulties, requiring us to create a working vocabulary which allowed effective communication (Siemens, 2009). Through this process, we were exposed to different perspectives and forced to work through our differences to find common ground and commitment to the collaboration as a whole (Siemens and the INKE Research Group, 2009). Many of these face-to-face meetings combined formal discussions with informal ones over meals, which allowed us to get to know each other on a personal as well as professional level. The trust that is developed through these interactions can sustain a team through the usual stresses and strains of collaboration (Siemens, 2008; Kraut and Galegher, 1990). For any research project, but particularly for one of this magnitude in terms of budget, membership, and research scale, the development of the collaboration cannot be rushed if it can hope to be successful (Bagshaw, Lepp and Zorn, 2007; Massey et al., 2001).

---

26   Northcraft and Neale (1993); Bagshaw, Lepp and Zorn (2007); Bruhn (1995).

27   Bracken and Oughton (2006); Lutz and Neis (2008).

28   The attribution of academic credit and authorship is a particularly important issue facing multidisciplinary teams, particularly given the different conventions among disciplines (Kraut, Galegher and Egido, 1987–88; Choi and Pak, 2007). For example, publications in the sciences tend to list all contributors to a project—not merely the authors—while in the humanities, credit is generally granted to the first author, who is the individual deemed to have done the most work (Kraut, Galegher and Egido, 1987–88; Fanderclai, 2004). If teams do not discuss and resolve this issue of attribution in advance, they often face conflict (Bagshaw, Lepp and Zorn, 2007).

29   Bagshaw, Lepp and Zorn (2007); McGinn et al. (2005).

Second, given the variety of disciplines represented within our group and the resulting potential for conflict, our research team articulated an authorship strategy fairly early in the collaboration. Our negotiated convention of authorship comprises of an acknowledgement of two or three key individuals as named authors, along with the attribution "INKE Research Group," which clearly signals the nature of this particular working relationship. Any published work and data represents the collaboration of the whole team, past and present, not the work of any sole researcher.

Finally, beyond our discussions of research questions, objectives, and approaches during and after our grant application development, we also formally articulated roles, expectations, and task interdependence through a project charter (for the grant application stage) and administrative governance documents (for the grant working stage). The charter was supplemented by a Gantt chart which outlined key tasks, timing, and research area responsibility. Further, the collaboration was portrayed as a figure eight diagram, which showed the integrative flow of research across our four research areas and the involvement of partners and stakeholders in the project. These documents reduced any potential for future conflict, and also provided an opportunity for us to "get to know each other and to build trust" (McGinn et al., 2005: 564). Other digital humanities and digital libraries teams have also found formal documentation to be necessary for effective team research. As one participant in an earlier study on collaboration in these communities stated: "formal documents sound cheesy, but in a multi-ethnic, multi-lingual, multi-generational, multi-talented work group (as every work group is) they are essential for setting a baseline understanding of what the project is and who is supposed to do what" (Siemens et al., 2009).

While our research team is still in the early phases of its seven-year research project, it has been a team in fact for almost six years. Throughout this time, we have been building the necessary relationships and processes that we will need to navigate the challenges associated with multidisciplinary research collaborations.

References

Amabile, Teresa M. et al., 'Academic–Practitioner Collaboration in Management Research: A Case of Cross-Profession Collaboration', *Academy of Management Journal* 44.2 (2001): 418–31.

Astleitner, H. and D. Leutner, 'Learning Strategies for Unstructured Hypermedia – A Framework for Theory, Research, and Practice', *Journal of Educational Computing Research* 13.4 (1995): 387–400.

Bagshaw, Dale, Margret Lepp and Cecelia R. Zorn, 'International Research Collaboration: Building Teams and Managing Conflicts', *Conflict Resolution Quarterly* 24.4 (2007): 433–46.

Barrett, A., 'The Information-Seeking Habits of Graduate Student Researchers in the Humanities', *Journal of Academic Librarianship* 31.4 (2005): 324–31.

Barthes, R., *S/Z*, trans. R. Millar (New York: Hill and Wang, 1974).

Bates, M.J., 'The Cascade of Interactions in the Digital Library Interface', *Information Processing and Management* 38.3 (2002): 381–400.

Beagrie, N. and M. Jones, *Preservation Management of Digital Materials: A Handbook* (York: Digital Preservation Coalition, 2002).

Best, Michael, 'Introduction: A Booth at the Fair', *Monitoring Electronic Shakespeares*, special issue of *Early Modern Literary Studies* 9.3 (2004), available at: <http://extra.shu.ac.uk/emls/09-3/bestintr.htm>.

Best, Michael (ed.), *The Internet Shakespeare: Opportunities in a New Medium*, special issue of *Early Modern Literary Studies* 3.3 (1998), available at: <http://extra.shu.ac.uk/emls/si-02/si-02toc.html>.

Blandford, A., J. Rimmer and C. Warwick, 'Experiences of the Library in the Digital Age', *Proceedings of the Third International Conference on 'Cultural Covergence and Digital Technology'*, Athens, 2006.

Bolter, Jay David, *Writing Space: Computers, Hypertext, and the Remediation of Print*, 2nd edn (Mahwah, NJ: Lawrence Erlbaum, 2001).

Bracken, L.J. and E.A. Oughton, '"What Do You Mean?" The Importance of Language in Developing Interdisciplinary Research', *Transactions of the Institute of British Geographers* 31.3 (2006): 371–82.

British Academy, *E-resources for Research in the Humanities and Social Sciences – A British Academy Policy Review* (2005), available at: <http://www.britac.ac.uk/reports/eresources/report/sect3.html#part5>.

Bruhn, John G., 'Beyond Discipline: Creating a Culture for Interdisciplinary Research', *Integrative Physiological and Behavioral Science* 30.4 (1995): 331–42.

Bruhn, John G., 'Interdisciplinary Research: A Philosophy, Art Form, Artifact or Antidote?' *Integrative Physiological and Behavioral Science* 35.1 (2000): 58–66.

Buzzetti, Dino and Jerome McGann, 'Electronic Textual Editing: Critical Editing in a Digital Horizon', *Electronic Textual Editing* (Text Encoding Initiative Consortium, 2005), available at: <http://www.tei-c.org/Activities/ETE/Preview/mcgann.xml>.

Caplan, P., 'Preservation metadata', *Digital Curation Manual*, available at: <http://www.dcc.ac.uk/resource/curation-manual/chapters/preservation-metadata/preservation-metadata.pdf>.

Carroll, John M., 'Introduction: Human–Computer Interaction, the Past and the Present', in John Carroll (ed.), *Human–Computer Interaction in the New Millennium* (New York: ACM Press, 2002).

Cech, Thomas R. and Gerald M. Rubin, 'Nurturing Interdisciplinary Research', *Nature Structural and Molecular Biology* 11.12 (2004): 1166–9.

Chartier, Roger, *The Order of Books*, trans. Lydia G. Cochrane (Stanford: Polity Press, 1994).

Chatman, S., *Story and Discourse: Narrative Structure in Fiction and Film* (New York: Cornell University Press, 1978).

Cheypesh, Oksana et al., 'Centering the Mind and Calming the Heart: Mandalas as Interfaces', *Society for Digital Humanities (SDH/SEMI)* (York University, Toronto, 2006).

Choi, Bernard C.K. and Anita W.P. Pak, 'Multidisciplinarity, Interdisciplinarity, and Transdisciplinarity in Health Research, Services, Education and Policy: 2. Promotors, Barriers, and Strategies of Enhancement', *Clinical and Investigative Medicine* 30 (2007): E224–E32.

Chu, C.M., 'Literary Critics at Work and their Information Needs: A Research-Phases Model', *Library and Information Science Research* 21.2 (1999): 247–73.

Cuneo, Carl, 'Interdisciplinary Teams – Let's Make Them Work', *University Affairs* (November, 2003): 18–21.

Dalcher, D. and A. Genus, 'Introduction: Avoiding IS/IT Implementation Failure', *Technology Analysis and Strategic Management* 15.4 (2003): 403–7.

Dalton, M.S. and L. Charnigo, 'Historians and their Information Sources', *College and Research Libraries* 65.5 (2004): 400–425.

Day, M., 'Metadata', *Digital Curation Manual* (2005), available at: <http://www.dcc.ac.uk/resource/curation-manual/chapters/metadata/metadata.pdf>.

DeRose, Steven J., David G. Durand, Elli Mylonas and Allen H. Renear, 'What Is Text, Really?' *Journal of Computing in Higher Education* 1.2 (1990): 3–26.

Derrida, Jacques, *Of Grammatology* (Baltimore: Johns Hopkins University Press, 1976).

Derrida, Jacques, *Dissemination*, trans. Barbara Johnson (Chicago: University Press, 1981).

Derry, Sharon J., Lori Adams DuRussel and Angela M. O'Donnell, 'Individual and Distributed Cognitions in Interdisciplinary Teamworks', *Educational Psychology Review* 10.1 (1998): 25.

Dillon, Andrew, *Designing Usable Electronic Text*, 2nd edn (Boca Raton: CRC Press, (2004).

Dobson, T.M., 'For the Love of a Good Narrative: Digitality and Textuality', *English Teaching: Practice and Critique* 5.2 (2006): 56–68.

Dobson, T.M. and R. Luce-Kapler, 'Stitching Texts: Gender and Geography in Frankenstein and Patchwork Girl', *Changing English* 12.2 (2005): 265–77.

Dobson, T.M. and D.S. Miall, 'Orienting the Reader? A Study of Literary Hypertexts', *SPIEL* 17.2 (1998): 249–62.

Douglas, J.Y., *The End of Books – Or Books Without End? Reading Interactive Narratives* (Ann Arbor: University of Michigan Press, 2000).

Duff, W., 'Metadata in Digital Preservation: Foundations, Functions and Issues', in F.M. Bischoff, H. Hofman and S. Ross (eds), *Metadata in Preservation: Selected Papers from an ERPANET Seminar at the Archives School Marburg* (Marburg: Archivschule Marburg, 2003).

Eco, Umberto, *Interpretation and Overinterpretation*, ed. S. Collini (Cambridge: Cambridge University Press, 1992).

Ellis, D. and H. Oldman, 'The English Literature Researcher in the Age of the Internet', *Journal of Information Science* 31.1 (2005): 29–36.

ELO, *Electronic Literature Collection* Volume 1 (College Park, MD: Electronic Literature Organization, 2006), available at: <http://collection.eliterature. org/1/>.

Fanderclai, Tari, 'Collaborative Research, Collaborative Thinking: Lessons from the Linux Community', in James A. Inman, Cheryl Reed and Peter Sands (eds), *Electronic Collaboration in the Humanities: Issues and Options* (Mahwah, NJ: Lawrence Erlbaum Associates, 2004).

Fitzgerald, J. and T. Shanahan, 'Reading and Writing Relations and their Development', *Educational Psychologist* 35.1 (2000): 39–50.

Flowers, S., *Software Failure: Management Failure: Amazing Stories and Cautionary Tales* (Chichester, NY: John Wiley, 1996).

Foss, C., 'Tools for Reading and Browsing Hypertext', *Information Processing and Management* 25.4 (1989): 407–18.

Frascara, J., *User-Centred Graphic Design* (London: Taylor and Francis, 1997).

Galey, Alan, 'Dizzying the Arithmetic of Memory: Shakespearean Source Documents as Text, Image, and Code', *Early Modern Literary Studies* 9.3, Special Issue 12 (2004): 4.1–28, available at: <http://purl.oclc.org/emls/09-3/ galedizz.htm>.

Ganong, W.F., *Review of Medical Physiology*, 21st edn (New York: Lange Medical Books, 2003).

Garrett, Jesse James, 'Ajax: A New Approach to Web Applications', *Adaptive Path*, available at: <http://www.adaptivepath.com/publications/essays/archives/>.

Gibson, J.J., *The Ecological Approach to Visual Perception* (Boston: Houghton-Mifflin, 1979).

Granger, S., 'Emulation as a Digital Preservation Strategy', *D-Lib Magazine* 6.10 (2000).

Green, R., 'Locating Sources in Humanities Scholarship: The Efficacy of Following Bibliographic References', *Library Quarterly* 70.2 (2000): 201–29.

Greetham, D.C., *Textual Scholarship: An Introduction* (New York: Garland, 1994).

Greetham, D.C., *The Margins of the Text* (Ann Arbor: University of Michigan Press, 1997).

Hansen, W.J., 'User Engineering Principles for Interactive Systems', *Proceedings of AFIPS Fall Joint Computer Conference* 39 (1971): 523–32.

Hara, Noriko et al., 'An Emerging View of Scientific Collaboration: Scientists' Perspectives on Collaboration and Factors that Impact Collaboration', *Journal of the American Society for Information Science and Technology* 54.10 (2003): 952–65.

Hedstrom, M.L. et al, '"The Old Version Flickers More": Digital Preservation from the User's Perspective', *American Archivist* 69 (2006): 159–87.

Ingwersen, P. and K. Jarvelin, *The Turn: Integration of Information Seeking and Retrieval in Context*, vol. 18 (Berlin: Springer, 2005).

Iser, W., *The Act of Reading: A Theory of Aesthetic Response* (Baltimore: Johns Hopkins University Press, 1978).

Johns, Adrian, *The Nature of the Book: Print and Knowledge in the Making* (Chicago: University of Chicago Press, 1998).

Kim, H. and S.C. Hirtle, 'Spatial Metaphors and Disorientation in Hypertext Browsing', *Behaviour and Information Technology* 14.4 (1995): 239–50.

Kintsch, W., 'The Role of Knowledge in Discourse Comprehension: A Construction Integration Model', *Psychological Review* 95.2 (1988): 163–82.

Kirschenbaum, Matthew G., 'Extreme Inscription: Towards a Grammatology of the Hard Drive', *TEXT Technology* 13.2 (2004a): 91–125.

Kirschenbaum, Matthew G., '"So the Colors Cover the Wires": Interface, Aesthetics, and Usability', in Susan Schreibman, Ray Siemens and John Unsworth (eds), *A Companion to Digital Humanities* (Malden, MA: Blackwell, 2004b): 523–42.

Kraut, Robert E. and Jolene Galegher, 'Patterns of Contact and Communication in Scientific Research Collaboration', in Jolene Galegher, Robert Kraut and Carmen Egido (eds), *Intellectual Teamwork: Social and Technological Foundations of Cooperative Work* (Hillsdale, NJ: Erlbaum, 1990).

Kraut, Robert E., Jolene Galegher and Carmen Egido, 'Relationships and Tasks in Scientific Research Collaboration', *Human–Computer Interaction* 3.1 (1987–88): 31–58.

Landow, George, *Hyper/Text/Theory* (Baltimore and London: Johns Hopkins University Press, 1994).

Landow, George, *Hypertext 2.0: The Convergence of Contemporary Critical Theory and Technology*, rev. edn (Baltimore: Johns Hopkins University Press, 1997).

Lavoie, B.F. and R. Gartner, *Preservation Metadata* (No. 05-01) (York: Digital Preservation Coalition, 2005).

Lazinger, S., *Digital Preservation and Metadata* (Englewood: Greenwood, 2001).

Lehmann, S. and P. Renfro, 'Humanists and Electronic Information Services: Acceptance and Resistance', *College and Research Libraries* 52 (1991): 403–13.

Leventhal, L.M., B. Teasley, K. Instone, D. Rohlman, and J. Farhat, 'Sleuthing in HyperHolmes: An Evaluation of Using Hypertext vs. a Book to Answer Questions', *Behaviour and Information Technology* 12 (1993): 149–64.

Linden, J. et al., *The Large Scale Archival Storage of Digital Objects* (York: Digital Preservation Coalition, 2005).

Liu, Yin and Jeff Smith, 'Aligning the Agendas of Humanities and Computer Science Research: A Risk/Reward Analysis', *SDH-SEMI 2007*.

Luce-Kapler, R. and T.M. Dobson, 'In Search of a Story: Reading and Writing e-Literature', *Reading Online* 8.6 (2005): np.

Lutz, John Sutton and Barbara Neis, 'Introduction', in John Sutton Lutz and Barbara Neis (eds), *Making and Moving Knowledge: Interdisciplinary and Community-Based Research in a World on the Edge* (Montreal, Quebec: McGill-Queen's University Press, 2008).

Maclean, Marie, 'Pretexts and Paratexts: The Art of the Peripheral', *New Literary History* 22.2 (1991): 273–9.

Makri, S. et al., 'A Library or Just Another Information Resource? A Case Study of Users' Mental Models of Traditional and Digital Libraries', *Journal of the American Society of Information Science and Technology* 58.3 (2007): 433–45.

Massey, Anne P. et al., 'When Culture and Style Aren't About Clothes: Perceptions of Task-Technology "Fit" In Global Virtual Teams', *Proceedings of the 2001 International ACM SIGGROUP Conference on Supporting Group Work* (2001).

McGinn, Michelle K. et al., 'Living Ethics: A Narrative of Collaboration and Belonging in a Research Team', *Reflective Practice* 6.4 (2005): 551–67.

McKenzie, D.F., 'The Broken Phial: Non-Book Texts', in *Bibliography and the Sociology of Texts* (Cambridge: Cambridge University Press, 1999): 31–53.

Miall, D.S. and T.M. Dobson, 'Reading Hypertext and the Experience of Literature', *Journal of Digital Information* 2.1 (2001).

Miall, D.S. and D. Kuiken, 'Beyond Text Theory: Understanding Literary Response', *Discourse Processes* 17 (1994): 337–52.

Newell, Sue and Jacky Swan, 'Trust and Inter-Organizational Networking', *Human Relations* 53.10 (2000): 1287–328.

Northcraft, Gregory B. and Margaret A. Neale, 'Negotiating Successful Research Collaboration', in J. Keith Murnighan (ed.), *Social Psychology in Organizations: Advances in Theory and Research* (Englewood Cliffs, NJ: Prentice Hall, 1993).

Rabinowitz, P.J., *Before Reading: Narrative Conventions and the Politics of Interpretation* (Ithaca, NY: Cornell University Press, 1987).

Renear, Allen, 'Out of Praxis: Three (Meta)Theories of Textuality', in Kathryn Sutherland (ed.), *Electronic Text: Investigations in Method and Theory* (Oxford: Clarendon, 1987): 107–26.

Rose, Jonathan, 'Worker's Journals', in J. Don Vann and Rosemary T. VanArsdel (eds), *Victorian Periodicals and Victorian Society* (Toronto: University of Toronto Press, 1995): 301–10.

Rosenberg, M.E., 'Physics and Hypertext: Liberation and Complicity in Art and Pedagogy', in George Landow (ed.), *Hyper/Text/Theory* (Baltimore: Johns Hopkins University Press, 1994): 268–98.

Rosenblatt, L., *Literature as Exploration* (New York: Noble and Noble, 1938/1968).

Ross, S., 'How to Preserve and Prove the Integrity of Digital Objects?' *DigiCULT Thematic Issue: Integrity and Authenticity of Digital Cultural Heritage Objects* (2002).

Rouet, J.F. and J.J. Levonen, 'Studying and Learning with Hypertext: Empirical Studies and their Implications', in J.F. Rouet et al. (eds), *Hypertext and Cognition* (Mahwah, NJ: Lawrence Erlbaum, 1996): 9–23.

Ruecker, Stan, *Affordances of Prospect for Academic Users of Interpretively-Tagged Text Collections*, unpublished PhD Dissertation (Edmonton: University of Alberta, 2003).

Ruecker, Stan, 'The Electronic Book Table of Contents as a Research Tool', *Congress of the Humanities and Social Sciences: Consortium for Computers in the Humanities/Consortium pour Ordinateurs en Sciences Humaines (COCH/COSH) Annual Conference*, London, Ontario, 2005.

Ruecker, Stan, 'Proposing an Affordance Strength Model to Study New Interface Tools', *Digital Humanities 2006* (Paris, 2006).

Ruecker, Stan et al., 'The Clear Browser: Visually Positioning an Interface for Data Mining by Humanities Scholars', *Digital Humanities 2006* (Paris, 2006).

Russell, Martha Garrett, 'Administering Interdisciplinary Collaboration', in B.W. Mar, William T. Newell and Borje O. Saxberg (eds), *Managing High Technology: An Interdisciplinary Perspective* (Amsterdam: Elsevier, 1985).

Schreibman, Susan, 'Computer-Mediated Texts and Textuality: Theory and Practice', *Computers and the Humanities* 36 (2002): 283–93.

Shneiderman, B. and C. Plaisant, *Designing the User Interface: Strategies for Effective Human–Computer Interaction*, 4th edn (Reading, MA: Pearson – Addison Wesley, 2005).

Siegfried, S., M.J. Bates and D.N. Wilde, 'A Profile of End-User Searching Behavior by Humanities Scholars: The Getty Online Searching Project Report no. 2', *Journal of the American Society for Information Science* 44.5 (1993): 273–91.

Siemens, Lynne, 'The Balance Between On-line and In-person Interactions: Methods for the Development of Digital Humanities Collaboration', *SDH-SEMI 2008*.

Siemens, Lynne and the INKE Research Group, 'From Writing the Grant to Working the Grant: An Exploration of Processes and Procedures in Transition', *INKE 2009*.

Siemens, Lynne et al., '"It Challenges Members to Think of their Work Through Another Kind of Specialist's Eyes": Exploration of the Benefits and Challenges of Diversity in Digital Project Teams', *Thriving on Diversity – Information Opportunities in a Pluralistic World*, ASIS&T 2009 Annual Meeting.

Siemens, R.G., 'Cultures Separated by a Common Language? Homography/Homophony and Collaborative Understanding, in Discipline and Context', *Enhancing International Research Collaborations, Strengthening Quality, Connections and Impacts: A SSHRC Congress 2009 Session*.

Siemens, R.G. et al., 'The Credibility of Electronic Publishing: A Report to the Humanities and Social Sciences Federation of Canada', *TEXT Technology* 11.1 (2002): 1–128.

Sless, D. and R. Wiseman, *Writing About Medicines for People*, 2nd edn (Melbourne: Communication Research Institute of Australia, 1997).

Slights, William W.E., *Managing Readers: Printed Marginalia in English Renaissance Books* (Ann Arbor: University of Michigan Press, 2001).

Social Sciences and Humanities Research Council of Canada (SSHRC), *From Granting Council to Knowledge Council: Renewing the Social Sciences and*

Humanities in Canada (Ottawa, Ontario: Social Sciences and Humanities Research Council of Canada, 2004).

Spufford, Margaret, *Small Books and Pleasant Histories: Popular Fiction and its Readership in Seventeenth Century England* (Athens, GA: University of Georgia Press, 1982).

Steemson, M., 'DigiCult Experts Search for e-Archive Permanence', *DigiCULT Thematic Issue: Integrity and Authenticity of Digital Cultural Heritage Objects* (2002).

Stone, S., 'Humanities Scholars: Information Needs and Uses', *Journal of Documentation* 38.4 (1982): 292–313.

Stotsky, S., 'Research on Reading/Writing Relationships: A Synthesis and Suggested Directions', *Language Arts* 60 (1983): 627–43.

Talja, S. and J. Maula, 'Reasons for the Use and Non-Use of Electronic Journals and Databases – A Domain Analytic Study in Four Scholarly Disciplines', *Journal of Documentation* 59.6 (2003): 273–91.

Thérien, G., *Sémiologies* (Montreal: Université du Québec à Montréal, 1985).

Van Peer, W. and S. Chatman (eds), *New Perspectives on Narrative Perspective* (New York: SUNY, 2001).

Warwick, Claire, 'Print Scholarship and Digital Resources', in Susan Schreibman, Ray Siemens and John Unsworth (eds), *A Companion to Digital Humanities* (London: Blackwell, 2004): 366–82.

Warwick, C., A. Blandford and G. Buchanan, 'User Centred Interactive Search: A Study of Humanities Users in a Digital Library Environment', *Association for Computers and the Humanities – Association for Literary and Linguistic Computing 2005* (University of Victoria, Canada, 2005).

Warwick, C. et al., '"If You Build It Will They Come?" The LAIRAH Study: Quantifying the Use of Online Resources in the Arts and Humanities Through Statistical Analysis of UserLog Data', *Proceedings of Digital Humanities 2006* (Paris: Universite de Paris-Sorbonne, 2006): 225–8.

Warwick, C. et al., *The LAIRAH Survey, A Report to the Arts and Humanities Research Council: AHRC ICT Strategy Scheme* (2007).

Waters, D. and J. Garret, *Preserving Digital Information: Report of the Task Force on Archiving of Digital Information Commissioned by the Commission on Preservation and Access and the Research Libraries Group* (Washington, DC: Commission on Preservation and Access, 1996).

Watson-Boone, R., 'The Information Needs and Habits of Humanities Scholars', *Reference Quarterly* 34 (1994): 203–16.

Watt, Tessa, *Cheap Print and Popular Piety, 1550–1640* (Cambridge: Cambridge University Press, 1991).

Whitmire, E., 'Disciplinary Differences and Undergraduates' Information-Seeking Behaviour', *Journal of the American Society for Information Science and Technology* 53.8 (2002): 631–8.

Wiberley, S.E., 'Subject Access in the Humanities and the Precision of the Humanist's Vocabulary', *Library Quarterly* 53 (1983): 420–33.

Wiberley, S.E., 'Names in Space and Time: The Indexing Vocabulary of the Humanities', *Library Quarterly* 58 (1988): 1–28.

Wiberley, S., 'Time and Technology', *College and Research Libraries* 61.5 (2000): 421–31.

Zwaan, R.A., J. Magliano and A.C. Graesser, 'Dimensions of Situation Model Construction in Narrative Comprehension', *Journal of Experimental Psychology: Learning, Memory, and Cognition* 21.1 (1995): 386–97.

Chapter 12

The Author's Hand: From Page to Screen

Kathryn Sutherland and Elena Pierazzo

1. Introduction

The digital capture and delivery of manuscripts for scholarly study and for general access is currently opening new or under-explored areas of our literary culture; at the same time it is challenging assumptions within the digital community about what text is and how to represent it adequately. The digital representation and delivery of Jane Austen's fiction manuscripts are a case in point. In what follows we present some of the findings and the problems from our joint work. For both of us this has been an unexpectedly invigorating collaboration. Textual scholars trained in the principles of textual criticism and palaeography, one of us is an expert in a particular subject area (Jane Austen studies) and the other an expert in digital technologies. The combination has led us to fresh insights for Austen scholarship and for the encoding and representation of modern working manuscripts.

2. The Jane Austen's Fiction Manuscripts Project

Jane Austen's fiction manuscripts are the first substantial bodies of autograph writings surviving for any British novelist. Some 1,100 pages, they represent every stage of her writing career, roughly 1787 to 1817 (the year she died), and a variety of physical states: working drafts, fair copies and handwritten 'publications' for private circulation. The manuscripts were held in a single collection until 1845 when, at her sister Cassandra's death, they were dispersed among family members, with a second major dispersal, to public institutions and private collections, in the 1920s. As a record of the creative mind of one of English literature's most famous writers, they are priceless. Yet until now they have been unavailable except to a very few privileged scholars; even then, never as a single collection. No manuscripts remain for the famous six novels. The manuscript evidence therefore represents a different Jane Austen: different in the range of fiction they contain from the novels we know only from print; and different in what they reveal about the workings of her imagination. Because of the variety of their pre-print states and because of the way they extend the time span of her writing life (far longer than the single decade of the printed novels), these manuscript writings can claim a special place in our understanding of the evolution of the famous fictions.

In 2006 the Arts and Humanities Research Council granted three-year funding for a project to digitize the manuscripts. The aims of the digital project have been three-fold: the virtual reunification of this significant collection by means of high-quality digital images; the linking of the images to fully encoded and searchable diplomatic transcriptions; and the creation of as complete a record as possible of the provenance, conservation history and physical state of these frail documents. Throughout, our focus has been on the manuscripts as physical objects, as well as linguistic texts recorded on those objects. Through virtual reunification, scholars, curators and other interested users are provided for the first time with the opportunity to make simultaneous ocular comparison of the dispersed manuscripts' different physical and conceptual states, allowing intimate and systematic study of Jane Austen's working practices across her career.

Our work on the digital edition has been impelled by two particular kinds of enquiry: how might the resources of the digital medium (facsimile representations of manuscript images and complex encoding of manuscript content) model and describe the way Jane Austen may have worked as a writer? And how might the particular features of Austen's working practices as laid out in the manuscript space test the transcription systems at our disposal as digital editors? A consequence of our collaboration that increasingly informs our thinking has been the challenge to revise, for the digital medium, the assumptions we bring from paper-based editing.

3.1 Digital Editing: What Changes and What Does Not

Is digital editing any different from the kinds of editing necessary to produce a printed edition? The answer to this question, as to many others, is yes and no. According to Daniel O'Donnell (2008: 11), we should first establish what we mean by 'digital': the use of digital tools in the production of an edition or the publication of an edition in digital format. One can indeed use digital methodologies and tools to produce either a print or a digital edition, or both; and, as a matter of fact, the Jane Austen's Fiction Manuscripts Digital Edition will have a dual output, one digital in the form of a website, and the other a multi-volume print edition from Oxford University Press. So the question now refined becomes: does the methodology to produce the edition change, does the output or do both?

The use of digital technology for editorial work changes the working methodology whatever the planned output – print or electronic – with more radical change when there is a digital output. This is because the shift in medium leads to a reconsideration of the kind of editorial product it is possible to publish. Furthermore, as the work becomes more and more collaborative, editors witness both the shrinking of their responsibilities (many people are now involved in what was once a solitary enterprise) and the enlargement of their field of competence, as they are required to design new elements: for example, websites, browsing and searching interfaces.

When it comes to evaluating digital editions, Mats Dahlström (2009: 29) warns about not 'mixing apples and pears' by setting 'digital editions versus, say, eclectic editions'; that is, not confusing the types and purpose of editions with the methodology used to produce them. But in an important sense digital editions are of essence hybrids – apples and pears at the same time – their methodologies simultaneously realizing several different critical approaches to text that in turn demand a reconsideration of traditionally distinct categories. Many digital editions are fundamentally multi-perspective: that is, they are able to display the text in diplomatic, semi-diplomatic and reading views, among others, all generated from the same source data, usually encoded in XML. To produce such diversity of choice, the text must be annotated comprehensively for the many possible outputs without privileging any one of them. In this way, the source file can potentially realize several kinds of edition; and, while it is all of them, it is none, since each must be made real by some further processing. So, if we should not compare digital editions with eclectic editions, nor can we easily compare printed diplomatic editions with digital diplomatic editions, especially if the latter are offered alongside other possible editions (views) of the text capable of being generated from the same source file. According to Tim McLoughlin (2010), in moving from print to digital, the purpose of the edition is also transformed, with the final product changing, from a text to be read to an 'object' to be used. The claim is overstated: the book too, especially at the service of the critical edition, is both reading device and storage and retrieval machine of great complexity. Nevertheless, the shift from print to digital redistributes a range of activities, forcing the editor to undertake unexpected tasks, most of which are likely to be unwelcome: most obviously, 'editor as encoder'. At the same time, the new editorial model is full of surprises: the flexibility and openness of the encoding schemas; the need to guess what users are likely to want *to do* with the 'material'.

Complicated by such qualifications, it becomes clear that the use of digital methods and tools can change both the way scholars manipulate their texts and the way they think about them. On the other hand, what does not change in digital editing is the prerequisite skills of traditional scholarship: the underlying cultural tools necessary to edit. Reading and transcribing a manuscript is not an easy task: it requires trained eyes, palaeographic expertise, codicological knowledge and editorial competencies, as well as understanding of the specific author one is editing. What has changed is the *way* we transcribe and the features we choose to include in our transcription. Digital images can facilitate and enhance our reading capabilities, while other tools can help in keeping editorial practices under control. What has also changed is the way our implied recipients read or use (are they readers or users?) our texts, with the consequence that we also have to change the way we deliver those texts. Most of all, what has changed is the way we work: digital editions are essentially collaborative ('It takes a village' to use Peter Shillingsburg's words (2006: 94–8)); and this development brings the greatest challenges to editorial work.

Even if scholars must acquire essential new skills to use digital techniques and languages, it is very rare to find one person with all the skills necessary for the preparation and publication of digital editions. Texts need to be digitized, checked, annotated, encoded and transformed; facsimile images need to be annotated, elaborated and transformed into suitable formats. If the edition is to have an electronic output, then an interface must be designed, including both functionality and graphics; search engines and browsing facilities must be designed and deployed; infrastructural support is needed, such as networking and maintenance of servers; and so on. For centuries, editorial work was more or less the province of a single scholar able to control and supervise all stages of the process up to the point when the manuscript was delivered to a publisher; the publisher was then in charge of typesetting, preparing the layout, copy-editing the manuscript, and so on. With the advent of digital publication, the scholar is forced to co-operate with other experts from the very beginning; s/he is also asked to be involved in tasks conventionally undertaken by a publishing house; again these tasks are now to be performed in co-operation with other experts, most probably from other disciplines. We might say that the new medium revives an old challenge by shifting to the scholar's study many of the functions that, over the centuries, devolved to the printing house and later the publisher.

The experience of collaboration is not always positive. Lynne Siemens (2009) has provided a good description of the tensions one can find within the team of a digital humanities project, the main difficulty being one of reciprocal understanding across disciplines. By contrast, and perhaps unusually, those involved in the Austen digital edition experienced little of the incomprehension and misunderstanding outlined by Siemens, and this is because both sides of the team, domain experts and digital experts, spoke the same language, the language of scholarly editorial practice.

3.2 Modelling

The first activity in preparing a digital edition is modelling, by which we mean the analytical process of establishing the kind and purpose of the edition, its implied community of users and what features best represent their various needs (see McCarty, 2005: 20–72). Although it is true that this is not a new activity – editors regularly determined the type and purpose of their editions long before the advent of computers – nevertheless modelling has acquired a new importance and role in digital editing due to 'the fundamental dependence of any computing system on an explicit, delimited conception of the world or "model" of it' (McCarty, 2005: 21). What is also different is the way such a model is expressed: a declaration of intents and editorial practices in traditional editorial work, some kind of computer-friendly formalism in the case of digital editing. A digital edition is both an 'image', a representation of the text, and also 'textual data to be processed' (Buzzetti, 2009: 47). In fact, in order to be processable, data must be modelled in a way that is suited to the purpose for which it has been created. In other words, the model of an edition must foresee all the possible questions which editors and end users are likely to pose, and must embed the knowledge necessary to answer such questions.

As Willard McCarty (2005: 26) states, modelling is an iterative, learning process, the result of which is a better knowledge of the object to be studied; it requires a sound knowledge of the object (in this case, texts) to be modelled and of the processing to be applied. In addition, modelling is an ongoing process: as knowledge of the object deepens within the context of the project in general and the editorial work in particular, so it is to be expected that the initial model will need to be refined many times over. From experience, the best way to build a model of a digital edition is to design the end product first (usually a website). Again from experience, the best way to do this is to use a visual aid, a so-called 'wireframe', which is a skeletal drawing of a fully functional final product (the website). In spite of the traditional mistrust of humanities scholars towards visual representations (Jessop, 2008a: 47), the graphic support of wireframes has proved a fundamental aid to thinking across many digital humanities projects. It is a way to embody visions and imagine the future, with the additional advantage, from a computing point of view, of putting a firm plan in place before the development of the real website. In this respect, Martyn Jessop is right when he declares that the 'greatest value' of digital visualization is for 'synthesis and modelling' (2008b: 288).

Once the final product has been designed in all its foreseeable details, then the modelling proceeds backwards: which kind of features must the model contain in order to enable the desired output? Which technology will be best suited to manage the kind of interactivity that is expected? As one might imagine, the answers to such questions require long discussion and at least two discussants: a domain expert and a digital humanities expert. A process very similar to the one just described took place for the Jane Austen's Fiction Manuscripts Digital Edition, and it is discussed in detail below.

3.3 Print Editions of Jane Austen's Fiction Manuscripts

The history to date of the critical editing of Austen's fiction manuscripts has been bounded by the possibilities of the printed book; at the same time, it displays little consistency of treatment. The Austen we are most of us familiar with is the writer of six classic novels, recoverable only as products of the printing press. The manuscripts, unpublished in her lifetime, literally present a different face. Where the finished novels have been through the normalizing processes (whether authorial or editorial) that attend print – from the removal of signs of erasure and revision, to the introduction of paragraphing and expansion of abbreviations – the blots, interlinear insertions and false starts of the irregular writing and rewriting hand appear integral to the meaning of modern manuscript. The best recourse for the editor might seem complete photo-facsimile reproduction of the primary documents accompanied by detailed diplomatic transcriptions: that is, something that looks like the real thing together with an informed interpretation of its inked marks and shapes. But even in Austen's case, where the manuscript evidence is modest in size (only 1,100 pages), this remained through the twentieth century an expensive option as regards the facsimiles and, in the case of transcriptions, a challenge to the typography and design of the printed page. Perhaps unsurprisingly, the two major print editions of the complete Austen manuscripts – R.W. Chapman's Oxford edition, prepared piecemeal over a long period (roughly from 1925 to 1954) and the recent Cambridge edition (2006–08) under the general editorship of Janet Todd – though separated by more than half a century, display a comparable irresolution over the status and treatment of their materials.

Chapman turned to Austen's manuscripts after completing his edition of the printed works in 1923, and it is clear that he identified the manuscript state with inferior artistic production. For him these documents fell into two distinct groups: juvenile compositions (and therefore inferior); abandoned or unfinished drafts (and therefore inferior). Issued over many years as transcriptions in individual volumes, they were eventually collected together in a single volume entitled 'Minor Works'. He nowhere articulates his principles or method in presenting the manuscripts to a wider readership. For the unfinished working drafts, his preference was for clean transcriptions, preserving contractions and orthographic idiosyncrasies but removing all signs of struggle – corrections and erasures, whether of single words or longer passages – to a series of textual notes at the back of each volume. The detail in these notes is difficult to interpret, shorn of the immediate context that would illuminate their synoptic representation. Uniquely for only one manuscript (the two discarded chapters of *Persuasion*), he provided a photo-facsimile, preceding the clean transcription. When it came to the juvenile compositions, he made no attempt to represent their eccentric features of layout or formal styling – features that form part of their subtle bibliographic comedy. In sum, across the 30 years of his engagement with the manuscripts, he saw no need for diplomatic transcriptions that would preserve line and page breaks, orthographic features (like Austen's long 's'), underlinings, and so on. On the other hand, he generally respected other alien features of the originals: for example, grammatical contractions, superscript letters and the absence of paragraphing. It might be objected that his choices represent neither the characteristics of the writing hand nor the developed conventions of the critical edition since what he offers are neither diplomatic transcriptions nor fully edited reading texts. Yet Chapman (1925: unpaginated 'Preface') was clear that his method was scrupulous, observing of his work on *Sanditon*, the final manuscript: 'This edition ... is, for all critical purposes, virtually a facsimile of all that Miss Austen wrote and did not erase.'

The Cambridge Edition of the Works of Jane Austen presents the manuscripts across three volumes. *The Juvenilia*, edited by Peter Sabor, is a print transcription which seeks to preserve the 'idiosyncrasies and inconsistencies, which form part of the texture of her prose, and which can help establish the date of a particular item' (Sabor, 2006: lxviii). In practice, this means observing Austen's spelling, capitalization, paragraphing and punctuation; but it also means replacing her long 's' and ampersand, transforming underlinings into italics and ignoring most of the eccentric and pseudo-bibliographic features of this set of manuscripts. Revisions, deletions and corrections are removed from the text and recorded in notes at the foot of each page. There is no attempt to replicate the layout of Austen's page or to record line or page breaks. In other words, like Chapman's, this is a clean transcription readied towards print but away from the bookish parody of the originals. The volume containing the print novel *Persuasion*, edited by Janet Todd and Antje Blank, becomes home for the cancelled manuscript chapters of that novel, which are laid out in an appendix in two versions: as a 'clean text' transcription, shorn of all their considerable evidence of revision and erasure; and as a set of photo-facsimile pages, to which the interested reader is directed (2006: 278–325). There is no textual or critical elucidation provided for these discarded chapters. A third volume, *Later Manuscripts*, edited by Janet Todd and Linda Bree (2008), contains all the extant Austen manuscripts apart from the juvenilia and the fragment of *Persuasion*. Here the editorial method changes again, in favour of 'discreetly edited' 'reading' versions; transcriptions are consigned to appendices. Only two of the manuscripts represented in the volume are transcribed: *The Watsons* and *Sanditon*. Unlike Chapman's or Sabor's modified transcriptions, these are diplomatic transcriptions; but their relegated status, as appendices, shifts focus to the 'reading' versions, 'edited to reflect basic publishing conventions of the early nineteenth century' (2008: xvi).[1]

We might speculate why editors of Austen manuscripts have chosen diplomatic transcription so rarely and why they apply its principles so inconsistently. It is not because the partial alternative of photo-facsimile reproduction has been preferred. In both these major editions, facsimile reproduction is purely illustrative, an embellishment and not an integral critical tool. Chapman's choice is historically conditioned and needs to be seen in terms of the editorial ideals of the early twentieth century, with their rejection of the fragmentary or unformed: the processes of composition as distinct from the product. For him and in Austen's case most particularly, tactfully tidied transcription clearly seemed allowable if it brokered a relationship between author and reader consistent with the expectations raised by the finished and published novels: Chapman was embarrassed by the experimental apprenticeship writings and by the mess and struggle on display in the maturer drafts. The Cambridge editors' inconsistencies in dealing with the range of textual challenges posed by the documentary forms can perhaps be put down to a greater commitment to commentary and contextual annotation, and an uncertainty over the targeted readership for their edition. Chapman early in the twentieth century and Sabor, Todd, Blank and Bree at the

---

1 Todd and Bree do not say so, but they appear to find justification in Chapman's treatment, 80 years earlier, of the *Sanditon* fragment (see Chapman, 1925, unpaginated 'Preface': 'Some explanation may be thought necessary of the way in which the fragment is printed. It approximates to the manner of 1817 …')

start of the twenty-first century can be excused by the absence of a well-defined Anglo-American editorial theory and practice for dealing with manuscript fiction, and especially with working drafts, as opposed to poetry; and all can take as partial defence the difficulties inherent in the print medium.

3.4 Constraints of Digital Technologies and How They Are Different from the Constraints of Paper

When designing a digital edition (that is, an edition with digital output), scholars must recognize that while the different medium overcomes some of the constraints of the printed page, it nevertheless introduces new constraints and limitations, which in turn affect our new perception of the object in complex and subtle ways. As Shillingsburg (2006: 146) notes: 'Meanings are generated by readers who have learned to deal with symbols and formats. Change the symbol and the meaning changes; change the format and the implications are changed; change the contexts of interactions with texts and the importance and significance of the text changes.' One of the biggest advantages of a digital edition is that the web has fewer space restrictions than a printed book: a text can be presented in different views (diplomatic, semi-diplomatic, reading, interlineated, genetic, and so on); a critical apparatus can be more capacious; more ancillary or explanatory materials can be added. Above all, the publication of large quantities of facsimile images becomes more affordable than ever before. A digital edition can indeed include those many features and components described by Shillingsburg as transforming it into a 'knowledge site' (2006: 101–2).

In comparison to the printed page, the virtual space has a more flexible layout and, when it comes to diplomatic editions, can represent easily more features than in print. One consequence of this is the rise of a new publication format, the so-called 'ultra diplomatic transcription', which integrates transcription and facsimile.[2] Other interesting examples of the kind of flexibility offered by the web can be found in website projects for the Codex Sinaiticus and the Vincent Van Gogh Letters:[3] in both, the main page is structured as boxes containing images, transcriptions (in different formats), annotations, translations, and so on; these in combination offer the user a completely different reading and studying experience.

But digital environments have their constraints too, the most important being that people do not read easily from the screen. It has been demonstrated that reading a lengthy and complex text requires much more effort from a computer screen than

---

2   Ultra diplomatic transcriptions are used by the HyperNietsche Project, an example of which is to be found in Gabler (2007: 205). A similar approach can be found in Elsshot (2007).

3   See respectively <http://www.codexsinaiticus.org/> and <http://vangoghletters.org/vg/> (accessed 13 July 2010).

from paper. The introductory paragraph of *Writing for the Web*, a tutorial by Jacob Nielsen et al., declares:

> Writing for the Web is very **different from writing for print**:
>
> * 79% of users **scan the page** instead of reading word-for-word
> * Reading from computer screens is 25% slower than from paper
> * Web content should have **50% of the word count** of its paper equivalent[4]

To face such limitations, a set of rules has been envisaged for so-called 'web-writing'. These rules advise writing short sentences, breaking the text into lists and tables wherever possible, avoiding italics and favouring bold-faced words. The above quotation exemplifies these principles in an iconic way.

This is no trivial constraint, especially when the website may have as its main goal an edition of a long text, the product of sophisticated pre-electronic literacy, and when it would falsify that text to break it or change the fount face at pleasure. If one listens to the 'usability gurus',[5] one might conclude that the web is not the right environment for a scholarly edition at all. On the other side, it is very difficult to discard the many advantages offered by the digital medium. One might further counter that digital editions are not reading devices at all but objects to be used (searched, browsed, skimmed, and so on). We will return to this point shortly. Books and digital resources also differ in the sequence in which one reads/uses them. A book has a default access order; a website does not. As Malte Rehbein (2010: 65) remarks:

> In a printed text, there is a cover, clearly indicating its beginning and its end, there is a predetermined sequence of pages, usually numbered, indices at a certain position in the book and a table of contents. The very nature of the book draws the reader's attention and directs him accurately. ... The electronic edition usually has a starting 'page', but does not have a clearly visible end; there is no closing page, no back cover. The user often does not know how much of the material he has already seen, how much of the data he has accessed.

While the quantity of information potentially available to web users is much greater than can be squeezed between covers, one never knows which part of a

---

4 Nielsen, Schemenaur and Fox, *Writing for the Web*. Bold face as in the original. At present (13 July 2010) the resource is no longer available from the web (with the exception of web archives like we.archive.org where a copy of the tutorial is still available from <http://web.archive.org/web/20080530074621/http://www.sun.com/980713/webwriting/>(accessed 13 July 2010)). It also remains available through quotation; see, for instance, Whithaus (2005: 5).

5 See note 4 above, the reference to Nielsen et al.; see also J. Nielsen, *How Users Read on the Web*, 1 October 1997, Web resource: http://www.useit.com/alertbox/9710a.html [accessed: 23-01-2012].

website a user will choose to read/use. The design must therefore account for different interests and types of usage, with the risk of excluding the traditional reader looking for a full, organized product to be read 'from cover to cover'.

Last but not least, while it is more or less always possible to predict how a printed text will look in the hands of the reader,[6] it is not easy when it comes to websites. Any web designer knows that, in spite of declarations from software developers that they all follow the same web standards, it is a painful and almost prohibitive task to make the website look more or less the same on all internet browsers. This is so even before one considers the release of new versions of browsers, an event that happens at an alarmingly fast rate and which may change completely the way the text is displayed. Such changes may generate new bugs and problems in pre-existing websites, and the resources to fix those problems may or may not be available at any particular moment. Further, with the diffusion of such small portable devices as smart-phones, netbooks and e-readers, users can face very different experiences in accessing the digital resource, sometimes with the risk of misunderstanding it entirely. For example, a transcription may have been designed only to be read alongside an image, but many portable devices are unable to display both image and text on the screen at a readable size. So far, print culture has produced objects that are stable from many points of view: they have in-built durability; they cannot be changed overnight;[7] and they look the same in the hands of different readers in different countries and at different times. By contrast, digital culture still has a long way to go in all these respects: longevity, reliability and stability are still distant goals.

3.5 The Role of Facsimiles

Despite such caveats, the incorporation of digital images, whether of printed books or manuscripts, is currently considered among the major benefits of electronic editions. The high standard of imaging technologies makes the case for the usefulness and value of visual evidence as a form of authentication and even as a check on the mediating role of the editor; in addition, the presence of the image serves a dominant view of editing that emphasizes the importance of documentary forms (what Jerome McGann has called 'bibliographic codes') to the meaning of texts. Though in Anglo-American company, this editorial case is more often made in the interests of the social text and the meaningful extra-authorial processes that attend the construction of the book, the documentary evidence of

---

6   A century (if not more) of scholarship in analytic bibliography has taught us that this affirmation is not always true, but we ask the reader to concede our simplification for the sake of argument.

7   While the possibility of easily updating a website can be considered one of the big advantages of digital publication, it also potentially jeopardizes its status as a stable scholarly resource to be quoted and referenced.

original manuscripts serves an equally valid view of text as the sum of the creative processes of the individual author. This is especially so where, as with Austen's manuscripts, their texts were not submitted to the socializing processes of print until a hundred years after her death.

For the present edition, the Austen manuscripts have been digitally photographed to the highest possible standard with the most advanced equipment currently available.[8] Yet, at the risk of stating the obvious, even the most exact reproduction cannot duplicate all the features and properties of its original. In the case of a digital image of a manuscript, the medium itself is lost: we have the visual impression of paper and ink but not the physical materials of the original. In the Austen digital edition, we have tried to remain mindful of this distinction while profiting from its paradoxical potential. For example, great care has been taken to limit certain kinds of enhancement (cropping, scale distortion, erasure of blemishes, flattening, and so on) all too frequent (and all too ignored) in the substitution of digital facsimile for original. At the same time, other enhancements and distortions are positively embraced: notably the capacity to magnify difficult words or passages and through distortion to focus upon a manuscript's graphic values; even aspects of the materiality of the manuscripts (details of watermarks in paper) can be more readily amenable to examination in virtual form. But, as Diana Kichuk has noted, the mounting availability and apparent superiority of facsimile reproduction in the digital medium risks seducing expert and inexpert user alike into believing that the medium provides a precise equivalent of the original. She concludes that 'successful remediation [the substitution of image for original] depends on the witting and unwitting complicity of the viewer' (2007: 297). It is an unexpected and as yet underestimated fact that a digital edition incorporating facsimile images makes greater interpretative demands on its compilers and users: fidelity to an original can no longer be taken for granted but must always be under critical scrutiny.

The suggestion that photo-facsimiles raise the critical stakes acknowledges the trend in recent editorial thinking to extol what Randall McLeod has called the 'un-editing' potential of such images. Writing of the photographic reproduction

---

8   The same equipment and photographer (on loan to us from the Digital Image Archive of Medieval Music) were also used by the Israeli Antiquities Authority during 2008 for the digitization of some of the Dead Sea Scrolls. Scanning of the Austen materials was done in 24 bit colour. In the early stages of the project, a Phase One PowerPhase scanning back was used, capturing images at 144 million pixels and yielding images of up to 350 Mb. With this equipment, each manuscript image took up to two minutes to capture. More recently, Phase One developed a single shot camera which captures up to 40 million pixels, yielding images of approximately 44 Mb. This became our camera of choice, being faster and more portable, yet sacrificing nothing in terms of quality, since most of our materials are relatively small in size. Many of the holding libraries could not take images at the high standards we have established, which is why we used our own photographer and equipment.

of the earliest print editions of Shakespeare's plays, McLeod (1981–82: 37) observes:

> to witness the vast difference between the evidence of text conveyed by photofacsimiles and what stands revealed as editorial rumors and irrelevant improvements of it, is immediately to unedit Shakespeare.
>
> Thus the camera anchors our perception of Shakespeare's text in historical evidence untrammeled with ideal projections of its meaning.

And a few lines later he sums up: 'Our editorial tradition has normalized text; facsimiles function rather to abnormalize readers.' There is much to take issue with in this fashionable swipe at the whole discipline of editing: from the suspicion cast on the expert reader (the editor) to the confidence placed in the 'abnormalized' common reader. But we would agree that the provision of facsimile evidence changes the model in fundamental ways. Not least, now that the document itself has been raised in status, its presence as visual description (note: not as the real thing) within the edition appears to argue against certain kinds of re-interpretative licence traditional and indeed necessary among print editions. Now the document is more than a vehicle for text, and, though strictly non-reproducible,[9] it is nevertheless meaningfully indivisible, through that visual description, from its text. If the argument can be made for facsimile editions of early printed works, it seems even more compelling when applied to the unique manuscript.

In a non-facsimile printed scholarly edition, the diplomatic transcription normally stands in for the manuscript, ensuring that it is not the manuscript that provides authority for the edition but the implied precision of the editor's translation. By contrast, in the image-based digital edition, the editor is continually on trial, open to account and correction. With the image always available for close inspection, some hard decisions become harder: is the expectation greater or smaller that a transcription will resemble what it transcribes? Which expressive equivalents (that is, which matchings of part to part) are necessary or achievable? And, with the image of the manuscript available, do any expressive equivalents become redundant? Presumably a totally exact match would be pointless since the element of interpretation would be reduced to nil: an erasure would remain an erasure; a blotted passage would stay blotted; shifts in scriptural style and the expressive qualities of letter shapes and relative sizes would be reproduced exactly. On the other hand, a degree of interpretative play would never be closed off because never engaged: being largely uninterpreted, the transcription would remain almost as open to interpretation as the original – and, to that extent, transcription would be useless.

Print provides fewer choices than handwriting. If it is undoubtedly the case that facsimile images should not be accepted as the original, the print transcription of the written word is subject to far greater standards of conformity, improvement

---

9   Cf. Joseph Dane's sharp rejoinder to the advocates of social text editing, 'A "book" is a material object ... by its very nature non-reproducible' (1995: 32).

and distortion. As Walter Ong memorably put it, 'print is comfortable only with finality': 'Print is curiously intolerant of physical incompleteness. It can convey the impression, unintentionally and subtly, but very really, that the material the text deals with is similarly complete or self-consistent' (Ong, 1982: 132–3). Handwriting happily accommodates within the range of its communication the quirks and inconsistencies of individual manner, taste and personality; print largely confines such quirks to the semantics of style. In print, where the transcription both substitutes for and interprets the written original, we largely take on trust the reliability of that substitution. We may, if availability permits, check the one against the other, but not continually. In the digital facsimile edition, image and transcription can have a continuous relationship. Available side by side, as in the Austen edition, the one patrols or parodies the other. And with the original always open before us, we trust the transcription less – less often and for fewer purposes. Why take on trust what we can see (and correct) for ourselves? At the same time, we are constrained by the superabundance of visual signals (transcription *and* original) to level their relationship and to look for excessive visual identity. This may be particularly so when it comes to the representation of the look of the manuscript page. A print transcription, we take it, will be faithful to the linguistic elements of the text – its words and punctuation. But to shapes, to spatial relations, to the graphic 'noise' of dashes of varying length and sub-semiotic marks? Ironically, the availability of facsimile images can lead to an intensified demand for fidelity of transcription.[10]

Facsimile editions, then, may be a major benefit of digital editing but it would be foolish to assume that they do not also issue new critical challenges by appearing to fulfil certain expectations. In doing so, they revise our understanding of the purposes of transcription at a fundamental level. We should accordingly be wary of suggesting that the 'un-editing' initiated by the facsimile does not require an even closer (and more suspicious) critical engagement with the textual object. The sustained availability of facsimile images of necessity renders the relationship between text and document meaningful in more ways than the purely aesthetic: the Austen digital edition is an edition of a series of objects as well as of their texts. This, more than any function of the digital, sets it apart from previous Austen manuscript editions, changing its relationship to the materials.

4.1 Modelling the Jane Austen's Fiction Manuscripts Digital Edition

Malte Rehbein (2010: 65) has successfully described the process of modelling a digital edition as the collaboration between a 'classical scholar' and a 'digital humanist'. In his article, Rehbein outlines the discussions which led to the modelling of the digital edition of the correspondence of James Barry, edited by Tim McLoughlin. This process can be summarized emblematically in the encoding

---

10   This seems to be implied in the fascinating account of the procedure for making diplomatic transcriptions of Emily Dickinson's fragments given by Werner (2007: 35–7).

of an uncertain date. Here the 'common editorial practice' of putting the uncertain date in square brackets, an example of 'output-driven editing', is compared with the text encoding alternative ('input- and user-driven editing'). Rehbein argues for the superiority of the latter because it describes the editorial principles rather than the output. Despite Rehbein's convincing argument, McLoughlin (2010: 46) answers by lamenting the verbosity of the TEI encoding and the increased workload it brings, noting that his 'experience has been that an editor might need an additional 30% or more time for the project'. This leaves open the question whether or not such frustrations were compensated by the value of the end product.

The modelling of the digital edition of the Austen manuscripts has been a similarly dialectic process, and the use of output-driven approaches versus functional markup was recursively debated, but in our case those discussions have led to some different results from those described by Rehbein. Output-driven considerations have sometimes won the field, helped by the fact that one of the purposes of the edition was to transcribe and present the text with a layout as close as possible to the original. This meant that the transcribed text had to look good on the screen while reproducing as faithfully as possible the author's way of working. The encoding tried to pursue this task of visual rendition, mediating it with the need to generalize phenomena from a semantic point of view, as described in the TEI principles of best practice. The choices we made for the encoding of Austen's fictional manuscripts are summarized in Table 12.1, grouped by categories of editorial interest.

Table 12.1   Features encoded in the transcription of the Austen's manuscripts

Feature categories	Encoding choices
Document features	• manuscript description • manuscript structure • patches
Topography	• layout • indentation • interlinear insertions • approximate positioning of interlinear insertions
Handwriting	• long 's' • length of dashes
Orthography	• peculiar spellings
Reading facilitators/ segmentators	• capitalization • line-break markers • expansion of abbreviations
Genetic	• revisions
Textuality	• novels, drama, verses
Decoration	• drawings

Encoding with such a complex model has been extremely challenging and not entirely successful (see sections 4.2 and 4.3 below). While it has revealed the implicit limits of an output-driven way of thinking, it has also highlighted the immaturity of web publication when compared to the stability of print. Figure 12.2 shows the encoding of a particularly tormented line in *The Watsons* (Figure 12.1) which presents three levels of interlinear insertions.

Figure 12.1   The Watsons, 10 (p.6), Bodleian Library, University of Oxford

```
among them as po<g ref="#ls"/>sible, Emma was <au:revision>
    <del rend="overstrike">eager<g ref="#c_o"/> to<lb xml:id="qmwats-del106"/>take <choice>
        <abbr>Eliz:'s</abbr>
        <expan>Elizabeth's</expan>
    </choice> usual place with<g ref="#c_o"/> in their <w rend="capital">Father's</w> r<g
        ref="#c_o"/>oom,</del>
<add place="superlinear" type="rewriting" n="1" rend="-15 gl">delighted with the alternative
    of <au:revision>
        <add place="superlinear" n="2" rend="-12 gl">
            <del rend="overstrike">glad to</del>
        </add>
        <add place="superlinear" n="3" rend="-10 gl">
            <del rend="overstrike"> each <choice>
                <abbr>eveng</abbr>
                <expan>evening</expan>
            </choice>
            </del>
        </add>
    </au:revision></add>
</au:revision>
```

Figure 12.2   Encoding sample

Encoding to reproduce the look of Austen's page, on the one hand, and trying to describe the stages of the authoring process, on the other, has shown the limits of the TEI *Guidelines*. This experience has inspired the creation of a working group within the TEI Special Interest Group on Manuscripts, with the precise goal of enhancing the TEI in currently defective areas: namely, representing genetic process, complex page layout and compositional phenomena, and documentary view.[11] The international working group has proposed new modules and the enhancement of existing ones, suggesting a dozen new elements which should allow users to encode their source manuscripts from three perspectives: documentary (what is on the page), process (how the page was progressively filled with words and signs) and textual (what those signs on the page actually mean. We consider this contribution to the international community to be an important outcome of the Austen digital edition, made possible by the discussions and critical thinking generated by its recursive modelling. The lengthy process can perhaps be listed under the 'meaningful surprises' of modelling mentioned

---

11   See Manuscripts SIG: Documents and Genetic Criticism TEI Style. Since December 2011 the proposal has been fully integrated into the TEI.

by McCarty; but also, and more optimistically, under a new category: 'fruits of collaboration'.

4.2 Stratification, Evolution, Time: An Ongoing Problem of Representation

The tension between the competing fields of visual and semantic representation is especially evident in encoding genetic evolution. Surprisingly, given the huge industry that burgeoned around Austen during the twentieth century, critics have speculated very little about her working methods as a writer. Hers was a highly repetitive, tightly revised art; a matter of tracing and retracing the same ground. We know from the characteristic materials of the famous six novels that she revisited the same ideas, themes and subjects from one novel to the next, examining them from different critical angles. Yet Austen's print reputation as a polished stylist and a cool social appraiser has obscured both the congested ground of her imagination and the messiness of the surviving manuscript pages, with their narrative of internal change. One of the irresistible opportunities suggested by digitization is the possibility of encoding and displaying in some form the layering and evolution of Austen's writing process: her first, second and even third attempts to settle a word, phrase or passage. More broadly, a genetic approach holds out the possibility of a new understanding of Austen's imagination.

The manuscripts themselves provide examples of several kinds of genetic development or reworking over time. These range from immediate rethinking of a passage, where the pattern of erasures and substitutions suggests speed, instinct and economy – a spontaneous redrafting in which first and second or final thoughts are the work of a single session – to changes that are impossible to date: whether to a single session or later period of revision. Elsewhere, we find Austen using patches of paper cut carefully to size and pinned or pasted in place to hide and replace a heavily erased or reworked passage or to provide a substantial insertion to extend a passage. In such instances of sustained reworking, the expansion or revision of the linguistic text is signalled by the extreme refashioning of the physical structure of the document. Other examples include the return after several years to update a detail at a particular point in a manuscript, suggesting a concern to refresh the currency of the story long after it appears to be finished, and the use of a notebook over a considerable period of time to collect materials from different stages of creative development.

One of the challenges we set for the Austen digital edition was to distinguish and encode for systematic analysis the different processes of revision, and to represent their appearance on the space of the screen. Until you leave behind the protocols of print representation, however, any contradiction between these two objectives is easily overlooked. In print and on the space of the static page, changes in fount or colour conventionally represent different stages in the process of writing; through encoding, a logic other than that of the page comes into play, allowing the process and the appearance of revision to be registered in time as well as in space. Logically, as we know, a correction follows in time the word, phrase or passage which it replaces, but the space of the document may contradict temporal logic. Such contradiction is both a function of the limited dimensions of paper and a regular characteristic of the dynamics of working manuscripts, where rewriting (revisions, expansions, substitutions and erasures of all kinds) transgresses the orderly zones of finished copy, spilling over into margins, interlinear spaces and supplementary leaves. For example, a revision, representing a second or third thought, may by one logic (of intention and time) be accurately encoded as following a deleted word, and by another logic (of visual appearance and the page) may in fact be set down in a space before the deleted word; a patch containing a passage of sustained rewriting may lie precisely across an earlier version, obscuring its existence, though parts or all of the earlier passage may remain in play; a sublinear insertion may be written, revised and finally replaced by a third element constituted from parts of an earlier form and parts of the rejected revised form, all squeezed into a space above and before the earlier revision. How do we encode for analysis the processes of rewriting in their correct order while also preserving the visual link between the output transcription and the digital image of the manuscript passage?

4.3 Compromises

Encoding the transcriptions has been a lengthy and difficult process, absorbing the greatest part of the project's three years. It was clear from the beginning that the initial requirement of encoding 'everything' to show the transcribed text in type-facsimile would not be an easy task. The manuscript page is in fact a highly flexible environment, in spite of being physically and spatially limited. The dimensions of the script change continuously when writing, with some lines accommodating more glyphs than others and some pages more lines than others; interlinear insertions can be very dense without affecting the spacing of the main lines of writing, and margins can be used in unpredictable and imaginative ways. By contrast with such versatility and whatever the final output, when the transcription is prepared using any mechanical device, the editor has to accommodate the transcribed text in a more standardized environment; this holds especially for a computer, but even, to a certain extent, for a typewriter or typesetter. As a result, a certain distance between the physical object and the transcribed object is inevitable. In fact, no transcription, however accurate, will ever be able to represent the source document entirely. Why, then, did we bother to attempt a type-facsimile edition? Many scholars have in fact objected to the usefulness of such an aim. Michael Hunter (2007: 75), for example, does not hide his impatience with type-facsimile editions in his review of Brian Southam's edition of the Austenian transcription, *Sir Charles Grandison*:

For, painstaking as this is, it fails to replicate all features of the original – not only different handwritings and letter forms, but also ink blots, different methods of striking through words, or exact details of layout, for which only a pictorial facsimile suffices. The chief thing which a type-facsimile *can* do is to distinguish words in pen or pencil, or in different hands, but even this might be better achieved by a commentary on a photographic or digital reproduction.

On the contrary, only by attempting to transcribe and reproduce as much as we can of the manuscript are we able to investigate and understand the authorial process, and so gain a deeper and more complete insight into Austen's way of working and ultimately into the text itself. This understanding (of text as process rather than product) is best shared with users by means of a type-facsimile edition, because such an edition is both interpretation or commentary on the thing reproduced and subject to the disciplinary frame of the thing itself.

The placing of interlinear insertions has been particularly problematic. From a semantic point of view, we needed to insert interlinear additions where they belong in the flow of the text, according to our opinion or guided by the author's conventions. On the other hand, we also wanted every insertion to be displayed as closely as possible to the position where Austen put it. For example, in Figure 12.2 both the semantics and the author's caret require that the interlinear insertion 'delighted with the alternative ...' be *transcribed* immediately after the deleted 'eager', but in order to reproduce the page layout it must be *displayed* on top of the last part of 'possible', two words earlier. Another difficulty has been the representation of concepts such as 'align to the right', or 'align to the centre'. Because such concepts can only be understood relative to a given physical space, once the space changes or migrates to a different medium, the concepts themselves will need to be revised. For instance, a segment which is 'align to the right' of the manuscript page will need to be displayed seven centimetres to the right of the left margin for some manuscript pages, and nine for others, but never aligned to the right of the screen. In this and in the former case, the end result (that is, the website) has not always been satisfactory. Nevertheless we believe that what we have achieved represents a reasonable compromise, especially as the transcribed text is always presented alongside the facsimile. The type-facsimile edition is indeed not the same as the manuscript: it is neither a substitute for it nor a surrogate, but rather a visual representation of functions and a set of editorial interpretations of what is on the manuscript page.

5. Digital Publishing: A User's Perspective

5.1 Users vs Readers

As Tim McLoughlin (2010: 40) points out, in the electronic medium we become users who no longer read texts but 'browse', 'search' and 'navigate' digital 'objects'. In reply, Rehbein (2010: 63–4) insists that searching and browsing are not exclusive to digital devices, but that they characterize our use of certain kinds of printed books; he gives the example of dictionaries. This is certainly true, but it is hard to disagree that digital objects seem more suited to information seeking than to continuous reading: the web 'usability gurus' unanimously agree on that,[12] as do many scholars. Indeed the regularly declared unsuitability of digital texts for continuous reading has been considered the main reason for hybrid (print and digital) publication of editions. Hans Walter Gabler (2006: 344) writes: '… the electronic medium is not a particularly comfortable site for sustained sequential reading. This might suggest the need for a double provision when an edition goes electronic.' Ciula and Lopez (2009: 133) seem to be of the same opinion, describing the dual output of the Henry III Fine Rolls Project in the following terms: 'For a scholar interested in the historical record, the reading of the Fine Rolls edition and the seeking of information related to it is a comprehensive process that does not stop when the book is closed or the browser is shut.' Here 'reading' appears to refer to the book, and 'seeking of information' to the browser. However, despite this body of opinion, very few studies have been undertaken to test whether our intuition about the use of digital and analogue objects is actually supported by evidence. This is one of the purposes of the INKE (Implementing New Knowledge Environments) project,[13] which is entirely devoted to the analysis of the experience of reading analogue and digital outputs in order to understand how we read/use texts in different media and whether there is some technique we can apply to enhance the reading experience on the web.

Even if it is our conviction that a website does not offer the best environment for continuous sequential reading, in designing the Austen digital edition we have tried to accommodate both users and, to some extent, readers. The choice consciously to privilege users is more or less forced by the nature of the texts we have transcribed. Draft manuscripts, especially when presented as type-facsimile and facsimile editions, do not allow for continuous reading: the countless paradigmatic variations force the reader to stop every few words and re-read the same passage over and over again in order to accommodate the different versions of the text proposed by the author. In such instances, the text offered cannot but be a scholarly object rather than a text sought out for the pleasure of reading. We are therefore unapologetic in saying that the website contains objects to be used.

---

12   See note 4 above, the reference to Nielsen et al.; see also Nielsen 2007.

13   A major research project supported by the Social Sciences and Humanities Research Council of Canada (SSHRC); see <http://www.inke.ca/> (accessed 13 July 2010). The project is an evolution of the HCI-Book (Human-Computer Interface and the Electronic Book) project; see <http://www.hci-book.org/cluster/index.php> (accessed 13 July 2010). See also the contribution of Siemens et al. in this volume.

5.2 New Users/Old Users

Where they exist in any quantity, authors' manuscripts have regularly posed a challenge to the ordered print lives of texts, altering our angle of vision and questioning our sense of what constitutes a literary work. Whether we view this anterior life before print as the mess from which print rescues text or as opening a perspective onto its deeper identity, manuscripts exert a fascination for scholars and non-specialists alike. At the same time, conservation issues and the status of manuscripts as unique documents make the case for their digitization compelling. The textual content of a manuscript may or may not be significantly different from that of a printed book, but restrictions on the use of the actual document mark a huge distinction that intrudes on the value of that content in a way that happens more rarely in print. Even without the challenges of fully encoded representations of their texts, the virtual reunification of Austen's scattered originals offers clear institutional and wider cultural advantages in the shape of accessible surrogates. Almost everyone, scholar and amateur enthusiast alike, who views these images will be a new user, to whom images of the actual documents are completely fresh and their reconnection inconceivable without digital technology.

References

Buzzetti, D., 'Digital Editions and Text Processing', in M. Deegan and K. Sutherland (eds), *Text Editing, Print and the Digital World* (Aldershot: Ashgate, 2009): 45–61.

Chapman, R.W. (ed.), *Jane Austen, Fragment of a Novel* (Oxford: Clarendon Press, 1925).

Ciula, A. and T. Lopez, 'Reflecting on a Dual Publication: Henry III Fine Rolls Print and Web', *Literary and Linguistic Computing* 24.2 (2009): 129–41.

Codex Sinaiticus, available at: <http://www.codexsinaiticus.org/> (accessed 13 July 2010).

Dahlström, M., 'The Compleat Edition', in M. Deegan and K. Sutherland (eds), *Text Editing, Print and the Digital World* (Aldershot: Ashgate, 2009): 27–44.

Dane, J., '"Ideal Copy" versus "Ideal Texts": The Application of Bibliographical Description to Facsimiles', *Papers of the Bibliographical Society of Canada* 33 (1995): 31–50.

Elsshot, W., *Achter de Schermen*, ed. Peter de Bruijn, Vincent Neyt and Dirk Van Hulle (Antwerp: Center for Manuscript Genetics, Huygens Instituut, 2007).

Gabler, H.W., 'Moving a Print-Based Editorial Project into Electronic Form', in L. Burnard, K. O'Brien O'Keffe and J. Unsworth (eds), *Electronic Textual Editing* (New York: Modern Language Association of America, 2006): 339–45.

Gabler, H.W., 'The Primacy of the Document in Editing', *Ecdotica* 4 (2007), 197–207.

Hunter, M., *Editing Early Modern Texts: An Introduction to Principles and Practice* (New York: Palgrave Macmillan, 2007).

Jessop, M.,,. 'The Inhibition of Geographical Information in Digital Humanities Scholarship', *Literary and Linguistic Computing* 23.1 (2008a): 39–50.

Jessop, M., 'Digital Visualization as a Scholarly Activity', *Literary and Linguistic Computing* 23.3 (2008b): 281–93.

Kichuk, D., 'Metamorphosis: Remediation in *Early English Books Online (EEBO)*', *Literary and Linguistic Computing* 22 (2007): 291–303.

McCarty, W., *Humanities Computing* (Basingstoke: Palgrave Macmillan, 2005).

McLeod, Randall, 'Un "Editing" Shak-speare', *SubStance* 10 (1981–82): 26–55.

McLoughlin, T., 'Bridging the Gap', *Computerphilolgie* 10, ed. M. Rehbein and S. Ryder (2010): 35–54, available at: <http://computerphilologie.tu-darmstadt.de/jg08/mclough.pdf> (accessed 13 June 2010).

Manuscripts SIG: Documents and Genetic Criticism TEI Style, web resource available at: <http://www.tei-c.org/SIG/Manuscripts/genetic.html> (accessed 13 July 2010).

Nielsen, J., P.J. Schemenaur and J. Fox, *Writing for the Web*, web resource available at: <http://www.sun.com/980713/webwriting/index.html> (accessed 06 April 2010).

O'Donnell, D.P., 'Resisting the Tyranny of the Screen, or, Must a Digital Edition Be Electronic', *The Heroic Age* 11 (2008), available at: <http://www.mun.ca/mst/heroicage/issues/11/em.php> (accessed 13 June 2010).

Ong, Walter J., *Orality and Literacy: The Technologizing of the Word* (London and New York: Routledge, 1982).

Rehbein, M., 'The Transition from Classical to Digital Thinking: Reflections on Tim McLoughlin, James Barry and Collaborative Work', *Computerphilolgie* 10 , ed. M. Rehbein and S. Ryder (2010): 55–67, available at: <http://computerphilologie.tu-darmstadt.de/jg08/rehbein.pdf> (accessed 13 June 2010).

Sabor, P. (ed.), *The Juvenilia*, The Cambridge Edition of the Works of Jane Austen (Cambridge: Cambridge University Press, 2006).

Shillingsburg, P.L., *From Gutenberg to Google* (Cambridge: Cambridge University Press, 2006).

Siemens, L., '"It's a Team if You Use 'Reply All'": An Exploration of Research Teams in Digital Humanities Environments', *Literary and Linguistic Computing* 24.2 (2009): 225–33.

Todd, J. and A. Blank (eds), *Persuasion*, The Cambridge Edition of the Works of Jane Austen (Cambridge: Cambridge University Press, 2006).

Todd, J. and L. Bree, *Later Manuscripts*, The Cambridge Edition of the Works of Jane Austen (Cambridge: Cambridge University Press, 2008).

Vincent Van Gogh Letters, available at: <http://vangoghletters.org/vg/> (accessed 13 July 2010).

Werner, Marta L., '"A Woe of Ecstasy": On the Electronic Editing of Emily Dickinson's Late Fragments', *The Emily Dickinson Journal* 16.2 (2007): 25–52.

Whithaus, C., *Teaching and Evaluating Writing in the Age of Computers and High-Stakes Testing* (Mahwah, NJ: Lawrence Erlbaum Associates, 2005).

Chapter 13

Being the Other: Interdisciplinary Work in Computational Science and the Humanities

Melissa Terras

> What is at stake when we encounter the knowledge of others, the reasoning of the other? ... Knowledge is itself a construct that requires the other ... Groups, institutions and communities are about engaging and living with others. Cooperation and communication ... presuppose recognising the other and learning how to take into account the perspective from where she proposes her psychological, social and historical truth.
>
> Jovchelovitch (2007): 109

Introduction

Research projects which require developments in both computing science and the humanities can undertake novel research that would otherwise prove impossible. Although not the most common of digital humanities projects,[1] interdisciplinary research and working practices can bridge computing or engineering science and more than one traditional aspect of humanities research. Individuals working in such interdisciplinary teams often find they are the 'Other' – working beyond a defined disciplinary cultural unit, with the need for the construction of roles and responsibilities that allow their skill sets to be admitted to a working team, rather than behaving, and treating each other, as if they come from foreign climes. This chapter discusses the role of disciplines when undertaking innovative cross-disciplinary research, and the resulting practical, theoretical, professional and personal issues that can come into play, which can affect the outcomes of advanced digital humanities projects.

Undertaking ambitious computational projects in the humanities and working in a cross-disciplinary environment is an exception from the lone scholar image traditionally associated with humanities research, even within the smallest of digital humanities projects:

---

1   It is the case that 'A central project of humanities computing is to help in the construction of a worldwide digital library of resources and tools' (McCarty, 2001: 173); however, there are outlier projects which do not work in the service area of digital libraries and digitised collections.

Given that the nature of research work involves computers and a variety of skills and expertise, Digital Humanities researchers are working collaboratively within their institutions and with others nationally and internationally to undertake research. This work typically involves the need to coordinate efforts between academics, undergraduate and graduate students, research assistants, computer programmers, libraries, and other individuals as well as the need to coordinate financial and other resources. (Siemens, 2009: 226)

The issue becomes even more complex when software development and the writing of new, bespoke computational algorithms becomes necessary (rather than just use of existing software for, say, digitisation and the creation of online resources):

Few research centres in Digital Humanities have the staff necessary for undertaking large application development projects, and even the ones that do quickly find that cross-departmental collaborations are needed to assemble the necessary expertise ... For most Digital Humanities practitioners, amassing a team of developers almost requires that the work be distributed across institutions and among a varied group of people. Any non-trivial application requires experts from a number of different development subspecialities, including such areas as interface design, relational database management, programming, software engineering, and server administration (to name only a few). (Ramsey, 2008: 20)

A humanist devoting their research time to working in the digital arena will have to face both logistical and personal issues of research across disciplines, which will affect both the project, their role in the project, their own personal skills development, and perhaps their own career. Yet there has been 'minimal research on the role of teams with academic communities, particularly within the Humanities' (Siemens, 2009: 225) and minimal consideration of how issues of interdisciplinarity – particularly the use of new and emergent technologies within a traditional academic discipline which can bring about explicit interdisciplinary confrontation of knowledge, skills, methodologies and tools – can affect the outcome of large-scale, multidisciplinary research projects.

The aim of this chapter is to sketch out the effects, benefits and problems of interdisciplinary research for the digital humanist, providing a brief overview of successful research projects to demonstrate the varied and complex nature of interactions between humanities scholars, engineers, computer scientists and other interested parties. Additionally, by summarising potential flashpoints which can arise in such projects (including disciplinary identity, developing and retaining skill sets, publication venues, administrative and management problems, and the production of successful research outcomes), this chapter aims to highlight areas which principal investigators and managers of projects which fall within the digital humanities domain should be prepared to deal with, should they arise within the course of their research.

Disciplines, Disciplinarity, Other

Being part of a discipline gives a scholar a sense of belonging, identity and kudos. But the idea of what constitutes a discipline is vague, and often depends upon the physical proof of a university department's existence:

> [A Discipline] can be enacted and negotiated in various ways: the international 'invisible' college; individuals exchanging preprints and reprints, conferences, workshops … But the most concrete and permanent enactment is the department; this is where a *discipline* becomes an institutional *subject*. The match between discipline and subject is always imperfect; this can cause practical difficulties when, for example, the (discipline-based) categories of research selectively do not fit the way the subject is ordered in a particular department. (Evans, 1995: 253–4)

Additionally, a 'discipline' is not an immutable topic of research or body of individuals: 'For nothing is more certain in the lives of the disciplines, whatever the field, whatever the institutional setting, than that they are forever changing' (Monroe, 2002: 2).

Disciplines gain status from becoming permanently established in the university subject roll-call. Academic culture can define a 'tribe' of scholars, whilst the span of disciplinary knowledge can be described as the 'territory' of the discipline (Becker and Trowler, 2001). 'Fields gradually develop distinctive methodological approaches, conceptual and theoretical frameworks and their own sets of internal schisms' (ibid: 14), and those of traditional humanities subjects are well entrenched into university culture. Although it is difficult to provide a definition of what a discipline may be, there are characteristics which are associated with disciplinary practice. Disciplines have identities and cultural attributes. They have measurable communities, which have public outputs, and:

> can be measured by the number and types of departments in universities, the change and increase in types of HE courses, the proliferation of disciplinary associations, the explosion in the number of journals and articles published, and the multiplication of recognised research topics and clusters. (Becker and Trowler, 2001: 14)

The community is defined and reinforced by being formally accepted as a university subject, but also instituting a publication record and means of output. More implicitly, disciplines have identifiable idols and jesters in their subject (Clark, 1980), heroes and mythology (Taylor, 1976) and sometimes artefacts specific to the subject domain (Becker and Trowler, 2001). Disciplines also become defined by 'the nurturance of myth, the identification of unifying symbols, the canonisation of exemplars, and the formation of guilds' (Dill, 1992).

The digital humanist, then, faces two challenges. There are those of forging an identity and gaining recognition for digital humanities as a discipline itself. What are the methodological approaches of a digital humanist (McCarty, 2001)? Is there a culture which binds the scholars together (Terras, 2006a)? Or is the digital humanities community merely that – a community of practice, which shares theories of meaning and power, collectivity and subjectivity (Wenger, 2002), but is little more than a group of academic scholars who share outlier methods, interests and skills, and apply them within their own individual, established, field of humanities discourse?

The second challenge, which presents both problems and opportunities for the digital humanist, arises for those scholars who choose to step outside the traditional humanistic fold and engage with experts in data management, manipulation, processing and visualisation, such as computer and engineering scientists: that is, behaving in a heightened example of interdisciplinary study (as opposed to, say, working across two individual humanities disciplines, which brings with it its own benefits and trials, but often shares fundamental methodological approaches). The concept of 'interdisciplinary' research, defined as 'of or pertaining to two or more disciplines or branches of learning; contributing to or benefiting from two or more disciplines' (OED, 1989), became popular towards the mid twentieth century, and has been increasing in popularity since.

> Unlike its nearest rivals – borderlands, interdepartmental, cooperative, coordinaged – 'interdisciplinary' has something to please everyone. Its base, *discipline*, is hoary and antiseptic; its prefix, *inter*, is hairy and friendly. Unlike fields, with their mud, cows, and corn, the Latinate *discipline* comes encased in stainless steel: it suggests something rigorous, aggressive, hazardous to master. *Inter* hints that knowledge is a warm, mutually developing, consultative thing ... (Frank, 1988: 100)

Although popular, the term is often ambiguous: 'It can suggest forging connections across the different disciplines; but it can also mean establishing a kind of undisciplined space in the interstices between disciplines, or even attempting to transcend disciplinary boundaries altogether' (Moran, 2002: 15). The traditions, cliques, publishing quirks, heroes, artefacts and in-jokes that combine to make a discipline are not easily and quickly learnt or understood. These differences are particularly pronounced when attempting to cross the divide of the 'two cultures' – the scientific and the humanistic, which were mapped by C.P. Snow long ago (Snow, 1959; see Collini, 1993, for the implications and afterlife of Snow's characterisation of the split between the arts and sciences). Those willing to work in such exceptionally interdisciplinary environments need to be aware of the logistical, practical, theoretical and methodological issues that can arise when becoming the 'Other' (Fabian, 1983): the different scholar in the team, without such pre-learned disciplinary strategies. Interdisciplinary projects need to engage with the 'alterity' of such team dynamics: the need to exchange one's own perspective for those who have vastly different learnt behaviour (which can often be implicit) (Nealon, 1998). There are undoubted difficulties that arise in cross-disciplinary research teams, but also benefits from cross-pollination of knowledge, processes and research strategies. What are the benefits of straddling the disciplinary divide, and what does this mean, both practically and theoretically, for the digital humanist?

It is useful here to provide an example of two interdisciplinary digital humanities projects, to show both the scope and reach of the research, and the scope and reach of the project team necessarily employed to successfully undertake such complex research. The author's personal experience on these and other projects is then used to highlight the logistical and personal issues which can face those undertaking interdisciplinary research as a digital humanist.

eSAD: eScience and Ancient Documents[2]

The analysis and understanding of ancient manuscripts and texts via specifically developed technological tools can aid both the classicist and the computer scientist, in the development of novel techniques which are applicable elsewhere. A demonstrative case is recent work done on building an intelligent image processing and artificial intelligence-based system to aid in the reading of the Roman stylus texts from Vindolanda (Terras, 2006b). This joint project between the Centre for the Study of Ancient Documents (CSAD)[3] and the Department of Engineering Science[4] at the University of Oxford between 1998 and 2002, funded by the UK's Engineering and Physical Science Research Council (EPSRC), resulted in a system which both aided the scholar in reading the Vindolanda texts (Terras and Robertson, 2005; Terras, 2006b) and developed innovative image processing algorithms (Molton et al., 2003; Schenk and Brady, 2003; Brady et al., 2005) which are proving useful in a range of applications, including medical imaging analysis.

Members of the original project team have since procured funding to carry on the research under the AHRC-EPSRC-JISC Arts and Humanities e-Science Initiative Programme, from September 2008 until September 2011. The project, now based between the Oxford e-Research Centre,[5] CSAD and UCL's Department of Information Studies,[6] is creating tools which can aid the reading of damaged texts like the stylus tablets from Vindolanda.[7] Furthermore, the project will explore how an interpretation support system (ISS) can be used in the day-to-day

---

2 <http://esad.classics.ox.ac.uk/>.
3 <http://www.csad.ox.ac.uk/>.
4 <http://www.eng.ox.ac.uk/>.
5 <www.oerc.ox.ac.uk>.
6 <http://www.infostudies.ucl.ac.uk/>.
7 <http://vindolanda.csad.ox.ac.uk/>.

reading of ancient documents and keep track of how the documents are interpreted and read. A combination of image processing tools (Tarte et al., 2008) and an ontology-based support system will be developed to facilitate experts by tracking their developing hypotheses (Roued-Olsen, 2010): this is based closely on work currently been undertaken by medical imaging researchers and physicians, and systems used to track and trace medical diagnosis and treatment of colorectal cancer (Austin et al., 2008). The eSAD system will suggest alternative readings (based on linguistic and palaeographic data) to experts as they undertake the complex reading process, aiming to speed the process of understanding a text. The project also aims to investigate how the resulting images, image tools and data sets can be shared between scholars.

Necessarily, the project involves classicists, engineering scientists and information scientists, with close input from those with specialities in humanities computing, medical imaging analysis, papyrology, user analysis and image processing. Various issues have emerged from this research, including how to model complex humanities research processes. Many of the approaches being considered, and appropriated, by the team are borrowed from colleagues at Oxford who are working within medical imaging and information engineering on the modelling of the diagnosis and treatment of disease, such as colorectal cancer. The resulting MDT (multidisciplinary team) tool they produced is 'designed to support complex group decision making under difficult conditions including time pressure, incomplete information, changing group members and ever expanding guidelines' (Austin et al., 2008: 1872). Ascertaining how – and if – the same approach could be applied to the reading of ancient texts has required liaising with classicists who may be the end users of the tool under development (no use-community can be guaranteed until there is a final product, although integrating users into the development phase is an important step to ensure that the tool developed matches users' needs). There was also a close relationship developed with engineers working on the logic of argumentation (Fox et al., 2010) to understand and begin to appropriate their methods. During the course of the project, other research questions became important, such as how to facilitate the annotation of digital surrogates of primary documentary evidence, and how to track and trace developing hypotheses which emerge from the analysis of digital images of texts (Tarte, forthcoming). To facilitate pursuit of the divergent research questions emerging from the project, various cross-disciplinary seminars were organised by the project to facilitate knowledge exchange between the different disciplinary experts involved.

eSAD is an ambitious project undertaking new research in both computing science and the humanities. As the project comes to an end, it has created new, advanced image processing algorithms to deal with the noisy, abraded images of ancient manuscripts (Tarte et al., 2008) and a prototype system which demonstrates the potential in using MDT type tools for the reading of ancient texts, which is superior to the current notation used by papyrologists to record uncertainty (Roued-Olsen, 2010). The system developed is only a prototype, though, and it remains to be seen how this tool can be further developed (and funded) to provide a system which becomes entrenched into established papyrological method. Although there are identifiable publication and algorithmic outputs from eSAD, the project also demonstrates a common problem with ambitious interdisciplinary research: research issues are often described and articulated in great detail, which can be very interesting, but it is rare that a successful computational tool is produced which is ready to be applied beyond the projects' specific narrow research limitations.

Multi-spectral Image Processing Methods for Separating Palimpsestic Text

On a smaller scale, a joint PhD studentship between the Department of Medical Physics and Bioengineering[8] and the Department of Information Studies[9] at UCL illustrates the cross-pollination that can occur between two very different disciplines. Running from 2010 to 2013, this project is applying benchmarkable methods developed within medical physics for the multi-spectral analysis of human tissue to images of documents, to investigate the development of computationally robust techniques to read palimpsest texts.

Multi-spectral imaging – where image data is captured at specific wavelengths across the electromagnetic spectrum – is a promising technology for research in the humanities, particularly when applied to damaged and abraded documents where ink is no longer visible to the naked eye. It has the potential to reveal many details about the physical composition of a document, including identifying the inks used within it (Senvaitienë et al., 2005), its present condition and information about its history (Tanner and Bearman, forthcoming). The process of capturing these images is relatively simple (although dependent on having access to specialist imaging hardware), and is already part of the repertoire of current digitisation efforts used in the cultural heritage spectrum. However, these techniques have so far been applied in an ad-hoc manner, depending on characteristics of individual documents. Medical physics, on the other hand, has a suite of computationally robust modelling procedures routinely used when undertaking multi-spectral imaging for diagnostic purposes. The aim of this current research is to develop protocols which will allow the multi-spectral imaging of documentary materials in a controlled, benchmarkable environment, developing a suite of tools which will allow those wishing to undertake such analysis to do so with confidence and ease (Giacometti, 2010).

The project is dependent on input from those in medical physics who routinely use advanced image processing methods for diagnostic analysis, as well as those working with ancient and medieval textual material, to provide a demonstrable test and use case for the computational approach that is being developed. The PhD student working on this material (Alejandro Giacometti) is jointly supervised by a medical physicist and a digital humanist, ensuring that the research concerns of

8   <http://www.ucl.ac.uk/medphys/>.

9   <http://www.infostudies.ucl.ac.uk/>.

both communities are addressed within the project. Interestingly, the issues already raised in undertaking imaging of manuscript material using medical imaging techniques require new developments of image processing techniques in medical physics – which then feeds back into the medical physics community. Areas for further research, which are being identified as the project develops, include how to communicate issues of benchmarking and robust image processing methods to those working on ancient texts, and how to make image processing algorithms as widely available as possible to facilitate uptake. The project is promising and demonstrates the strength in the research that can be undertaken when applying techniques from a very different discipline to a humanities research problem, although concrete research outcomes with any impact are yet to be produced.

The Digital Humanities as Interdiscipline

Of course, it is true that interdisciplinary scholarship exists in many areas of research, in the sciences, social sciences, arts and humanities. New interdisciplinary fields:

> not only fill existing gaps or take advantage of new possibilities but sometimes, quite overtly, seek to remedy, redress, respond to or in other ways compensate for lacks, problems, rigidities, blindspots, and incapacities inherent in existing or traditional disciplinary structures, omissions made evident by the unfilled needs at a specific historic moment. (Davidson, 2010: 209)

Why this issue is particularly pertinent to the digital humanist, though, is the fact that, to a certain extent, all digital humanities research is by definition operating on this scholarly divide between computational method and humanities investigation. This pivots around the technological and communication changes that occurred towards the close of the twentieth century: increasing access to and use of computational and internet technologies resulted in more scholars investigating how these could be appropriated to facilitate their own research. Early projects in digital humanities (see McCarty, 2005: 190–91) tended to investigate and adopt computational tools that had been developed by programmers and computer scientists, applying existing methods and tools described as 'core activities commonly assumed to belong to computer science' (Thaller, 2001) to distinct humanities problems, although 'the limits of computing define where humanities computing does its primary scholarly work' (McCarty, 2005: 188). Although adopting existing technology has yielded many insights, and created many digital resources for scholars, some of the most interesting and rewarding research in the digital humanities comes when new and novel techniques are developed in both the computational and humanities realm, to undertake research that would otherwise be unable to be carried out without the additional tools that computing can provide.

This approach was once relatively rare. (McCarty described such research as being a 'brilliant exception', highlighting the 'overall lack of success individual scholars have had in attracting the attention of computer science on their own terms' [2005: 192], and Davidson stresses the 'clear divide in digital humanities between the more technology-oriented scholars and others who are interested in the social and cultural implications of technology but have no interest or expertise in developing skills of their own' [2010: 213]). However, there is now a growing trend in undertaking cross-disciplinary research, fostered by funding from research councils keen to facilitate the adoption of scientific method by humanists. The most exciting and innovative projects provide difficult issues for computing science to solve, and real-world case scenarios that require redevelopment and rethinking of traditional computational approaches (although this can be viewed as one-way traffic: there is not the same impetus to bring methodology from the humanities and social sciences into scientific research, for example). Often the planned outputs of this research aim to be widely applicable beyond the scope of their funded area. For example, the recent international 'Digging into Data Challenge', launched by the Joint Information Systems Committee (JISC) from the United Kingdom, the National Endowment for the Humanities (NEH) and the National Science Foundation (NSF) from the United States, and the Social Sciences and Humanities Research Council (SSHRC) from Canada 'encourages humanities and social science research using large-scale data analysis, challenging scholars to develop international partnerships and explore vast digital resources, including electronic repositories of books, newspapers, and photographs to identify new opportunities for scholarship'. The challenge promoted by such funding schemes is dependent on appropriating and developing new computational techniques to enable humanities research tasks to be undertaken, and the tools being developed by projects range from those enabling spatio-temporal correlation, analysis and visualisation, and text mining to musical analysis and authorship attribution.

Likewise, the UK's Arts and Humanities Research Council, Engineering and Physical Sciences Research Council and Joint Information Systems Committee established an 'Arts and Humanities e-Science Initiative' which has funded projects of which a:

> central feature ... is the substantial involvement of computer scientists alongside arts and humanities researchers ... By developing new and advanced methods in areas such as the image-processing of ancient manuscripts, choreography in virtual space, the computer simulation of a famous medieval battle, and the use of 3-D scanning to analyze the surfaces of museum objects, the scheme will not only open up new avenues in arts and humanities research, but will also test and extend the present range of e-Science technologies, and thus ultimately enhance their use in other domains as well. (AHRC, 2007)

Other schemes, such as the AHRC's 'Digital Equipment and Database Enhancement for Impact' (DEDEFI) programme (2009), and the NEH's 'Digital Humanities

Start-Up Grants' programme (2010), explicitly encourage novel computational tools to be developed in conjunction with computing scientists: indeed, the NEH funding call explicitly states that 'Digital Humanities Start-Up Grants cannot be used for ... the implementation or assessment of existing digital applications in the humanities (however, exploration of or planning for a new direction or tool for an established project is allowed)' (ibid). Partly as a result of this encouragement from funding bodies, working with dedicated programmers and computing scientists in developing novel computational approaches is now becoming a more widespread aim for those in digital humanities. This is reflected in the call for papers of the major conference in the field: Digital Humanities 2009 emphasised that 'early adopters' doing innovative 'new work on tools, text analysis, electronic editing, virtual worlds, digital preservation, and cyberinfrastructure' should submit proposals (Warwick et al., 2008a), whilst Digital Humanities 2010 stressed that it required papers that cover 'recent developments ... significant new methodologies ... [encompassing] the common ground between information technology and problems in humanities research and teaching' (Nerbonne et al., 2009). However, it can be argued that, although these calls for papers demonstrate the interest in such work, there is yet to be demonstrable achievements or identifiable milestones from projects which can provide evidence of the recent funding schemes' successes.

Interdisciplinary Issues in Digital Humanities

As representative of the type of project that a digital humanist might work on, the two projects detailed above also hint at various issues that can emerge from working in such an interdisciplinary environment. The discussion below, although informed by personal experiences within the projects mentioned in this chapter, other research projects I have previously and am currently working on, and communication with related research communities, is not indicative of any particular issue within either project, nor problem with any project team member.

When Things Go Wrong

Failure in academic projects is not something that is often admitted to – although projects that work at the cusp of two disciplines, charting new research ground, are more susceptible to difficulties that can arise than those working in established norms. I have not alluded to any of the projects I have worked on here that have had sizable problems (and mentioning issues here does not mean that they happened in the projects above), but I have encountered my fair share of disasters. Shall I be honest? Things have gone horrendously wrong, often between individuals who are supposed to be working closely together, but cannot bridge the personality – or discipline – clash to understand each other's approach. Most failures in projects, in my experience, stem from a lack of communication. Perceived slights of status or disputed 'ownership' of published outcomes have ruined what promised to be an interesting and fruitful working relationship. Those employed to do complex computational tasks have not had the desired skill set after all, meaning deliverables are not delivered. It has emerged that those in charge of managing either side of the research have no real understanding of the other discipline and require repeated correction of the same facts (if I have to inform my engineering colleague one more time that, yes, codicology is a word, and yes, it exists as a field of study ...) which, cumulatively, can start to grate on working practices. There have been huge differences in what are perceived as acceptable outcomes from the project: is a working tool, or ruminations and theorising about a potential working tool, the desired goal? There was research which had to be abandoned after months of statistical analysis because a party forgot to mention a dataset that should have been included which they presumed everyone knew about. There was the time when the research assistant set out to sabotage a project because she did not believe in a professor's expertise, and the one about the research assistant who suddenly left because the pressure was too much, taking passwords with them. Payment for individuals, departments, travel and equipment has been locked for months within administrative mazes which are seemingly un-navigable. Different cultures of celebration have even caused perceived slights between team members, when individuals do not understand how important a milestone has been reached. There have been meetings which went on forever without any outcome, and labyrinthine email conversations which never came to any real conclusion.

Such personality clashes, management issues and communication problems are not limited to the digital humanities, though, but can be found across all working environments: 'narratives of success, failure, compromise, change, and complication are, of course, familiar to anyone pioneering interdisciplinary ... structures' (Davidson, 2010: 216). The biggest issue, though, with many ambitious digital humanities projects (and perhaps in other domains, too) is the lack of identifiable outcomes at the close of a project which had been promised at their inception.

From working within many interdisciplinary projects, I have learnt that the key to choosing and maintaining a good working team can often be to look out for potential scholars who display an understanding of 'alterity' (even if they have never heard of the sociological theory): willing to work with others and possessing an ability to understand the needs and viewpoints of their team mates. As well as an interest in working in digital humanities and across disciplinary divides, the individual has to have the personality to match this in practice. It stands to reason that managers of interdisciplinary digital humanities projects should also therefore possess communication skills that allow for the successful management of complex teams – and to behave as mediator if things go wrong. There are also defined areas, articulated below, regarding research expectations, publication, training and project management that, if appropriately navigated, can add to the chance of a research project succeeding.

Disciplinary Cultures and Expectations

Although many digital humanists have exceptional computational skills, and the younger generation of scholars who are coming through humanities programmes have increased knowledge of computational environments, given the pervasive nature of networked technologies, it is now often the case that advanced digital humanities projects are dependent on collaboration with computer scientists, engineers and computer programmers to develop tools, techniques and methods which may be applicable to the further understanding of humanities research issues (and computational approaches). This poses many problems for both the humanist aiming to utilise advanced computational techniques and the scientist aiming to use the humanistic research question as the 'real-world' problem: not only have they to find interested collaborators, but to engage with the discourse, habits and different focus of other disciplines in order to answer their own research questions.

The arts and humanities and the computational sciences are very different beasts, and it takes conscious efforts in communication to ensure that all team members both understand project developments and are understood themselves. There is the lack of a common language, leading to tensions between technical and non-technical members of a team. To function well in both disciplines, the scholar needs to understand both the subject and culture of both disciplines (which can take both time and excellent communication skills, which not everyone has), or a larger team needs individuals who can communicate effectively across these boundaries. Digital humanists need to be comfortable networking in both their 'home' humanistic domain and other disciplines.

There are also issues of an individual's perceived status in a project. There can be tensions between those who are employed on what is now becoming known as an 'alt-ac' (alternative academic) career: 'positions within or around the academy but outside of the ranks of the tenure-track teaching faculty' (Nowviskie, 2010), such as programmers working in teams who may very well have a PhD in Computer Science, but did not get – or chose not to pursue – the academic career route. Sensitivity to issues which can arise around academic status is crucial to maintaining harmony within interdisciplinary teams.

Management

Successful teams in digital humanities research have been defined as those who maintain a good working relationship, adopt clearly defined tasks, roles, milestones and obligations (which are to be discussed by the teams themselves), and work together to meet goals (Siemens, 2009: 231). There is interest in how successful digital humanities projects function (Ramsay, 2008). A large-scale survey project (Siemens et al., 2002) has highlighted collaboration issues in digital humanities projects: in particular, the need for face-to-face collaboration (Ruecker et al., 2008) and strong leadership.

Often managing projects in digital humanities can involve wrangling with university administrators, the administrative systems of funders, or their respective computing systems which are not routinely set up to deal with projects that occur within both the humanities and sciences. This can both affect the individual within a project (as secondary supervisor on the multi-spectral imaging project above, which is based in Medical Physics rather than my home department of Information Studies, my work on it does not 'count' towards my career progression within my institutional framework), and also impact wider areas, such as attracting funding (it can be difficult to persuade funders to support projects, and difficult for universities to process cross-faculty, or cross-institutional, funding bids and grants).

Training

Individuals 'with the adequate combination of research in a humanities discipline and technical expertise are rare and valuable' (Warwick et al., 2008b: 390) and it is unusual to find scholars trained in both humanistic and computational disciplines. There are a few master's level courses in digital humanities – for example, at the University of Alberta,[10] King's College London[11] and University College London[12] – but for the most part those working in digital humanities projects will have picked up their skill set through experience, trial and error, rather than formal teaching programmes, requiring careful management and training. There is an additional problem that, due to the short-term nature of many research projects, retaining trained staff can be problematic (Warwick et al., 2008b: 385).

Publishing

One of the most difficult issues to be encountered when working in a joint research team across various disciplines only rears its head well into the project, when there are outputs to be disseminated. Publication can be a hugely tricky area to negotiate. Problems often arise because of different academic expectations regarding publication in different domains: author order on papers, for example, varies hugely between disciplines. There can be issues about where to publish outcomes and an understanding is required of the different authorial tones needed for publication across a wide disciplinary range. Acceptance of these publications on a scholar's CV can also be problematic (does an article published in the *Journal of Hellenic Studies* 'count' for a tenure-track computing scientist?), and issues of how digital publication is perceived versus traditional print outputs still abound. Only by being open about intended publication outcomes at the start of projects can teams hope to successfully navigate what can become a divisive issue.

---

10   <http://huco.ualberta.ca/>.
11   <http://www.kcl.ac.uk/schools/humanities/depts/cch/digihum/>.
12   <http://www.ucl.ac.uk/dh/courses>.

Additionally, to counteract many of these problems, and to positively overcome cultural issues, it has been suggested that at the start of a project a 'charter' is drawn up between all project stakeholders, stipulating modes of communication, expected roles, expected means of conduct and expected means and modes of publication (Ruecker and Radzikowska, 2008). Making such issues explicit at the start of a project can foster openness of communication and alleviate any doubt for team members or managers regarding their individual roles, duties or expectations in the interdisciplinary environment. There have been times, in my experience, when producing this charter halfway into a project and reminding individuals what they have signed up to (specifically about the naming of authors on publications) has stopped a project imploding entirely.

When Things Go Right

Much of the work described as interdisciplinary digital humanities, involving input from computing science, engineering science and humanities scholars, is novel, even quirky, research. Often the outcomes are unexpected, or can generate useful spin-offs which feed back into engineering and computing science (such as the image processing algorithms mentioned above, developed to look at ancient documents but now also used by others looking at medical images). Humanities problems provide interesting use cases, and often require redefinition of the traditional mathematical approach and development of novel computational techniques. Moreover, working in the crossover between humanities and computing can be extremely personally rewarding, as Adam Gibson, Reader in Medical Physics and Bioengineering at University College London and the primary supervisor of the multi-spectral imaging project described above, attests:

> My research is in medical imaging, but I've recently started collaborating with workers in Digital Humanities, looking at ways of applying medical imaging techniques to ancient documents. Medical imaging is now a fairly mature subject, and there has been a great deal of work done on processing and improving images. It is refreshing to be able to apply some of these methods to challenges in a different area. The problem we are tackling is hard and the methods we use do need to be developed further to optimise them for this new field but it is fun and exciting to feel that you can contribute productively to a new area of study. (Gibson, 2010)

The opportunities which exist for research which crosses over the disciplinary bounds between the arts, humanities and culture, and the computational and engineering sciences are legion: developing partnerships and working in cross-disciplinary teams can be a rewarding personal experience for all involved. Translating this into identifiable tools and research outcomes will become increasingly important, though, to maintain interest in, and funding of, this type of original, ambitious research.

Conclusion

> For collaboration to be fully successful, one must begin from the assumption
> that one's own definition of what counts as 'knowledge' may not be the right
> or only definition. Such collaboration requires accepting that there are reasons
> (practical, historical, philosophical, or simply traditional) for the practices of
> another field, including those that seem most antithetical (or annoying) to one's
> own practices. (Davidson, 2010: 217)

This chapter has scoped out issues which present themselves when working in
interdisciplinary domains, and shown the benefits, usefulness and problems
of projects that require interdisciplinary collaboration between computing or
engineering science and the humanities. Such work, although still outlier in the
field of digital humanities, has the potential of feeding back useful techniques
and approaches to both the humanities and the computational sciences, although
given that much of the research presented is in its early stages, it is difficult as yet
to point to identifiable successes. As we learn more from the distinct cultures and
disciplines, dealing with such cross-disciplinary communication, management,
training and personnel issues should become more routine. The quest in digital
humanities 'is still for otherness, but it is an otherness often cloaked in familiarity'
(McCarty, 2005: 139), as digital humanities projects begin to exist across
computational and humanities domains.

References

Arts and Humanities Research Council, 'e-Science Research Grant Awards', <http://
www.ahrcict.rdg.ac.uk/activities/e-science/awards_2007.htm> (17 May 2007).
Arts and Humanities Research Council, 'Digital Equipment and Database Enhancement
for Impact (DEDEFI)' <http://www.ahrc.ac.uk/FundingOpportunities/Pages/
dedefi.aspx> (2009).
Austin, M., M. Kelly and M. Brady, 'The Benefits of an Ontological Patient Model
in Clinical Decision-Support', *Proceedings of the 23rd AAAI Conference on
Artificial Intelligence*, <http://www.aaai.org/Papers/AAAI/2008/AAAI08-325.
pdf>, (2008).
Becker, T. and P.R. Trowler, *Academic Tribes and Territories*, 2nd edn (Buckingham:
The Society for Research into Higher Education and Open University Press,
2001).
Brady, M., X. Pan, M. Terras and V. Schenk, 'Shadow Stereo, Image Filtering and
Constraint Propagation', in A.K. Bowman and M. Brady (eds), *Images and
Artefacts of the Ancient World* (Oxford: Oxford University Press, 2005): 15–30.
Clark, B., *Academic Culture*, Working Paper number 42 (New Haven, CT: Yale
University Higher Education Research Group, 1980).

Collini, S., 'Introduction', in C.P. Snow, *The Two Cultures* (Cambridge: Cambridge University Press, 1993): i–lxiii.

Davidson, C.N., 'Humanities and Technology in the Information Age', in R. Frodeman, J. Thompson Klein and C. Mitcham (eds), *The Oxford Handbook of Interdisciplinarity* (Oxford: Oxford University Press, 2010): 206–19.

Dill, D.D.,'Academic Administration', in B.R. Clark and G. Neave (eds), *The Encyclopedia of Higher Education*, vol. II (Oxford: Pergamon Press, 1992): 1318–29.

Evans, C., 'Choosing People: Recruitment and Selection as Leverage on Subjects and Disciplines', *Studies in Higher Education* 20.3 (1995): 253–65.

Fabian, J., *Time and the Other: How Anthropology Makes Its Object* (New York: Columbia University Press, 1983).

Fox, J., D. Glasspool, V. Patkar, M. Austin, L. Black, M. South, D. Robertson and C. Vincent, 'Commentary: Delivering Clinical Decision Support Services: There is Nothing as Practical as a Good Theory', *Journal of Biomedical Informatics* 43.5 (October 2010): 831–43.

Frank, R., 'Interdisciplinary, The First Half Century', in R. Burchfield, E.G. Stanley and T.H. Hoad (eds), *Words for Robert Burchfield's Sixty Fifth Birthday* (Woodbridge: Boydell & Brewer, 1988): 100.

Giacometti, A., 'Multi-spectral Image Processing Methods for Separating Palimpsestic Text', MPhil Transfer Report, Department of Medical Physics, University College London (2010).

Gibson, A., Personal Communication, 26 August 2010.

Jovchelovitch, S., *Knowledge in Context: Representations, Community and Culture* (Abingdon: Routledge, 2007).

McCarty, W., 'Looking Through an Unknown, Remembered Gate: Interdisciplinary Meditations on Humanities Computing', *Interdisciplinary Science Reviews* 26.3 (March 2001): 173–82.

McCarty, W., *Humanities Computing* (Houndmills: Routledge, 2005).

Molton, N., X. Pan, M. Brady, A.K. Bowman, C. Crowther and R. Tomlin, 'Visual Enhancement of Incised Text', *Pattern Recognition* 36 (2003): 1031–43.

Monroe, J., 'Introduction: The Shapes of Fields', in *Writing and Revising the Disciplines* (Ithaca: Cornell University Press, 2002): 1–12.

Moran, J., *Interdisciplinarity* (Oxford: Routledge, 2002).

National Endowment for the Humanities, 'Leading Research Agencies Announce New International Competition: "The Digging into Data Challenge"', <http://www.neh.gov/news/archive/20090116.html> (16 January 2009).

National Endowment for the Humanities, 'Digital Humanities Start-Up Grants', <http://www.neh.gov/grants/guidelines/digitalhumanitiesstartup.html> (6 August 2010).

Nealon, J., *Alterity Politics: Ethics and Performative Subjectivity* (Durham, NC: Duke University Press, 1998).

Nerbonne, J., E. Burr, R. Cunningham, J-C. Meister, E. Mylonas, B. Nelson, B. Nowviskie, J. Rybicki and J. Walsh, 'Digital Humanities 2010 CFP' (2009), retrieved from <http://lists.digitalhumanities.org/pipermail/humanist/2009-October/000781.html>.

Nowviskie, B., '#alt-ac: Alternate Academic Careers for Humanities Scholars', *Bethany Nowviskie's Blog* <http://nowviskie.org/2010/alt-ac/> (3 January 2010).

Oxford English Dictionary, 'Interdisciplinary', *The Oxford English Dictionary*, 2nd edn, OED Online (Oxford: Oxford University Press, 1989).

Ramsay, S., 'Rules of the Order: The Sociology of Large, Multi-Institutional Software Development Projects', paper presented at *Digital Humanities 2008*, Oulu, Finland, <http://www.ekl.oulu.fi/dh2008/Digital%20Humanities%20 2008%20Book%20of%20Abstracts.pdf> (2008): 20.

Roued-Olsen, H., 'Towards an Interpretation Support System for Reading Ancient Documents', *Literary and Linguistic Computing* 25.4 (2010): 365–79.

Ruecker, S. and M. Radzikowska, 'The Iterative Design of a Project Charter for Interdisciplinary Research', paper presented at *DIS 2008*, Cape Town, South Africa (2008).

Ruecker, S., M. Radzikowska and S. Sinclair, 'Hackfests, Designfests, and Writingfests: The Role of Intense Periods of Face-to-face Collaboration in International Research Teams', paper presented at *Digital Humanities 2008*, Oulu, Finland, <http://www.ekl.oulu.fi/dh2008/Digital%20Humanities%20 2008%20Book%20of%20Abstracts.pdf> (2008): 16.

Schenk, V.U.B. and M. Brady, 'Visual Identification of Fine Surface Incisions in Incised Roman Stylus Tablets', *ICAPR 2003, International Conference in Advances in Pattern Recognition* (2003).

Senvaitienë, J., A. Beganskienë, S. Tautkus, A. Padarauskas and A. Kareiva, 'Characterization of Historical Writing Inks by Different Analytical Techniques', *CHEMIJA* 16.3–4 (2005): 34–8.

Siemens, L., '"It's a Team if You Use 'Reply All'": An Exploration of Research Teams in Digital Humanities Environments', *Literary and Linguistic Computing* 24.2 (2009): 225–33, special issue: 'Selected Papers from Digital Humanities 2008, University of Oulu, Finland, June 25–29'.

Siemens, R., M. Best, E. Grove-White, A. Burk, J. Kerr, A. Pope, J-C. Guédon, R. Rockwell and L. Siemens, 'The Credibility of Electronic Publishing: A Report to the Humanities and Social Sciences Federation of Canada', *Text Technology* 11.1 (2002): 1–128, <http://web.viu.ca/hssfc/Final/Credibility.htm>.

Snow, C.P., *The Two Cultures and the Scientific Revolution* (New York: Cambridge University Press, 1959).

Tanner, S. and G. Bearman, *Digitizing the Dead Sea Scrolls* (forthcoming).

Tarte, S., 'Digitizing the Act of Papyrological Interpretation: Negotiating Spurious Exactitude and Genuine Uncertainty', submitted, based on paper given at *Digital Humanities 2010*, <http://dh2010.cch.kcl.ac.uk/academic-programme/ abstracts/papers/pdf/ab-808.pdf> (forthcoming).

Tarte, S.M., J.M. Brady, H. Roued-Olsen, M. Terras and A.K. Bowman, 'Image Acquisition and Analysis to Enhance the Legibility of Ancient Texts', *UK e-Science Programme All Hands Meeting 2008 (AHM2008)*, Edinburgh, September 2008.

Tarte, S., D.C.H. Wallom, P. Hu, K. Tang and T. Ma, 'An Image Processing Portal and Web-Service for the Study of Ancient Documents', *Fifth IEEE International Conference on e-Science and Grid Computing*, <http://www.computer.org/portal/web/csdl/doi/10.1109/e-Science.2009.10> (2009).

Taylor, P.J., 'An Interpretation of the Quantification Debate in British Geography', *Transactions of the Institute of British Geographers* N.S. 1 (1976): 129–42.

Terras, M., 'Disciplined: Using Educational Studies to Analyse "Humanities Computing"', *Literary and Linguistic Computing* 21 (2006a): 229–46.

Terras, M., *Image to Interpretation: An Intelligent System to Aid Historians in Reading the Vindolanda Texts*, Oxford Studies in Ancient Documents (Oxford: Oxford University Press, 2006b).

Terras, M. and P. Robertson, 'Image and Interpretation: Using Artificial Intelligence to Read Ancient Roman Texts', *HumanIT* 7.3 (2005), <http://www.hb.se/bhs/ith/3-7/mtpr.pdf>.

Thaller, M., 'Bridging the Gap; Splitting the Bridge? Studying Humanities Computer Science in Cologne', *Duisburg: Computers – Literature – Philosophy (CLiP) 2001*, <www.uni-duisburg.de/FB3/CLiP2001/abstracts/Thaller_en.htm> (2001).

Warwick, C., N. Fraistat and M. Kirschenbaum, 'Call for Papers: Alliance of Digital Humanities Organizations Digital Humanities 2009', <http://www.mith2.umd.edu/dh09/index.html%3Fpage_id=54.html> (2008a).

Warwick, C., I. Galina, M. Terras, P. Huntington and N. Pappa, 'The Master Builders: LAIRAH Research on Good Practice in the Construction of Digital Humanities Projects', *Literary and Linguistic Computing* 23.3 (2008b): 383–96.

Wenger, E., *Communities of Practice: Learning, Meaning, and Identity* (Cambridge: Cambridge University Press, 2002).

Chapter 14

Interview with John Unsworth, April 2011, carried out and transcribed by Charlotte Tupman

John Unsworth and Charlotte Tupman

Q: *You have been involved in collaborations of several different kinds over many years. What do you think these collaborations accomplish in addition to ensuring that a job no-one can do by him- or herself gets done? What new avenues of research are facilitated by these collaborations?*

I think most collaborative projects take that form because they are trying to address a problem that requires a range of expertise that is not found in a single person, or because the scale of what is being undertaken is more than one person can do in a reasonable period of time, or both. They open up the possibility of doing interdisciplinary and multidisciplinary research, and tackle problems that do not fall neatly into disciplinary divisions of knowledge.

Q: *You have been closely involved in designing and building infrastructural support for research across the disciplines, for example, as Chair of the Commission on Cyberinfrastructure for the Humanities and Social Sciences, American Council of Learned Societies. How is such support related to collaboration and to research? Is it in any way a kind of research in itself?*

First of all I would want to distinguish between designing and building infrastructural support for research, and promoting the funding of that kind of work, which in some ways is what we did in the Commission for Cyberinfrastructure for the Humanities and Social Sciences. That was an exercise not in building, but in funding. The infrastructure for supporting large interdisciplinary collaborative research activities is widely recognised as a subject of research in its own right. It is more widely recognised as such in the sciences: much of the research into the infrastructure and information support for collaborative work happens in library and information science, and is a social science problem as much as a technical problem. Sometimes it is tackled in computer science as a technical problem, but that is the easier part of the problem to solve. People in industry, for example, would agree that it is easier to procure and install a knowledge management system than it is to get people to use it. So a social science research agenda around cyberinfrastructure encompasses what it takes to get people to actually use it: what their real requirements are; what kinds of information they need out of that infrastructure; and what the impediments are to virtual collaborations that are geographically diverse and cover different disciplines.

Q: *How do you think the humanities are being affected by adopting structural models from the sciences? In the trade-off, what is being gained, and what lost?*

I don't think that those models have been widely adopted. If they were universally adopted and no-one did anything else, then we would have lost a type of research which is still valuable in the humanities: the work that can best be done by one person thinking carefully and writing alone. We had a symposium here a couple of years ago on digital humanities research methods, at which a historian argued that the big science model for humanities research is fine as long as it doesn't take away the small science opportunities. If the only kind of humanities in the future is big humanities, then something will have been lost. In humanities, we often emulate what we *think* the sciences do, but our emulation may not actually bear that much resemblance to the reality of what goes on in science. Often science looks more collaborative because a lot of people get together to write a grant proposal, but that does not mean that they have necessarily figured out how to work together. Just because there are many authors listed on a paper, that does not mean that they all collaborated in a meaningful way. The reality is very different across the different sciences too.

Q: *Do you feel, then, that models from the sciences are not adopted because humanities scholars do not always fully grasp them, or because there is resistance to them?*

Both are probably true: there is a resistance in humanities to scientism, and science envy. I think that's appropriate. Rather than thinking about this as 'adopting models from the sciences', we are better off identifying what we need and how we can create those models.

Q: *One effect on the humanities seems to be a methodisation of research. This is reflected in your much quoted essay, 'Scholarly Primitives: What Methods Do Humanities Researchers Have in Common, and How Might our Tools Reflect This?' What has changed since you wrote it, what new aspects have come forth that you had not anticipated, and in what ways have things remained essentially the same?*

I think a lot of the scholarly primitives are still valuable, but I recall feeling at the time that some of them could be further decomposed and therefore might actually not be legitimate primitives, so if I were doing this over I might make it a shorter list. But all the things that are on that list are still things that we need to do, and some of them are not much better supported by our general-purpose research environment than they were when I wrote [the article], which is a little surprising. Annotation, for example, is very basic and important but we don't yet have good facilities on the web for that: it is still a research problem. We have a collaborative research project on annotation with the Maryland Institute for Technology and the Humanities, which is grappling with basic issues such as how we can model the ontology of an annotation and then actually bring those models to bear in our working environments. The fact that a number of these things are still not well supported might suggest that our needs are unique, or it might say that our needs are broadly shared but extremely difficult to accommodate. It is hard to say. When I talk about our general research environment, I mean an environment consisting of Google, the web and a bunch of other things that are not produced by the digital humanities community. The solution to this is not to build a gated community for the digital humanities in which humanities-specific things can be supported: people do not want to work that way. People want to go where the information is, but the key is to work out how to influence the development of those more general-purpose environments.

Q: *ADHO [Alliance of Digital Humanities Organizations] has provided a global framework for the digital humanities. Would you tell us about the collaboration between you and Harold in setting up that umbrella organisation? What do you think is its long-term significance?*

This is an opportunity to say how important Harold's personal qualities are. The key to establishing the ADHO was a high level of trust between Harold and me: we trusted that each of us was interested in the greater good and willing to try to pursue that while still looking after the needs and interests of the organisations that we represented. But we also had to be willing to think broadly about what those interests might look like in a larger framework, and if Harold had not been the kind of open, honest, kind and trustworthy person that he is, then I don't think this would have happened. There was a fair amount of resistance and suspicion in the early days, which Harold probably had to deal with more than I did. This was because the income-producing activity at stake belonged to the ALLC [Association for Literary and Linguistic Computing]: the publication and the income from the *Literary and Linguistic Computing* journal. In ACH [Association for Computers and the Humanities], we gave up a journal that we had published for a long time, but at least from a financial point of view that was much less of a risk for us, because we had a terrible deal with the publisher and weren't making any money from that journal anyway. Part of the identity of the ACH was wrapped up in that publication, but financially speaking we had less at risk than ALLC. Harold therefore had more reassurance to do on his side, and I think those same qualities that made it possible for us to work together also helped him to persuade his ALLC colleagues that this could be done without harming the long-term interests of the ALLC.

The long-term significance of this arrangement is considerable: it has created a structure of affiliation. It is not just an agreement between two scholarly societies – societies that had, after all, been interacting for 20 years by this time; its importance is that it formalises a financial structure and a governance structure for other organisations who wish to affiliate. The first of those was the Canadian Society for Digital Humanities, but there are conversations going on now in Japan, Australia and Italy about the affiliation of other regional chapters. Therefore it is beginning to become a structure that can co-ordinate this scholarly activity around the world: if it can do that, it can represent the needs and interests of that community in a unitary way. This is actually profoundly important to the availability of research funding, and to the way this activity is reflected in university curricula: there are all sorts of reasons why aggregating, and making the aggregate activity visible, is important.

Q: *At Virginia you created an institutional form for the digital humanities that at its time represented a big step in the evolution of how the field was instantiated within universities. You have gone on to grow other forms of the digital humanities within a library school, and have had much to do with the institutional growth of the field in the United States. From that perspective, what do you think is the significance of Harold's contribution to this institutional evolution of the field?*

Harold has done a remarkable thing by taking what was essentially a support unit and turning it into an academic department. This is not the first time in history that it's been done: this is also where computer science came from. Here in Illinois we had one of the earliest computer science departments in the world. That department evolved out of an activity and an organisation that was set up to support one of the first university-owned computers. So it is an interesting parallel, but it is quite an accomplishment to have brought a unit through this transition, and in doing so, to have moved digital humanities generally closer to the heart of the university, which is, after all, about educating students, granting degrees and employing faculty.

Q: *What still needs to be changed to counter the perception of digital humanities as a support rather than a discipline? Do the digital humanities need more input into general humanities programmes taught in universities?*

It is interesting that by and large universities are organised around disciplinary structures that have not fundamentally changed in hundreds of years. The exception to this disciplinary form of organisation is the professional schools, which tend to be organised around areas of practice or categories of problems. These tend to draw on an interdisciplinary faculty. The other exception is research institutes, to the extent that they are involved in education. Those are also organised around problems rather than around disciplines. I think a department of digital humanities is a department of method in a real sense, and therefore orthogonal

Interview with John Unsworth 235

to disciplines. That is a strength, but in order for that strength to be realised, the methodological axis has to engage the disciplinary axis in some sustained way. So digital humanities still need to engage in meaningful ways with humanities departments of other kinds that are disciplinary in their organisation. In your local case of DDH [Department of Digital Humanities] still being thought of by some as a service organisation, it will just take time to change that view. It may take a long time: our Graduate School of Library and Information Science separated from the Library formally and administratively in 1971, but I am constantly being told that we have the third largest collection in the country, and my counterpart, the Dean of Libraries, is often told that she has the number one Masters programme, so people still cannot tell us apart after 40 years. These things can take a long time to go away!

Q: *How is Harold's Centre – now the Department of Digital Humanities – perceived worldwide?*

I think it is viewed as a central institution to the field and a premier programme in the field. Less formally, I think it is viewed as quite a remarkable empire, and I am sure by some people it is regarded as essentially being the Borg, and absorbing all kinds of things! That would be closer to home. But out in the field, I think people essentially aspire to the kind of success that Harold has had at King's.

Q: *Can other institutions learn about institutional models for digital humanities from the experiences at Virginia and at King's? Has the institutionalisation of digital humanities moved as fast as you hoped or believed it might?*

The experience at Virginia and the experience at King's are actually quite different. Virginia hasn't coalesced in the same way it has at King's. There are many interesting things going on at Virginia, but they go on more or less in parallel, some waxing and some waning, and they have never coalesced into a degree-granting programme. One of the last things I did when I was there was to get a Masters in Digital Humanities created and approved by the State Council of Higher Education, but it has never been offered. I spoke to the Chair of Media Studies there (which is where the degree was to be housed) and he said that they just did not have the faculties in Media Studies to be able to mount that programme. So Virginia, at least at one point, was aiming to do the kinds of things that Harold has done at King's, but I don't think we actually got there. In the larger field, interest in digital humanities has grown in recent years and the visibility of this activity has increased considerably. I am not sure that is only due to its institutionalisation. I think it is partly due to the increase in digital data, and to the fact that we now have coming into the profession a generation of people who have grown up doing their basic work in an online environment, which was not widely true of the generation before them. So we are now seeing digital humanities dissertations coming out of places where there are no digital humanities programmes *per se*. The interests of the students are shaping the projects. I see a recent groundswell of interest in digital humanities that actually exceeds the institutional organisation we have at present, which is probably a good thing. Certainly there is a real possibility of developing more institutional structure around this interest and activity.

Q: *As roles become more defined, how can we avoid the industrialisation of the digital humanities? How do we keep the questioning alive? What sort of institutional structures would best promote the core unknowingness of research?*

I am grappling with the idea of the industrialisation of digital humanities and I don't think we are there yet. If you did a survey of types of institutional structures that exist for digital humanities now, you would find that research centres far outnumber academic programmes or departments. Those centres exist in order to keep interesting questions alive and to support research. So I would be less worried about the industrialisation of digital humanities than I would be about universities doing away with traditional humanities, in which case our methodological dimension will not have much to work with. And right now we really need to find a way to use whatever caché the digital humanities now have with the media, administrators and students to help to rescue those programmes. This is not just because it is nice to help our colleagues, but because we need the expertise that they bring to the table and we cannot do our work without them.

Q: *From your current perspective as dean of a major school of library and information science, what do you think is or could be the relationship between digital humanists, librarians and information scientists? What do collaborations among them reveal about possibilities for the future?*

Researchers in library and information science programmes are in many cases dependent on collaboration with people in different domains, so I think there is a lot of potential for collaboration between library and information science faculty and humanities and digital humanities faculty on funded research. Librarians are sometimes on a tenure track (in a minority of universities), and in those cases there is an expectation that they will do research. That is the case at Illinois, and we collaborate quite a lot with the library faculty around externally funded research. Our annotation collaboration with the Maryland Institute for Technology and the Humanities [MITH] is one research project that we have in that area, and there are other projects that also involve people in the humanities. MITH has provided some good examples of externally funded collaborations that involve digital humanities and library and/or library faculty, as has Nebraska's Center for Digital Research in the Humanities. I think both examples have had some of their funding from the Institute of Museum and Library Services. There are lots of unexploited opportunities, and from the Ischool side [see www.ischools.org], the deans of schools of information are interested in seeing more of that activity. I don't think it would be difficult to promote, I just think we need to have the intention to do it.

We are in the final stages of preparation for the launch of a research centre that will be jointly hosted at Indiana and Illinois, the purpose of which will be to provide researchers with computational access to all the material in the HathiTrust. The HathiTrust is a shared digital repository for all the material that CIC (Big Ten) university libraries (and now many others) contributed to Google Books, plus all the other material that those libraries have digitised in other programs. It is not all available yet, but it is certainly in the pipeline, and there are about three billion pages in the repository. It will ultimately include material that is in copyright as well as orphan works and material that is out of copyright, so there will be some serious security and auditing requirements around using at least certain parts of the collection. However, I think that this body of data will provide a great boost to the kinds of research collaborations that we are discussing. It will be an enormous test bed, but more than that, it may finally do for the humanities what the infusion of enormous amounts of digital data has done in other disciplines, which is to force them to reconsider their methods. This has happened in different disciplines at different times; for example, around 1994 it happened for astronomy with the Sloan Digitized Sky Survey; I think this is going to be our Sky Survey and I think a shift to computational research methods will result.

Q: *Looking now at the emerging institutionalisation of the digital humanities, what do you see as the principal challenges and opportunities? One challenge is certainly finding people to fill the positions now opening up. Presumably this is just a temporary problem that will be solved by the current crop of doctoral students, for example, at King's. But where do you think the next generation of leaders in the digital humanities will come from? What sort of people will they be, with what sort of backgrounds?*

There are two challenges, I think, and they are closely related: you could almost say that our two problems are defining, and not defining, the digital humanities. Regarding the first challenge of defining digital humanities, the students I have counselled when doing job searches often have a very vague idea of what they are looking for. It is not only vague, but it is politically contested within the search committee. It is difficult to counsel or educate students to succeed in presenting themselves for job opportunities that are not well thought out, or that represent arguments that have not been concluded. So we need clearer definition for that reason, and we also need a form of labelling that is clear to our non-digital humanities colleagues, because they are often the people who create these search criteria. But the problem that is raised by definition is exclusion. For example, we don't really have a place comfortably worked out in digital humanities for people who come from the arts. We tend to divide the world into analytical and creative endeavours, and we tend to think of what we do in the humanities and in the digital humanities as being on the analytical side. This is why creative programmes exist uneasily alongside the rest of an English department, because they are on the other side of that same divide. We see the same issue in other subjects, for example, studio art and art history. It is reflected in many parts of the university, but actually I think it operates to the detriment of digital humanities, because we *need* to be collaborative and interdisciplinary. Certainly a quick look at many digital humanities projects would demonstrate the need for people with artistic sensibility and people with interest in design. It is one example of potentially harmful exclusion. These two things are in tension with one another, and they will probably continue to be in tension. I am not sure what we can do about it except to be conscious of it and try to do more good than harm.

Q: *Who do you think will be the future scholars of digital humanities? Where will they come from?*

I think the future scholars of digital humanities will come from humanities backgrounds or even from library and information science. The most important kind of credibility will ultimately be credibility with disciplinary colleagues. It will not be enough to be sound and interesting on a methodological level: it will be necessary that the questions you pursue are recognised as being interesting and important in the humanities. It is great that undergraduates are now being introduced to digital humanities, but I see this subject as being more a graduate or professional stage of education. A good parallel in another field is bioinformatics, in which the most common degree is probably a Masters degree, but people taking a Masters in bioinformatics often have a PhD in the life sciences. They realise that they need this methodological education in order either to re-tool themselves professionally or tackle different kinds of problems as a researcher. The methodological expertise is important, but it must be exercised on top of some kind of disciplinary depth.

Q: *You have been involved in evolving publishing models in the digital world, as Harold has. How do you see the future of publishing? Monographs? Journals? E-books? Do you see new opportunities for HE and publishers to work together to evolve new Open Access publication models, and if so, how will this influence scholarship in the future?*

Publishing for academic audiences is done in two fundamentally different ways in this part of the world: commercial publishing and non-profit publishing. The non-profit version is done by university presses and increasingly by libraries; the commercial version is done by commercial publishers, many of whom are European, and many focused on journals. If you set aside the digital for the moment and look at humanities publishing, we see in the non-profit world that humanities programmes are being ditched right and left, so important university presses are shutting down their operations in this area. That is not a hopeful circumstance if you want them to use their shrinking capital to experiment with new ways of doing things. I am afraid that the non-profit world is not, by and large, where the experimentation is going to happen. Commercial publishers are still publishing for a humanities audience, but only in certain areas. On the other hand, they are more willing to experiment than I think people realise, especially those publishers who have big investments in creating digital resources that are of interest to the humanities. Because those publishers have already sunk their money into building the collections, they have an incentive to find new things that people can do with those collections: for them, the cost of the additional research is a marginal cost compared to the cost of creating the resource.

I think that in the non-profit world, humanities publishing will be done in libraries, and university presses in general are going to be forced into the library. That might produce a similar sort of dynamic, as some of those libraries do create their own digital resources, and do invest a fair amount of money in them. However, those libraries that publish on a large scale are few and far between. I think we will have all of the following: books, journals, electronic publications, Open Access and commercial publishing. The important future opportunities are likely to be around the support of data communities: communities of scholars who congregate around a particular kind of resource, who need tools for working with these resources and who want to publish and share results with each other. If universities and university libraries can support those data communities, they might have a chance of competing with commercial publishers, but I am not terribly optimistic about that. The whole funding situation in public higher education in the industrialised world is so grim that experimentation that is relatively expensive and a bit ahead of the curve seems unlikely to happen in the university setting. It is happening in the commercial setting, but it is not being driven by the humanities.

Q: *Is there anything else you would like to add?*

Harold has been the best sort of person to work with that you could possibly ask for. He is a good friend and an utterly dependable colleague. In digital humanities, I think he deserves (and gets) a great deal of credit for building the field. It is appropriate that a lot of the questions in this interview have been about institution-building, because that is what Harold does. He doesn't do it for personal aggrandisement: he does it because he likes to build things that last, things that are sustainable and things that produce good results. He has done that under some extremely trying circumstances, and he is to be lauded and thanked for what he has accomplished.

Charlotte Tupman would like to thank her colleagues John Bradley, Marilyn Deegan, Willard McCarty and Simon Tanner for their help in formulating the interview questions.

Index

Bold page numbers indicate figures, *italic* numbers indicate tables.